SPREE KILLERS
HUMAN TIME BOMBS

Their explosive violence erupts without warning.

Often, they don't even know their innocent victims before they butcher them.

Small town or large city, quiet suburb or rural farm — no place is immune from their savage attacks.

SPREE KILLERS — men and women who suddenly go berserk, murdering unsuspecting people in a frenzy of blind destruction.

Here, from the exhaustive files of TRUE DETECTIVE MAGAZINE, are twenty shocking true crime accounts of the deadliest Spree Killers in the annals of modern law enforcement history.

No one can predict when they'll strike. Read and beware.

SPREE KILLERS

Edited by
ART CROCKETT

PINNACLE BOOKS
WINDSOR PUBLISHING CORP.

ACKNOWLEDGEMENT

This volume could not have been compiled without the invaluable assistance and editorial insights of Rose G. Mandelsberg.

PINNACLE BOOKS

are published by

Windsor Publishing Corp.
475 Park Avenue South
New York, NY 10016

Copyright © 1950, 1966, 1973, 1981, 1986, 1987, 1988, 1989, 1990 by RGH PUBLICATIONS

For complete copyright information, see Appendix

First Printing: January, 1991

Printed in the United States of America

TABLE OF CONTENTS

CHARLES WHITMAN:
"MASSACRE AT THE UNIVERSITY OF TEXAS"
by Zarko Franks 7

STEVE JUDY:
"2800 VOLTS FOR INDIANA'S MULTIPLE KILLER"
by Lee Gary 26

RICHARD SPECK:
"EIGHT GIRLS, ALL PRETTY, ALL NURSES, ALL SLAIN"
by W. T. Brannon 45

JUAN GONZALES:
"HOLIDAY HORROR ON A FERRY BOAT"
by Don Unatin 87

WAYNE NANCE:
"THE SERIAL KILLER SNUFFED TWO MORE!"
by Franklyn Sharpe 104

MICHAEL WAYNE JOHNSON:
"STOP THE MADMAN'S MURDER MISSION!"
by Barry Benedict 131

JOHN LIST:
"17-YEAR TRACK OF THE FAMILY SLAYER!"
by Bill Ryder 149

TEOFILO MEDINA:
"FOUR EXECUTIONS BY THE RAMPAGING PSYCHO!"
by Turk Ryder 167

PATRICK SHERRILL:
"A MANIAC'S RAGE CLAIMED 15 LIVES!"
by Bill Ryder 184

JERRY "ANIMAL" MCFADDEN:
"THE 'ANIMAL' IS LOOSE! HE'S A RAPIST!
HE HAS A WOMAN HOSTAGE!"
by Bill G. Cox 205

CARLTON GARY:
"HUNT FOR THE PHANTOM STRANGLER OF SEVEN!"
by Bob Spurlin   239

JAMES SCHNICK:
"WEIRD TWIST IN THE MARSHFIELD MASSACRE!"
by Barry Benedict   269

WILLIAM CRUSE:
"THE MAN WITH A RAGE TO KILL!"
by Don Unatin   286

JAMES HUBERTY:
"I'M GOING HUNTING HUMANS!"
by Tom Basinski   304

WILLIAM RYAN:
"HORROR OF THE HUNGERFORD MASSACRE!"
by Brian Marriner   327

BRANDEN THOLMER:
"RAMPAGING SEX STARVED STRANGLER!"
by Turk Ryder   349

JOSEPH "CUJO" REISS:
"I'VE JUST SHOT FIVE PEOPLE!"
by M. J. McCarthy   366

KENNETH ERSKINE:
"7 VICTIMS OF THE WHISPERING STRANGLER!"
by Philip Westwood   384

HOWARD FRANK STEWART:
"TWO-GUN STALKER ON A MURDER MISSION!"
by Bill G. Cox   406

HOWARD UNRUH:
"FANTASY OF DEATH"
by David Redstone   427

CHARLES STARKWEATHER:
"11 MURDER VICTIMS FOR THE YOUNG LOVERS!"
by Randall Shanley   442

APPENDIX   471

CHARLES WHITMAN:
"MASSACRE AT THE UNIVERSITY OF TEXAS"
by Zarko Franks

A sniper in gray nylon coveralls ducked behind the limestone parapet of the Tower observation deck to reload his 6mm Remington rifle with a 4-power scope. By this time he had sown most of his seeds of death and anguish on the innocents below.

Above him in the bell-clock tower, a giant hammer bonged 12 times against a 3½-ton bell. The chimes announced it was high noon in Austin, Texas, on that August 1st, a lazy summer day with the temperature at 98 degrees in the shade.

Below him lay the University of Texas campus and the rolling green countryside stretching to the LBJ Ranch on the Pedernales 65 miles away.

Momentarily, the great chimes drowned out the agonized cries of the dying and the wounded, those on the 27th floor below him and those he had picked off as they strolled on the campus and streets adjoining the University Administration Tower, a 4-sided stone shaft rising 307 feet into blue Texas skies. As for the yet uncounted dead, they would never cry again.

White puffs burst from the parapet shielding the sniper. The puffs, tiny explosions, were chips of the limestone hit by slugs fired by police from the ground far below.

But the sniper's position was well-nigh impregnable. A helicopter, carrying an armed police lieutenant, had sought to maneuver close to the sniper's stronghold. The pilot was forced to retreat because of the sniper's accurate fire.

Later, a lightning-fast decision would be made: Storm the sniper's citadel. The earlier orders issued by Austin Police Chief Robert Miles had been explicit: Shoot to kill!

If ever there was one, the situation was a classic, clear-cut example of the policeman's duty to protect the community, a desperate extremity in which the rifleman *must* be stopped at all costs. Chief Miles recognized this at once. He could not indulge the luxury of reflecting on possible future charges of police brutality or the use of what bleeding-heart liberals like to call "excessive force."

The deadly accurate sniper had killed 15 persons and wounded 31 others in an utterly unprecedented orgy of mass murder.

Who was this mass killer, this sniper with a clubfoot in his brain? Why had he suddenly gone berserk and started blasting at "anything that moved"? Why had he chosen the normally peaceful sanctuary of a university campus for his vendetta against the world? What twisted intelligence had driven him to select

8

the 300-foot tower as his impregnable fortress?

These were but a minute sampling of the questions that police and a stunned citizenry from coast to coast began asking as soon as the horrifying news of slaughter was announced in a series of bulletins which interrupted scheduled radio and television programs with increasing frequency during the last half of that never-to-be-forgotten Monday that began the month of August, 1966.

The slaughter, relatively speaking, took a pathetically short time. The answers to questions that were being asked by everyone in America, up to and including President Lyndon Johnson, would be much slower in coming, but come they did. . . .

At 9 a.m. that day, a University of Texas student named Charles Joseph Whitman, aged 25, an architectural engineering junior, drove his 1966 Chevrolet Impala to a hardware store in downtown Austin and bought a second-hand .30-caliber M-1 carbine.

Then he drove to Chuck's Gun Shop, bought three clips for the carbine, and several hundred rounds of ammunition for it and other rifles. Mrs. C. K. Maretzky, a store employee, remembered the handsome young blond Whitman. He was the ex-Marine who had been in the gun shop with his father, C. J. Whitman, a plumbing contractor from Lake Worth, Florida, the year before.

At 9:30 a.m. Whitman bought a 12-gauge shotgun from Sears, Roebuck & Co. on credit. He returned to his apartment on Jewell Street, and sawed off part of the shotgun's stock and barrel.

In his U.S. Marine footlocker beneath a blanket he concealed the new sawed-off shotgun, along with a

.35 caliber Remington pump rifle, a 6 mm Remington bolt action rifle with a 4-power scope; the 30-cal. M-1 carbine; a .25-cal. pistol; a 9 mm Luger and a .357 Smith & Wesson Magnum pistol.

Also in the footlocker he packed three hunting knives, a pocket knife and about 1,000 rounds of ammunition for the arsenal.

Earlier, he had stored in the locker two cans of pork and beans, a can of spiced meat, two cans of sausage, a can of fruit cocktail, cans of pineapple, beef ravioli, six packages of raisins, a thermos jug of coffee and toilet tissue.

His other supplies included a can of charcoal lighter fluid, sunglasses, a flashlight and extra batteries, matches, a clock, adhesive tape, binoculars, several hundred feet of strong nylon rope, an extension cord, a Stilson wrench, two pairs of cotton gloves, a canteen, a 3-gallon jug of water and a 3-gallon can of gasoline.

From a supply house earlier that day he had rented a 3-wheeled dolly. Before leaving his apartment he dressed in blue jeans, white shirt and tennis shoes. Over the jeans and shirt he wore a gray nylon jump-type suit with lots of pockets.

He trundled the dolly into his Impala and drove to the University campus. At the Administration Tower building he obtained a permit to park in the loading zone at the northwest corner of the Tower.

He told a receptionist he was a maintenance repair man. He wheeled the dolly bearing the footlocker down the main hall leading to the Tower's two automatic elevators.

He rode the elevator to the 27th story level, as high

as it went, unloaded his dolly there, then walked the two flights of stairs to the reception room on the observation deck.

Mrs. Edna Townsley, 51, a divorcee, was on duty. During the past eight years, Mrs. Townsley, whose life centered around her two sons, Danny, 16, and Terry, 12, had greeted thousands of visitors, students and tourists, from her desk.

This blond, smiling man in nylon coveralls was different. He carried two rifles. What, if anything, was said before he smashed her skull with a rifle butt, will never be known. The killer quickly dragged the dying woman behind a couch in the reception room.

Later, he would fire a slug into her head.

Footsteps approached from the observation deck. Two sightseers, Don Walden, 22, of San Antonio, and his date, Cheryl Botts, 18, of Rockdale, Texas, entered the room. They saw a blond young man bending over the couch. He stooped to pick up two rifles.

Cheryl Botts smiled at him and said, "Hello."

The young man smiled back and said, "Hi. How are you?"

Walden suppressed an inclination to ask the young man if he was going to shoot pigeons from the tower.

Cheryl noticed a dark stain on the rug near the reception desk. She told her date to step around it. After the exchange of pleasantries, the young couple left without incident.

Charles Joseph Whitman followed them down as they boarded the elevator. Moments later, Mrs. Vera Palmer arrived on the other elevator. She was to re-

11

lieve Mrs. Townsley at the reception desk.

"Don't you dare get off that elevator," Whitman warned her. Shaken, she rode back down, but forgot about the incident until the alarm spread of the sniper in the tower.

After she left, Whitman shouldered the footlocker, walked up the two flights and carried it to the tower observation deck, 231 feet above the ground level.

At about 11:40 a.m., a group of sightseers got off the elevator at the 27th floor. The group included M. J. Gabour, 47, a service station operator from Texarkana; his wife, Mary Frances, 41; their two sons, Mike, 19, a cadet at the Air Force Academy, and Mark, 15; and Mr. and Mrs. William Lamport of Austin. Mrs. Lamport was Mr. Gabour's sister.

The Gabours were on vacation and en route to Houston to see the North-South Texas All-Star High School football game in that city. They had decided to stop over at Austin to visit Gabour's sister and her husband, the Lamports.

Young Mark and his brother, Mike, ran up the flight of iron stairs. Their mother and aunt were several steps behind them. Gabour and his brother-in-law, Lamport, trailed behind.

A shotgun roared as young Mark opened the door to the reception room on the observation deck level on the 29th floor.

The boy screamed, fell back on the staircase. The shotgun roared twice more. Mike, wounded in the head, fell backwards. The two women, caught in the hail of pellets, also toppled backwards and down the stairs.

The elder Gabour turned over the body of his son,

Mark. "I knew it was no good," he said later. "He was dead."

Mrs. Lamport, mortally wounded, died later at the foot of the stairs. Mrs. Gabour, at this writing, was in grave condition at an Austin Hospital. Her son, Mike, was expected to recover.

Below, at the 26th-story level, nine employees of the classics department, after hearing the shotgun charges, huddled in fear. They barricaded the door to their office and waited out the ordeal.

Now the sniper was alone in his rocky fortress. He pushed a desk and chair against the door opening to the reception room.

It was about 11:45 a.m. Directly below, in the bright sunshine, was the campus mall. A few students had begun to trickle out of the University's red Spanish-tile roof buildings. Directly ahead in the distance, loomed the dome of the State Capitol.

Summer classes would not let out until 12:20 p.m. As lunchtime approached, however, the trickle of students soon turned into a torrent.

The sniper's first target probably was Alec Hernandez, 17, a newsboy on a bicycle making his deliveries of the *Austin American-Statesman*. The regular delivery boy was ill that day, and Hernandez was substituting for him.

A rifle bullet drilled through his groin and leg. He teetered, fell from his bike. Passers-by, exposing themselves to the sniper's fire, dragged him to safety.

From her office window, Mrs. Charlotte Darehshori, a pretty secretary in the graduate dean's office, saw three students stagger and fall. She ran out to find out why they had mysteriously been stricken.

13

One was dead. His blood-splattered chest told her what had happened. The rifle slugs whining around her told her to flee. She dashed behind the cover of the concrete base of the South Mall flagpole. There she was isolated and safe. For 90 minutes she huddled behind the concrete base.

She was one of the lucky ones. She lived to tell of her ordeal. Policeman Billy Paul Speed, 22, a traffic cop, did not. He was responding to an 11:30 a.m. police call to investigate an accident east of the campus. On the way he heard a report of the sniper firing from the tower. Speed joined about 50 other policemen closing in on the tower. As the rifle slugs splattered and sought every moving target, Speed took refuge behind a balustrade below a statue of Jefferson Davis, the father of the Confederacy.

Big stone pillars support the balustrade. A rifle slug whizzed between two of the pillars and struck the temporarily exposed cop. Leland Ammons, who was near Speed, watched the policeman's eye turn glassy. "Then he died right there," said Ammons, a law student.

South beyond the Jefferson Davis statue, Roy Dell Schmidt, 29, a city electrical serviceman, sat in his parked truck. A police blockade near the university had stopped him from making a service call in the area.

"A sniper's firing from the tower," an officer told him. "Get out of here." Schmidt had left his truck briefly.

Schmidt started to return to his panel truck when a slug tore into his chest. He died in the street.

Paul Sonntag, 18, a summer life guard, was stroll-

14

ing along the West Mall with his sweetheart, Claudia Rutt, 18. The young lovers were holding hands. He had earlier picked up his $75.12 paycheck for a week's work at the Red Municipal Pool.

A rifle slug whined. Claudia Rutt, clutching her torn chest, cried: "Help me! Somebody help me!"

Paul Sonntag leaned over the body of his coed sweetheart. Another shot rang out. He fell across her body. They died together there on the West Mall. On her finger was his senior High School ring.

Across the Drag, the student name for the college catering district of Guadalupe Street, is the University newsstand operated by Arthur H. Merchant.

Harry Walchuk, 38, a graduate student working towards his doctorate, was browsing through the newsstand. Walchuk was an instructor in government at Alpena College, Michigan.

As he turned to leave the newsstand he told Merchant: "The magazine I wanted wasn't there."

At that moment a girl screamed on the sidewalk. Merchant opened his mouth to say more magazines would arrive Tuesday, but the words never came. Walchuk gasped, clutched at his throat, then fell, mortally wounded, near the comic book rack. He lay there until he died at 3 p.m. that day.

Thomas Karr, 24, hometown Fort Worth, had come to study at the University because he wanted to be a career diplomat in South America. An honor student at Arlington State, he had come to Texas University because Arlington did not offer a Latin-American studies program. He was taking two summer courses. He finished a quiz on contemporary Spanish and American prose about 11:50 a.m., left

15

Batts Hall, southeast of the Tower, when a rifle slug hit him in the chest. He fell dead instantly.

Thomas Aquinas Ashton, 22, of Redlands, California, was on his way to meet a beautiful brunette, a Peace Corps trainee colleague. He had joined the Peace Corps the summer after graduating from the University of Southern California. There he had studied politics, economics and geology.

Other students knew him as a "real easy-going guy" with a burr haircut and black horn-rim glasses. Earlier that morning he had attended a class in the techniques of teaching English to Iranian students.

Other members of his class headed north along "The Drag" for lunch at the Student Union. After they saw and heard the danger from the Tower, they ducked behind buildings. Tom Ashton ignored their warnings to seek cover. His last words to his fellow students were: "I'm going to meet her. She's beautiful." He headed east.

No one knows, not even the ambulance driver, who picked up the body later, where Ashton was when the sniper killed him. The bullet struck his head.

Mrs. Claire Wilson, 18, eight months pregnant, had just left a freshman cultural anthropology class with Thomas Frederick Eckman, 18, who also was enrolled in the course. This was Mrs. Wilson's and Eckman's first summer on the campus.

A bullet shattered the skull of her unborn child after it struck her in the lower abdomen. The child was stillborn and was listed as one of the casualties. She was listed in grave condition. A third slug from the rifleman on the Tower struck Eckman in the

16

chest. He was dead on arrival at Austin's Breckenridge Hospital.

Dr. Robert Boyer, 33, had arrived in Austin the day before the sniper's wrath. He was scheduled to leave a day later. He had come to settle some financial affairs left over from 1965 when he had taught at the university for a year. At that time he was on leave from his duties as a research physicist and lecturer in applied mathematics at the University of Liverpool, England.

He was staying in Austin at the home of Dr. Robert Palter of the university's philosophy department.

Late that Monday morning Dr. Boyer, an expert on relativity, went to the administrative offices of the main building, under the Tower, on his financial matter. He had a few minutes to kill before meeting his friend, Dr. Palter, for lunch.

He walked out onto the South Mall to the top of a flight of steps dropping down between the statues of Jefferson Davis and Woodrow Wilson. He suddenly collapsed. A rifle bullet was found in his body later. He had been shot in the back as he walked away from the Tower.

Those are the names of the dead, tombstones today, the ones the sniper killed or wounded in the Tower itself or on the mall and streets below. Most of the 31 others he wounded were treated, then released.

Texas Governor John Connally issued a statement later in the week that the sniper had committed most of his violence, in fact 99 per cent of it, within the first 20 minutes after he started shooting from the

17

tower.

Police fired hundreds of rounds of ammunition at him from ground positions, but the sniper was too well protected by his stone parapet.

After the helicopter attempt failed, Police Chief Miles issued a call for every available officer.

Ramiro Martinez, 29, a mild-mannered Spanish-American who never before had drawn his police gun in anger, was home cooking steaks when he was alerted to come to the Tower. Martinez thought at first that a group of students were in a fight.

He buckled on his pistol belt and drove to the embattled tower. There he met fellow officers Houston McCoy, Jerry Day and Philip Connor and a civilian named Allen Crum, a squat man who once had been a tail-gunner in the Air Force.

Each had reached the Tower Building by zigzagging across the open spaces to evade the sniper's fire.

Officer Day punched the button on the elevator panel.

Allen Crum, the civilian, hollered at him: "If you're going up there, you're not going alone. I'm going with you."

By this time Martinez had arrived along with the others. Crum was given a .30-cal. rifle by a state investigator named W. A. Cowan. Then Crum was deputized on the spot.

The silent men rode the elevator to the 26th-story level "because we didn't want to take a chance of running into him (the sniper) if he was waiting for us on the 27th floor," Crum explained later.

They climbed the stairs to the 27th floor and there

found the bodies of Mark Gabour and his aunt, Mrs. Lamport, and the seriously wounded Mrs. Gabour and her son, Mike, both shot in the head.

Gabour, the dead boy's father, burst out of an office and lunged for Martinez's gun.

"I'm going after him myself," the grief-stricken father declared.

The officers restrained Gabour, who was then escorted down the stairs by Officer Day. Officer Connor went in search of help for the wounded left on the 27th-level stairway.

The state investigator, Cowan, had remained at a phone on the 26th floor to coordinate with officers outside the Tower.

Martinez, McCoy and the civilian Crum inched their way up the two flights of stairs leading to the observation deck which the sniper had made his fortress. Each covered for the other during the painstaking progress.

At the top of the stairs they found the door leading to the small reception room barricaded. Martinez cautiously pushed with one foot until he had cleared the door of the desk and chair behind it.

Behind a couch of the reception room on the observation deck level they found the body of Mrs. Townsley, her head split.

Officer Martinez, nearest to the door leading to the observation deck, crawled outside. Officer McCoy followed him. On hands and knees, Martinez armed with a pistol, McCoy with a shotgun, crawled to their left. Allen Crum, armed with the rifle, went right. This way they were certain to confront the sniper.

They stayed on hands and knees as they crawled forward because the parapet is only chest high and police fire from below was still chipping away at the limestone.

As he reached the west corner of the observation deck, Crum heard footsteps running toward the corner he was facing. He knew it had to be the sniper. Martinez and McCoy would be advancing slowly, measuring each inch of their way.

Crum fired a random shot into the west wall of the parapet.

Officer Martinez, at the opposite corner from Crum, now saw the sniper for the first time. A blond young man with a stretch-type sweat-band around his head. Gray nylon coveralls. An M-1 carbine in his hands.

Drum's shot had attracted the sniper's attention. He turned momentarily in Crum's direction. In that split second Martinez fired his pistol. The sniper jerked around and fired wildly once. Martinez emptied his .38 police special.

The sniper, whose back had been against the parapet, now thrashed on the deck. He still held the carbine. McCoy fired his shotgun twice at the wounded man, still dangerous as long as he clung to his weapon.

Still the figure in nylon coveralls jerked and flailed. Martinez snatched the shotgun from McCoy and fired point-blank at the sniper's head.

Charles Joseph Whitman, age 25, one-time Eagle Scout, altar boy and honor student, twitched no longer.

The men walked up to the still figure, took the gun

from his hands and saw that he was dead.

About an hour after his body was removed, the stature of his crime assumed new dimensions. The bodies of his wife, Kathy, 21, a one-time beauty queen in her hometown of Needville, Texas, and his mother, Mrs. Margaret Whitman, 44, a plumpish, graying woman, were found in their separate apartments.

He had stabbed his wife to death with a hunting knife. He had stabbed and shot his mother to death.

The notes he left gave a partial clue to his behavior. One long note, which authorities refused to release in full, told of an inordinate hatred for his father. He hated him, he said, "with a mortal passion."

He spoke of love and admiration for his wife and mother. He killed them, he wrote, to spare them shame and embarrassment for what he had set out to do.

One of his notes said he couldn't understand "the pressures bearing down" and "had decided to fight it out alone."

He surely knew he would be killed after his wrath with a rifle in the Tower.

"I am prepared to die. After my death I wish an autopsy to be performed to see if there's any mental disturbance," he had written in one of his notes.

An autopsy disclosed he was an excellent physical specimen but that he had a small tumor in the brain. Some medical experts say it could have affected his behavior. Others say it could not.

Austin authorities said the notes he left "definitely show he was very mentally disturbed."

His parents had separated about six months ago and Charles Joseph had gone to his hometown of Lake Worth, Florida (pop. 15,000). He was visibly shaken by the separation. He returned with his mother to Austin where she got a job as a cashier in a cafeteria.

The father called the son by long-distance telephone on numerous occasions trying to effect a reconciliation with his wife.

Neighbors in Austin described Mrs. Whitman as "courteous but timid." However, she was robust-looking and healthy.

Mrs. Whitman, a Catholic, had raised her three sons (Charles Joseph, the oldest, then Patrick, 21, and John 17) in the same faith. "She was very interested in Charles Joseph's opinions and he was concerned about giving them to her," said the manager of the apartment where Mrs. Whitman lived. "He took very good care of her and tried to see that she wasn't overworked. She was always over at Charlie's and Kathy's."

In his hometown, Charles Whitman was the prototype of the all-American boy you'd want your daughter to marry.

Police recall he had a "few minor traffic violations and that's all."

The all-America image didn't carry over during his Marine Corps days. He was a so-so Marine, records show. He was court-martialed once for loaning money for interest and gambling against regulations.

He qualified as a sharpshooter, a peg below expert, on the rifle range. he had scored 215 points out of a possible 250.

His father, C. J. Whitman, said: "I taught all my boys how to use guns. All of them are good."

In Needville, his wife's hometown, a 12-year-old boy who had hunted with Whitman recalled that "Charlie could hit a quail on the fly with a .22 rifle."

Charles Whitman's gambling urge apparently carried over to his college days. A former Texas student, Brooks Porter, says he still carries a $190 hot check Whitman gave him in a poker game four years ago.

On March 29th Charles Joseph Whitman, perhaps realizing the demons raging in him would destroy him, visited a University of Texas psychiatrist, Dr. Maurice Dean Heatly.

After he spent an hour with the young man, Dr. Heatly wrote:

"This massive, muscular youth seemed to be oozing with hostility as he initiated the hour with the statement that something was happening to him and he didn't seem to be himself. Past history revealed a youth who grew up in Florida where the father was a very successful plumbing contractor without an education, who had achieved considerable wealth. He identified his father as brutal, domineering and extremely demanding of other members of the family."

The psychiatrist's report continued:

"He expressed himself as being very fond of his wife, but admitted that his tactics were similar to his father's and that he had on occasion assaulted his wife physically. He said she had become more comfortable with him, that she really has less fear of him now than in the past because he had made a more intense effort to avoid losing his temper . . ."

Also in the report:

"The real precipitating factor for this initial visit after being on the campus several years seemed to stem from the separation of his parents some 30 days ago. He says that his father has averaged calling every 48 hours for several weeks petitioning him to persuade his mother to return."

And to the psychiatrist, Charles Joseph Whitman told of an urge "to go up on the tower with a deer rifle and start shooting at people."

Charles Whitman was told to make an appointment for next week. Should he feel a need to talk with the doctor sooner, he was asked to call.

Charles Whitman never came back to see the psychiatrist. He decided, as he wrote later, "to fight it out alone."

The psychiatrist saw no sign of psychosis at that time, he said later, nor did he see any indication that Whitman might be a danger to himself or society.

"I didn't feel he would do anything violent," said Dr. Heatly. He said he regarded Whitman's references to violence as transient and he said he was not particularly concerned by Whitman's mention of shooting people from the tower.

It's common on the University campus for a student he sees to refer to the tower as the site of "some desperate action" which they don't take, the psychiatrist said.

Many of the nation's top medical men, including psychiatrists, are scheduled to meet at Houston's M.D. Anderson Hospital at a date to·be announced later.

The purpose: To study the brain of Charles Joseph Whitman, the human chameleon who loved deeply and hated deeply.

Whatever the findings of these learned men, it will make little difference to pretty Karen D. Griffith, a 17-year-old Austin girl who for eight long days clung tenuously to life in Breckenridge Hospital as surgeons fought to repair the damage done by chest wounds from the sniper's rifle.

On August 8th, she and they lost the uneven battle and the once vibrant youngster died. Statistics, cold and unfeeling, will record her as victim No. 16 of the demented University of Texas sniper.

STEVE JUDY
"2800 VOLTS FOR INDIANA'S MULTIPLE KILLER"
by Lee Gary

Residents of the Indianapolis, Indiana area are of two minds about White Lick Creek, a narrow stream that meanders for miles southwest of the city before emptying into the White River. The creek is a favorite among fishermen and wild-mushroom fanciers but considered a treacherous nuisance by nearby property owners. Most of the year the White Lick is a sluggish, weed-choked tributary not more than 25 feet wide and three to five feet deep. But heavy rains often send the muddy creek churning out of its banks and over surrounding roads and homesites. In April, when stormy weather fronts carry moisture-laden clouds from the Gulf of Mexico across Indiana, folks living near the White Lick keep a wary eye on the unpredictable creek. They have learned to expect the unexpected—but no one was prepared for the shocking surprise the White Lick offered up the overcast morning of April 28, 1979.

Shortly before 9 o'clock that Saturday morning an automobile crossed the steel arch bridge that carries northbound Indiana Highway 67 across White Lick Creek. The bridge is about 14 miles southwest of Indianapolis, in Morgan County, and about five miles east of the small town of Mooresville. After crossing the bridge, the car turned right and parked on a primitive rutted access road which angles eastward from the highway.

The temperature was only 42 degrees, and there was a bone-chilling mist in the air. Two men got out of the auto and zipped their jackets against the damp cold as they followed a muddy path through sycamore, willow and ash trees growing near the water's edge. They were in search of wild mushrooms, a fungus that thrives along waterways where sandy soil is shaded by heavy brush and trees. About one hundred feet downstream one of the mushroom hunters suddenly stopped and called to his companion:

"I think there's a body over here," the man said, pointing to an area heavily overgrown with brush on the north bank of the creek. Both men moved closer and noticed several articles of clothing scattered on the bank about five feet above the object in the water. At this distance, the men could see that the form below them was that of a nearly nude woman. She was lying face down, her torso and head submerged just below the creek's surface, her legs sprawled up on the rocky bank. The men turned and ran for help.

Within a half-hour more than 15 police cars had arrived at White Lick Creek. Indiana State Troopers directed traffic and stood guard at various locations to insure the security of the cordoned-off area. Mooresville Chief of Police John Clark and Patrolman Harold Martin had been the first police officers on the scene. Next came Indiana State Police Detective Sgt. Jerry Conner from the Putnamville I.S.P. post. Clark and Martin introduced Conner to the mushroom hunters who again related the story of how they found the body.

I.S.P. Detective Sgt. Gary Hood, a veteran crime scene technician, arrived and began the tedious job of processing the area for evidence. Hood photographed the dead woman from every angle, taking pictures from the bridge and the bank opposite the body. Aerial photographs would be taken later. While Hood was at work, Det. Conner walked downstream from the body, carefully watching each footfall, searching for evidence. At this point, Conner and the other detectives had no idea of the enormity of the crime they would be expected to solve.

Morgan County Deputy Coroner Tom Neal arrived and officially pronounced the woman in the water dead and, as far as Conner knew, the still unidentified female was the only victim.

Det. Conner had slowly walked about 75 paces downstream from the woman's body when he noticed a splotch of color in the murky water. A gusting northwest wind was now kicking up washerboard waves on the creek surface, and the bright object, tangled in driftwood and weeds about four feet off the north bank, was distorted by the refracted light. At first Conner believed he had found part of the dead woman's clothing. He poked at the object with a stick and was horrified to see the body of a child bob to the surface! Conner shouted his discovery to the others and was soon joined by I.S.P. Detective Sgt. Jack Hanlon and Sgt. Frank Love. The second body discovered was that of a little girl, about five or six years old. Deputy Coroner Neal came up, briefly examined the body and declared the child dead.

Shouts were heard from two Morgan County deputies who had been searching the creek bank farther downstream. Detectives Conner, Love and Hanlon made their way toward the deputies, pushing wet brush aside and crouching to walk beneath drooping willow branches. They came upon the sheriff's men standing just beyond a looping bend in the creek. There, on a sandy outcrop, lay the lifeless body of another child, a small boy. The deputies pointed to a spot in the direction of an iron railroad bridge. There, face down, floated still another tiny body. Sgt. Conner remembers that after the bodies were retrieved and laid out on the shore, he had a sick feeling in the pit of his stomach and a sour taste in his mouth.

Deputy Coroner Neal's preliminary examination concluded that the woman had been strangled, gagged with a strip of material torn from her own clothing and probably raped. The children—two boys and a girl, all probably under six years of age—had apparently drowned in the creek. There were no visible injuries on the children's bodies.

Everything pointed to the unthinkable. Some person or persons unknown had brutally strangled the woman and then thrown the children into the creek, knowing the toddlers would quickly perish in the icy water. Another possibility, still more horrible, was

29

that the kids had drowned in the creek before the woman was killed. Either way, investigators would treat the horror at White Lick Creek as a mass murder.

The investigators needed to identify the victims as quickly as possible. Television news camera crews and newspaper reporters had gathered on the periphery of the murder site and the detectives were being repeatedly pressed for information. I.S.P. Lt. Merle McKenny, a 25-year state police veteran and criminal investigation coordinator for the agency, was dealing with reporters as best he could. McKenny had little information to offer except to confirm that four unidentified bodies, a woman and three children, had been discovered in the creek.

Sgt. Conner returned to the woman's body after ordering other detectives, troopers and deputies to continue the search downstream. The sergeant believed—hoped—that all the victims had been found, but there was no way to be certain until the four corpses had been identified.

Morgan County Prosecutor G. Thomas Gray was standing near the pile of clothing when Conner walked up. Gray didn't ordinarily inspect crime scenes, but upon hearing that a woman and three children were dead, the prosecutor assumed that this would be an extraordinary case. He was right. During the next two years Gray, a conservative country prosecutor, would appear on local and national television countless times and grant interviews to newsmen from around the world.

Sgt. Conner began to sift carefully through the clothing on the creek bank. The detective found a pair of shoes, a beige topcoat, a torn smock-type blouse of the kind worn by supermarket and restaurant workers, and undergarments. As Conner examined the clothing, Sgt. Hood photographed each item and placed it in a plastic evidence bag for analysis by the crime lab. Conner found two clues among the clothing that he hoped would save investigators a lot of time: attached to the pocket of the torn smock was a small tag bearing the single name: Terry. A few feet from the clothing pile Conner found a bank book. Inside was the name Terry Chasteen and an Indianapolis address. If the name tag and bank book belonged to the woman in the creek, investigators had an I.D. It seemed probable that the dead woman was connected in some direct way to the drowned children, a babysitter or perhaps their mother.

By early afternoon, Sgt. Conner and the other detectives had completed their preliminary investigative work at the murder site. Sgt. Hood had found several clear footprints and tire tracks in the area. Each one had been photographed and a few cast in plaster. Conner allowed the bodies to be removed to a nearby mortuary where attendants would prepare them for visual identification.

Lt. McKenny, with cooperation from Mooresville city officials, set up a murder investigation command post in the Mooresville city building. The name tag found by Sgt. Conner carried the logo of a well-known Indianapolis food store. Conner reached the manager of the store by telephone. The man confirmed that an employee named Terry Chasteen had failed to show up for work that morning. The woman, the manager said, had also not called in to explain her absence. The store manager went on to say that he believed the woman was the mother of three small children. Conner was given the absent worker's address and phone number from employee records.

Conner dialed the number, and the phone was answered by a man who identified himself as Blake Sizemore. During the conversation it was established that Sizemore was Terry Chasteen's live-in boyfriend. Sizemore said that Terry had left the house with her three kids at seven o'clock that morning. She routinely drove the children to a babysitter before going to work. Conner asked for Sizemore's address—it was the same as the one in Terry Chasteen's bank book—and told him to sit tight and wait for I.S.P. detectives. The man nervously agreed and hung up.

Conner noted that Sizemore sounded concerned, which was understandable, but not defensive or frightened. The detective had a hunch that he had no guilty knowledge of the fate of Terry Chasteen and her three children. But as a precaution, he immediately contacted Indianapolis city police, gave them Sizemore's address and asked them to keep an eye on the residence until I.S.P. officers could get there. At this point in the investigation, everybody was a suspect.

Sgt. Hanlon and Sgt. Love drove to the boyfriend's residence in northwest Indianapolis. As gently as possible, the detectives explained to Sizemore what had happened to his girlfriend and her three children. The man was visibly upset, shocked. It would be necessary, Hanlon explained, for Sizemore to accompany them to the mortuary and at-

32

tempt to make positive identification of the bodies. The officers also asked Sizemore for a list of Terry Chasteen's close relatives.

The fastest way from northwest Indianapolis to Mooresville is via Interstate 465, a four-lane expressway that encircles the city. The interstate passes near the famed Indianapolis 500 Speedway and, farther south, connects with Interstate 70 near Indianapolis International Airport. During the ride Sizemore explained that he had been living with Terry Chasteen for less than a year. The young woman had been divorced in 1978 from a Navy corpsman, the father of two of her three children.

As the I.S.P. patrol car approached the airport Blake Sizemore suddenly shouted, "I think that's Terry's car!"

Sizemore pointed to a bright red, late-model Ford parked on the shoulder of the southbound lane. Sgt. Love pulled the patrol car behind the empty Ford, and all three men walked up to examine the automobile.

"This is definitely Terry's car," Sizemore said.

Sgt. Love thought the discovery of the car was a nice piece of luck as he returned to the police car and radioed for assistance. Love told the dispatcher to notify Sgt. Conner of the discovery. In a few minutes, several I.S.P. units containing troopers, detectives and crime scene technicians were parked along the shoulder of 465. Terry Chasteen's abandoned automobile would be carefully searched for evidence on the spot and then impounded for meticulous examination by the crime lab.

Blake Sizemore, his eyes moist and voice breaking,

was able to identify the bodies at the mortuary as Terry Lee Chasteen, 21 years old, and her children, Misty Ann, five years old, Stephen Michael, four years old and Mark Lewis, two years old. Using Sizemore's identification, Sgt. Conner wrote the tiny victims' names in the appropriate location on a diagram of the murder site: Misty Ann Zollar's body had been snared by weeds about one hundred feet downstream from the body of her mother; another hundred feet farther down, at a bend in the creek, the current had washed four-year-old Stephen Michael Chasteen's body up on a sand bar; the body of tiny, two-year-old Mark Lewis Chasteen had snagged 50 feet away from his brother's corpse.

Back at the command post, Detectives Conner, Love and Hanlon huddled with Lt. McKenny and Prosecutor Gray. The men decided to call a news conference and ask for public assistance in the murder investigation. Late editions of Indianapolis newspapers and evening television and radio newscasts carried an appeal for anyone driving on Indiana Highway 67 near White Lick Creek between seven and nine o'clock that morning to contact I.S.P. headquarters. The response was immediate and massive. Indiana 67 is a heavily traveled north-south route. Hundreds of motorists passed the murder site during the specified time; scores called police. The callers were referred to the command post in Mooresville where Conner, Love, Hanlon and a dozen other investigators tried to sort out the callers with promising information.

One man had a particularly interesting story to tell. The caller told investigators that he and his son were passing the bridge over White Lick Creek shortly before eight o'clock when they noticed a pickup truck parked on the access road. The man's young son had pointed the truck out and commented on its "weird" paint job. The informant went on to describe how the pickup was painted a spectacular design in vivid red and silver.

All I.S.P. units and various police agencies across Indiana were alerted to be on the lookout for an odd-looking red and silver pickup truck. The investigators particularly wanted patrol officers in Indianapolis to have the pickup description as well as sheriff's patrol deputies in Marion and Morgan Counties.

The detectives got another lucky break the following day, Sunday, April 29th. Marion County Sheriff's Deputy Robert Yarnell was building a new home for his family in Indianapolis. By incredible coincidence, the young man who had spotted the red and silver pickup lived in the neighborhood. The youngster remembered seeing the same truck at the construction site. The young man's father called police and told them about the pickup. Sgt. Conner immediately contacted Deputy Yarnell. Yes, the deputy told Conner, the pickup truck belonged to a young man who had laid bricks for his new home. Yarnell identified the bricklayer as Steve Judy, who lived somewhere in southwest Indianapolis. Steve Judy! The name was very familiar to Indiana police.

The life of Steven T. Judy, 22 years old, was well-documented by various social agencies, mental institutions, police departments and courts and jails in the states of Indiana and Illinois. Judy was currently free on bond, having been arrested a little more than a week before on charges of holding up a grocery store; the armed robbery rap was the least of Judy's transgressions in a violent criminal history that stretched back ten years.

When Steve Judy was 12 years old, a cherubic-appearing youngster with a winning smile, he had posed as a Boy Scout and gone to a house near his home in Indianapolis. The boy asked the woman who answered the door if she would consider buying some Boy Scout cookies.

After being admitted to the house, the slim youth innocently asked if the woman's husband was home. The housewife had no reason to feel threatened by a mere child. But when she replied that she was alone in the house, Judy was suddenly upon her like a frenzied animal. The disbelieving young woman was forced into a bedroom where she was raped and stabbed repeatedly with a pocket knife. When the knife blade broke off in her sternum, the youngster went to the kitchen in search of a sturdier weapon. The terrified woman, in excruciating pain and bleeding profusely from 41 knife wounds, one of which completely severed her left index finger, managed to reach a bureau drawer where her husband kept a small hatchet.

Judy returned, seized the hatchet, and struck the woman four times across the head, laying open her skull. After weeks in the hospital and brain surgery, the victim survived the attack to testify at Judy's capital murder trial nine years later.

Indiana juvenile authorities sent Judy to Bahr Clinic, the youth division of Indiana Central State

Hospital in Indianapolis. Because of Judy's tender years and juvenile status at the time of his hospitalization, the records of his stay at Central State are confidential. The public may never know how the doctors diagnosed a 12-year-old who had committed a vicious sexual assault and attempted murder. It is known that Judy was released to live with foster parents in less than nine months, shortly after his 13th birthday. Judy would claim later, after he became a condemned killer, that he first cried out in vain for help during this period. But his foster parents, as seemingly demonstrated by their actions during Judy's legal problems, were attentive and loving to the end. Judy apparently recognized and returned their affection but had only bitter memories of his early childhood with his natural parents. "I remember my mom trying to shoot my dad . . . and my dad beating hell out of my mother," Judy said.

Judy's adult arrest was in the summer of 1975. He was convicted of nearly beating a woman to death in Naperville, Illinois, a far west Chicago suburb. Judy had the woman down on a street, repeatedly slamming her head with his fists. Passersby intervened, probably saving the victim's life. Judy, now 20 years old, served 20 months for the crime and was paroled in March, 1977.

Less than a month later, Judy was again violently molesting women. Back in Indianapolis, he jumped into a young woman's car and forced her to drive south, ironically taking almost the same route that the doomed Chasteen family would take two years later. At Waverly, Indiana, only eight miles southeast of the bridge over White Lick Creek, the young woman managed to jump from the vehicle. Judy was arrested a short time later and charged with kidnaping, vehicle theft and commission of a felony while armed. A trial ended in a hung jury; Judy pleaded guilty to a lesser charge of theft and was sentenced to one year in prison. Judy, however, was given credit for time served in jail awaiting trial, released from Indiana custody and sent to Illinois as a parole violator. There, through some bureaucratic snafu, Judy was set free a year early. He returned to Indianapolis.

Late Sunday afternoon, April 29th, Judy was arrested at his foster parents' home in southwest Indianapolis and transported to the Morgan County jail at Martinsville. Upon his arrest, Judy exhibited the combination of fatalism and cockiness that would characterize the young man's behavior to the end. According to his foster parents, Judy had returned to their home at midday Saturday, cleaned the inside of his colorful pickup truck and threw "some old wire or something" away. This information would fit the theory detectives ultimately developed about how Terry Chasteen and her three children met their deaths. The suspect himself would later confirm most of the details of the investigators' theory on the witness stand.

On Monday, April 30th, Sgt. Conner went to the Morgan County jail to interrogate Judy. By this time, Judy had been assigned a public defender and was keeping quiet on the lawyer's advice. Conner clearly remembers the meeting with Judy. The young murder suspect was "cocky," Conner recalls, and casual, confident. Judy did not look like a vicious killer, Conner thought. He was 5 foot, 9 inches tall, stocky and broad-shouldered; his brownish blond hair was conservatively trimmed, although unkempt. Judy's thin-lipped, toothy smile was marred by over-size incisors which gave his face an impish — devilish — aspect.

"I got nothing to say," the boyish suspect responded to each of Sgt. Conner's questions.

Conner left Judy in his cell. The investigator was confident that the seriousness of the charges against the young man would keep him there.

Now, just two days after the Chasteen bodies were found, Prosecutor Gray began to assemble the state's case against Steven Judy. With court orders, Judy's clothing would be seized, the young man would be compelled to give up hair and blood samples and his memorably outlandish pickup truck would be impounded and gone over bolt and screw by crime lab technicians.

There would be months of maneuvering by the prosecution and defense. Judy would fire his first court-appointed attorney and replace him with Steven L. Harris, considered one of the best lawyers in Morgan County. Harris hoped to prove Judy innocent by reason of insanity, a defense anticipated by Prosecutor Gray from the beginning.

Finally, in January, 1980, the murder trial of Steven Judy began in the remodeled main courtroom of the Morgan County Courthouse at Martinsville. Special Judge Jeffrey Boles of the Hendricks, Indiana Circuit Court presided over the four-week trial.

Gray and the investigators had amassed formidable technical and circumstantial evidence against

39

Judy. There were the eyewitnesses who had seen the pickup truck matching the description of Judy's vehicle parked near White Lick Creek at the approximate time of the murders; tests had determined that Judy's blood type matched semen stains found on Terry Chasteen's topcoat; threads found on Judy's confiscated clothing were microscopically identical to threads making up the material of Terry Chasteen's torn smock blouse; hairs found in Judy's truck were microscopically identical to the brown hair of Terry Chasteen; casts taken of tread marks at the scene matched the tires on Judy's pickup.

Much of the testimony given by the state's 56 witnesses would be highly technical. In an effort to avoid confusing or, worse, alienating the jury, the prosecutor carefully rehearsed several key witnesses, including I.S.P. crime lab chief Bill Kuhn.

But Steven Judy turned out to be the best prosecution witness of all. Judy began to exhibit publicly his determined death wish during the trial. The defendant took the stand in the last week of the proceedings and, in a soft, unemotional voice, he recounted for the jury, spectators and the news media exactly how he met and killed Terry Chasteen and her children.

Judy told the hushed courtroom of driving aimlessly around Indianapolis early the morning of April 28. He had dropped his girlfriend off a few hours earlier, he said, but didn't feel like going home to bed. On southbound Interstate 465 he spotted an attractive woman driving a nice red car. Judy said he pulled alongside the woman and pointed urgently to her tires, hoping she would believe she was about to have a flat. The trick worked.

Terry Chasteen pulled onto the shoulder of the highway and stopped. In the ensuing few minutes, Judy said he managed to raise the hood of Terry Chasteen's car and rip out the ignition coil. When the woman tried to leave, the car wouldn't start. Judy offered to drive Terry and her kids to a gas station. Terry, still trusting the good-looking Samaritan, accepted the offer, herded her three kids into Judy's pickup and crawled in beside them. As soon as Judy was gathering speed down I-465, he turned to the young woman and said, "I guess you know what's going to happen now?" The kindness had gone from his voice; his manner was no longer solicitous.

Terry Chasteen — probably because she feared for the children's safety — made little protest as Judy exited the Interstate and picked up southbound Indiana Highway 67. In a few minutes, the pickup was pulling into the muddy access road at White Lick Creek. Judy walked the woman down to the creek bank. The children, still not frightened, thanks to their mother's cool-headed courage, scurried happily in tow.

At a spot where the creek bank dropped sharply to the water's edge, Judy stopped and sent the kids downstream to play. He turned to the badly frightened but still composed young woman and ordered her to remove her clothes. She was forced to lie on her topcoat while Judy raped her. When Terry Chasteen could endure the torment and fear no longer, she began screaming. Judy tore her smock, gagged her with it and, when she continued screaming,

41

stilled her forever by strangling her.

The kids had come running at the sound of their mother's hysterics and stood around Judy, screaming and crying. Judy told the court: "It all seems so unreal . . . like my head was in a barrel . . ." There was no other sound in the courtroom except Judy's monotonous, droning voice as he described how he picked the children up one by one and threw them in the creek. He said he glanced over his shoulder once and saw one of the little boys struggling to stand up in the creek. "I walked away," he said.

Judy, incredibly, threatened both the judge and the jury from the witness stand: "You better put me to death," he said, "because next time it might be one of you . . . or your daughter."

At one point, the young woman Judy had savagely attacked when he was 12 years old was called to the witness stand. When Prosecutor Gray asked the woman if she still suffered from the ordeal, she raised her left hand and showed jurors the stub of her index finger. A woman juror became faint at the sight and had to be helped from the courtroom.

On Feb. 16, 1980, Steven Judy was found guilty of four counts of first degree murder and sentenced to die in Indiana's electric chair. On February 25th, Judy was transported to Death Row, housed in the monolithic, 100-year-old state prison at Michigan City, on the northern border of Indiana.

During the next year, Judy would thwart every effort to appeal his death sentence. Pros. Gray would defend the state's right to execute Judy and his belief in the justice of capital punishment in this case. Lawyers from the American Civil Liberties Union came to Indianapolis, attempted to file briefs on Judy's behalf and, failing, held news conferences and appeared on TV talk shows. Gray would debate ACLU lawyer Henry Schwartzchild on television the night before Judy's scheduled execution.

One hour before midnight on March 8, 1981, Judy sat down to a requested last meal of prime ribs, lobster tails, baked potatoes and chef's salad with French dressing. Prison officials refused Judy's request for four cans of beer. The condemned man's lawyer, Steven Harris, said Judy cried a little as the execution hour approached but calmed down after taking a Valium tablet provided for him by the prison doctor. While demonstrators — for and against the death penalty — marched outside the massive prison walls, Judy calmly walked the traditional 13 steps to the waiting, hand-made wooden electric chair. At 12:11 a.m. Central Standard Time, Warden Jack Ducksworth ordered the switch thrown. Witnesses stated that Judy lurched against the straps and his fists clenched as 2,300 volts of electricity surged through his body for ten seconds. This was immediately followed by a second jolt of 500 volts for twenty seconds. Steven Judy was dead.

Prison spokesman Tom Hanlon reported Judy's last words: "I don't hold no grudges. This is my doing. I'm sorry it happened."

A few weeks after his execution, Judy's foster mother reported that Judy had told her that he had raped and killed more women than he could remember. He allegedly said there was a "string of bodies" across Texas, Florida, Louisiana, Illinois and Indiana. Authorities are expected to investigate these

43

claims.

The woman told reporters at a press conference that Judy had "frequent urges to attack women" because he "considered them stupid and gullible. He said every woman he attacked he raped. Every woman he ever bothered, he either tricked them into pulling off the road, or he started to help them as they were stopped on the road."

While he was on the witness stand during his trial for the Chasteen murders, he admitted to 13 to 15 rapes.

His foster mother told newsmen that she wanted the world to know about Judy's confession because she was afraid other men might be executed for murders that Judy committed.

EDITOR'S NOTE:

Blake Sizemore is not the real name of the person so named in the foregoing story. A fictitious name has been used because there is no reason for public interest in the identity of this person.

RICHARD SPECK
"EIGHT GIRLS, ALL PRETTY, ALL NURSES, ALL SLAIN"
by W. T. Brannon

Shortly before 10 a.m., Thursday, July 14, 1966, the Chicago newspaper truck darted northward on Clark Street and jolted to a stop at the Belmont Avenue intersection just ahead of a bus. The bus driver grumbled a little, but halted behind the truck.

A bundle of papers was dropped off and the newsie hurried to open it. The headline was tall and black, visible even to the bus driver. He couldn't believe what he saw and he opened the door and got out for a better look.

Now, the bus riders were beginning to grumble. The driver, visibly shaken, held up a copy of the paper so that the passengers could see what had taken him away from his post behind the wheel.

Now the passengers, their gripes forgotten, streamed off the bus. They snatched up papers fast as the newsboy could pass them out. It was there in cold print, but they found it hard to believe. It was something they just couldn't take in.

Standing there on the street, before the open door of the bus, they read the sparse details. It had happened more than 20 miles away on the far southeast side in the 2300 block of East 100th Street. And the lone killer had escaped.

Somewhere on the streets of Chicago, he was at large, a menace to every woman who still lived. The men shuddered, some of the women wept as they filed back on the bus. They were like most other Chicagoans; they had become inured to the atmosphere of crime that had cloaked the city ever since the days of Capone.

They were blasé about gang killings and they had even learned to shrug off multiple slayings. But this was neither. It was mass murder—it was massacre. . . .

Harried Chicago police had their troubles. On Tuesday evening, July 12th, a fire hydrant was opened at Roosevelt Road and Throop Street, in a predominantly Negro district. As required by law, some policemen shut it off. A teenager opened it up again and he was arrested.

A minor riot erupted, some store fronts were kicked in and there was looting until police reinforcements restored order. The next night the weather had cooled—but tempers hadn't. The rioting flared anew, with bands of young hoodlums roving westside streets, breaking windows and looting.

After a hurried conference among top police officials, Deputy Superintendent James B. Conlisk ordered Plan 3 to go into effect at 6 p.m., Thursday. This meant that every man on the force would be working a 12-hour day, that the police department itself would operate on two 12-hour shifts instead of the usual three watches of eight hours.

Plans were quickly made for shifting 1,000 policemen to the riot-torn west side. In many areas, where the crime rate was low, one man would be withdrawn from every two-man squad. In most of the districts, this would make no difference.

Such a section was the neighborhood known as Jeffrey Manor, part of the larger area of the city called South Chicago. In Jeffrey Manor there are many single residences, homes of one and two stories.

It is a quiet area of friendly people where crime is unusual and violence is a virtual stranger. This was particularly true of the 2300 block of East 100th Street. On the south side of this block is a complex of town houses, six two-story units in one connected building.

Three of these—the one at the east end and the two adjoining it on the west—have been rented by South Chicago Community Hospital to house 24 student nurses, eight in each unit, because there was not enough room in the regular nurses' residence at the hospital. All 24 of the nurses were senior students or registered nurses taking graduate studies. In the third unit from the end lived a housemother, whose duty it was to supervise the coming and going of the young nurses, all in their early twenties.

Of all the streets in quiet Jeffrey Manor, this block probably was the most trouble-free, a section that seldom required police attention.

It was, that is, until Thursday, July 14th.

47

About six o'clock that morning, Commander Francis Flanagan, chief of Chicago homicide detectives, was getting ready to go to his office in the main police building on South State Street when the call came.

There was a lot of excitement in the town houses in the 2300 block of East 100th Street. At least one student nurse had been murdered. There had been several calls from residents of the area.

"What about the coroner?" Flanagan asked.

"He's been notified."

"And the crime lab?"

"They're on the way."

"Better call Dragel—he lives down this way," Flanagan said, referring to Director Daniel T. Dragel of the police crime lab. "I'm on my way."

Commander Flanagan himself lives in Jeffrey Manor and his home is only three blocks from the town houses. He knew the location well and he walked to the scene in about five minutes.

Already, two police cars were there and many residents, attracted by the unusual activity, had surrounded the end town house. As Flanagan started in the front door, he met Patrolman Daniel Kelly of the South Chicago District Station.

Kelly and Patrolman Leonard Ponne recognized Flanagan. Kelly pointed to a couch against the west wall of what was the downstairs living room. Face down lay the nude body of a young girl, a strip torn from a bedsheet tightly knotted about her neck.

"There are seven more upstairs," Kelly said.

"Seven more girls?"

"I know it's hard to believe," Kelly replied, strug-

48

gling to keep his composure. "Maybe you'd better take a look for yourself."

Flanagan did look. In the second floor hall outside the bathroom he found one body. The girl was in nightclothes that now were crimson. She apparently had been stabbed repeatedly and lay in a pool of her own blood.

Now in his twentieth year as a homicide detective, Flanagan is a veteran of 4,000 murder investigations in the city that has been called the crime capital of the world. After disputing that label for two decades, Flanagan wasn't so sure now.

Lines began creasing his normally good-natured features as he turned to his right and entered the bedroom at the end of the hall. Here he found three girls, stacked one upon another in the narrow floor space between the bunk bed and the door.

All these girls had been stabbed and a wide, irregular pool of blood surrounded them. Flanagan, who had been an Air Force pilot during World War II with 55 missions over Germany, was reminded of the gory slaughter in Nazi concentration camps.

The lines of his face deepening so that he was beginning to look much more than his 48 years, Flanagan backed out into the hall and turned left into the adjoining bedroom. Three more bodies of young women lay before his disbelieving eyes.

One was on a bed against the wall. Two others, piled one upon the other, were on the floor between the bed and the dresser. The girl on the bed had been strangled with a strip from a bedsheet and had been stabbed in the left breast.

One of the other girls had been strangled. The

49

other had been strangled, stabbed in the back, in the left eye and in the back of the neck.

Despite his wide experience, Commander Flanagan found this almost beyond belief. He turned away from the corpses, back to Patrolman Kelly. "Tell me all you know about it," he said.

Kelly gave this account:

Several persons in the neighborhood were up early that morning. In addition to the complex of six town houses in one building, there was a building at each end of the block containing three town house units. In one of these lived Mrs. Alfred Windmiller, who awoke about an hour earlier than usual that morning—around six o'clock.

She heard what she thought was a woman screaming and told her husband. He thought it was one of the neighborhood kids. But Mrs. Windmiller didn't agree and quickly dressed.

From the other end of the block, a nurse, Judy Dykton, who was acquainted with the students, heard the screaming, too. She ran to the end unit, looked in and saw the nude body on the couch in the living room and ran back to phone police and tell the house mother, Mrs. Laura Bisone.

When Mrs. Windmiller went downstairs, she encountered Robert Hall, 52, a supervisor at a steel mill and a resident of one of the townhouse units. He was out early walking his dog. Now, both heard the screaming and they hurried to the end unit of the six-unit complex.

A dark-haired girl in nightclothes stood on the second floor balcony-like ledge just outside a window from which the screen had been kicked out. She was screaming:

"Help me! Help me! They're all dead. Oh, God! I'm the last one alive on the sampan!" She kept repeating variations of this, sometimes in accented English, sometimes in English so broken it was difficult to understand. Only Miss Dykton knew that the girl was a Filipino and that some of what she was screaming was in her native dialect. Miss Dykton knew she was Corazón Amurao, 23.

"Don't jump!" Mrs. Windmiller cried. "Go back inside and take the stairs and come out the back door."

In addition to Miss Dykton, others in the neighborhood, hearing the girl's hysterical plea for help, had telephoned POlice 5-1313 and the alarm had gone out from the communications center.

Both Mrs. Windmiller and Mr. Hall ran back onto 100th Street and flagged down Patrolman Kelly, who happened to be passing. They quickly told him what little they knew and he, too, saw the girl cringing on the balcony. He shouted for her not to jump and told her he would come inside.

Pausing only to radio the South Chicago police station and ask for help, Kelly tried the front door and found it locked. As he hurried around to the rear, another police car, hailed by Hall, skidded to a stop. Patrolman Leonard Ponne got out.

Kelly had noticed that a screen had been removed from a rear window, but when he tried the back door, he found it unlocked. He entered a kitchen, where he noticed nothing unusual except a sink full of dirty dishes.

He went on through another door into the living

51

room. His glance quickly took it in. Across on the other side was the front door he had tried earlier. To the far right was the stairway leading to the second floor. To the right near the wall was a U-shaped writing desk. In one corner was a TV set.

But what caught Kelly's eye was against the left wall—a two-cushion, reddish orange davenport. Sprawled across it face down was the nude body of a girl. For a moment, Kelly just stood and stared in stunned silence.

Then he strode to the couch, checked to see if there was any chance of saving the girl's life. There was no pulse, the flesh was clammy, but he couldn't tell how long the girl had been dead.

Kelly's wife is a nurse at South Chicago Community Hospital. She was acquainted with all the students and Kelly himself knew some of them. Now, he lifted the head and suffered more shock. He recognized the dead girl as Gloria Jean Davy, 23. Before his marriage, he had dated her as well as her sister; he was acquainted with the family, whose home was in Dyer, Indiana, a small city a few miles across the state line and in the Chicago metropolitan area.

Was the killer still in the building? Was that why the girl was out on the balcony screaming? Patrolman Kelly drew his gun, then called to Patrolman Ponne whose voice he could hear outside.

"Get in here, Lennie," he shouted. "A girl's been killed. Maybe the guy's still in the building."

Ponne hurried into the room, took one look at the dead girl and his mouth dropped open. He, too, quickly drew his service revolver.

"I'll go upstairs, you take the basement," Kelly

said.

Both men moved cautiously in opposite directions. But when Kelly had discovered the other seven slain girls, he shouted in a hoarse voice for Ponne, who had found nothing in the basement.

The girl who had cried out the alarm now was framed in the window of one of the bedrooms. Kelly helped her inside.

"Do you know who did this?" he asked.

"One man," she replied in her accented English. She said he was a man she didn't know. But he had killed all her friends.

"Can you describe him? Tell me what he looks like?" Kelly pressed desperately, realizing that the girl was in shock, that she was near hysteria and might crack up at any moment.

She obviously tried hard and she came up with a description: The man was about 25, he weighed about 170 pounds and he had a crew cut. She wasn't sure about the color of his hair—it could have been brown to black. He wore a dark waist-length jacket and dark pants and a white T-shirt. She couldn't remember anything else. And she wanted to get away from this house of horror.

Patrolman Ponne escorted her to the town house unit two doors to the west, where she was turned over to the housemother, Mrs. Bisone. Kelly radioed the description to the communications center.

"I'll want to talk to her," said Commander Flanagan, "but first I'd better call in."

He went outside, where the gathering crowd was growing with each passing moment. The street now was jammed with police cars from which uniformed patrolmen and plainclothes detectives were hurrying toward the town house unit.

In the forefront was Lieutenant John Griffith, commander of the homicide and sex crime unit at Area 2 Detective Headquarters at 92nd and Cottage Grove Avenue, only a short distance away. With him were veteran homicide Detectives Byron Carlisle and Jack Wallenda.

The detectives and patrolmen gently but firmly urged the crowd back and quickly barricaded the area from the sidewalk in front, around the east side of the building to the driveway in the rear. Here, fresh skid marks were visible. Had the killer parked directly behind the town house unit he invaded, then made a fast getaway in a car?

Lieutenant Griffith quickly paired off detectives in teams and sent them to question people in the crowd and anybody who hadn't left his home in the immediate vicinity.

Meanwhile, from the nearest car radio, Commander Flanagan contacted Central Headquarters. He was told that Superintendent of Police Orlando W. Wilson had been notified at his home, as had Chief of Detectives Otto Kreuzer and Dr. Andrew J. Toman, Cook County coroner. Portable crime labs with 10 technicians were on the way.

As he broke the connection, Flanagan turned to Patrolman Kelly and said: "Let's talk to the girl."

She was in the town house two doors away, being comforted by the house mother, Mrs. Bisone. Realizing that she held a possible key to the killer's identity, the attractive, dark-haired, dark-eyed Filipino girl composed herself with some effort and gave

Flanagan this account of what had happened:

Late Wednesday evening—she didn't know the exact time, but it was around 11 o'clock—she had changed into her nightclothes and was ready for bed. She sat in the smallest bedroom with her friend and roommate, Merlita Gargullo, 23, who had just come from the hospital. There was a rap on the door and Miss Amurao got up to open it.

A tall young man stood there, a knife in one hand, a revolver in the other. "I'm not going to hurt you," he said. "I need your money to get to New Orleans."

Miss Amurao backed away as he stepped across the threshold.

"I'm not going to hurt you," he repeated. "I just want your money."

Gesturing with the gun and knife, he ordered the girls out into the hall and directed them to go into the next bedroom, where there were four other girls. All six were told to lie face down on the floor.

Faced with the gun and knife, the girls complied. He pulled a sheet off one of the beds and expertly tore it into strips, which were used to bind the girls' wrists. In addition to Miss Amurao and Miss Gargullo, the others tied up were Patricia Matusek, 20, whose home was in Chicago; Pamela Wilkening, 20, of suburban Lansing; Nina Schmale, 24, of Wheaton, a suburb to the west; and Valentina Pasion, 23, of the Philippines.

The intruder had barely finished tying up the six girls when there was a noise downstairs as the front door opened and closed. Then the captive girls could hear the voice of Gloria Jean Davy, 23, a brunette beauty who was president of the Student Nurses' Association of Illinois, as she talked on the house phone in the kitchen and told the house mother that she was home safe from a date.

She came upstairs, only to be greeted by the man with the knife and gun. He ordered her to lie down with the other girls. He did and he bound her wrists.

He talked to the girls in a slow, pleasant voice, again assuring them that he did not intend to harm them. While he was talking the front door opened and two more girls came in. One was Suzanne Farris, 22, who lived in the town house. The other was Mary Ann Jordan, also 22, a student nurse who was visiting.

There was more than the usual bond of friendship between the two girls. Mary Ann's brother was engaged to be married to Suzanne. Mary Ann normally slept in the nurses' residence near the hospital, but she had obtained permission to visit tonight with Suzanne in the town house. She would spend the night.

The girls went into the kitchen, phoned the house mother and told her they were in for the night. They went upstairs to their bedrooms and changed to nightclothes. Then the man with his knife and gun appeared and herded them in with the other girls — nine in all, now.

The young man seemed in no hurry. He told the girls again that he was not going to harm them, that he merely had tied them up until he could get their money, which he needed to make his way to New Orleans.

Whether they believed him or not, they kept quiet and didn't scream. Miss Amurao didn't believe him;

she was terrified and kept thinking of what she might do to escape.

The young man stood up, gestured to one of the girls, and led her out of the room. He was gone a few minutes, then came back and escorted a second girl out of the room. By this time, Miss Amurao was convinced that their lives were in danger. She managed to roll under the bunk bed, out of sight. She huddled there against the wall, scarcely daring to breathe. She was aware of the man as he made other trips out of the room, each time leading one of the girls.

She wondered when he would miss her and start looking. But miraculously, he didn't. She lay quiet, still too terrified to make a move, and the night passed. Was the man still in the house? What had happened to her friends?

In one of the rooms, an alarm clock went off. She knew it was five o'clock. It went off every morning at that time to awaken some of the students who had to report at the hospital early.

Miss Amurao thought if the man was still in the house that he surely would be frightened by the alarm clock. She listened as it ran down and stopped and she stayed under the bed for another half hour trying to detect some sound of movement.

But there was none and she decided now that it was safe to try to get out and find out what had happened. She struggled with her bonds and finally her wrists were free. She crawled out from under the bed and walked soundlessly out into the hall. The body of a nurse lay half in, half out of the bathroom door.

She looked into a bedroom and saw three more bodies. In the front bedroom were three more. She stepped over them, kicked out the screen and stepped out onto the balcony where she began crying for help.

She bit back the tears as she concluded her account, forcing herself to remain composed until Flanagan had finished writing his notes.

"Do you think you'll know this man if you ever see him again?" the homicide chief asked.

She said she was sure she would.

"Is there anything else you can think of?" Flanagan asked.

Yes, she said; she was sure that the man had been drinking heavily before he invaded the town house. The stale odor of alcohol created a stench every time the man talked.

She repeated the description she already had given Patrolman Kelly. There still was confusion about the color of the stranger's hair, perhaps because of the survivor's overwrought condition.

Meanwhile, hospital authorities had been notified of the savage slaughter and an official hurried to the scene. He said he thought Miss Amurao should be in a room in the hospital and that he would arrange for it.

"Okay, we'll get her over there," the homicide chief replied. "But since she is the only known witness, her life may be in danger. The killer may try to get at her, even in a hospital room. We must see that she's fully protected."

The hospital official explained why the girls had been in the town house, some seven blocks north of the hospital. He said that the nurses' residence was full and that some outside quarters had to be found. It had been decided to put only girls in their senior year or graduate students in the town houses, because they were more mature and they would be in less danger than younger girls.

However, because of the character of the neighborhood and its low crime rate, none of the hospital officials had suspected the girls were in danger. A house mother supervised the three units in each of which were eight students.

Among those living in the end unit, he said, were three Filipino girls. Each was a graduate of a nursing school in the Philippine Republic and each had come to Chicago for graduate study under the State Department's exchange program. Miss Amurao and the two others—both slain—in the end unit had begun their duties at the South Chicago Hospital on June 5th. He said there were many other Filipino nurses in Chicago, over 100 distributed among 10 hospitals.

When Commander Flanagan went back outside, he discovered that the area was crawling with policemen. Director Dan Dragel of the crime lab was there with 10 of his technicians and they already had started dusting likely surfaces for fingerprints.

From the evidence, said Dragel, it appeared that the killer had come in the back by removing a screen and had left via the rear door which Patrolman Kelly had found unlocked.

From the start, the technicians began to develop prints. They were all over the place and undoubtedly many had been made by the victims.

Their prints would be taken for later comparison

and elimination, but first, the hapless girls received the attention of Dr. Toman, and his battery of six pathologists—Drs. David Petty, John Belmonte, Edwin Hirsch, James W. Henry, Walter John Miller and Eugene H. Tapia.

They entered the building with Dr. Toman a hospital employee, and homicide Detectives Carlisle and Wallenda. They began a careful, professional preliminary examination after each girl had been identified by the hospital employee.

Meanwhile, Deputy Chief of Detectives Michael Spiotto, who would have overall direction, with Flanagan, of the entire investigation, had arrived. First, he took a look at the carnage. Then he went back outside to talk to Flanagan and plan the investigation.

Now, after a quick conference with Flanagan, it was decided that all leaves in the detective division would be canceled. Sixty men reporting for duty at Area 2 Detective Headquarters at eight o'clock that morning would be assigned to the case. They would be backed up by 80 other detectives to be detailed to Area 2 Headquarters from various other detective headquarters throughout the city.

It was also agreed that Spiotto and Flanagan would set up a command post in the Area 2 building. Here, on the sprawling second floor, additional telephones would be installed in the offices to be used by Spiotto and Flanagan as well as in other offices and the big assembly room that occupied a large part of the floor.

Already, reporters and photographers from five Chicago daily papers and from four television and radio networks were swelling the crowd outside the town house and the two veteran officials knew that more would be at the command post.

The place would be crowded, but they would make room. Both Flanagan and Spiotto, along with their boss, Superintendent Wilson, believe that a certain amount of publicity—bringing possible help from the public—is desirable. Wilson has proved this in his Crime-Stop program through which thousands of arrests have been made and as many crimes prevented with the help of alert citizens.

Perhaps publicity would help to solve this case, the worst slaughter in the modern-day history of Chicago, so they were prepared to release as much information as they could without jeopardizing their case.

Flanagan's order canceling leaves and Spiotto's order for 80 additional men to be sent to Area 2 were implemented in an incredibly short time.

When detectives appeared for morning roll call at eight o'clock—just two hours after the first news of the murders—20 of them were selected to canvass the immediate area.

Spiotto told them he believed that the killer was someone who knew there were eight girls in each town house unit.

"That's right," Flanagan agreed. "He was expecting eight—he didn't know an extra girl was going to come visiting and that's how he lost count. That's how one girl was able to survive."

Detectives Carlisle and Wallenda had talked to residents of the town house units and had been told that the walls were "paper thin." One woman had told them the walls were so thin she could hear her neighbor's TV as well as if it had been in her own room.

"The eight nurses who live in the second unit are on vacation and nobody's there," Carlisle added. "This fellow must have known that and picked the end unit deliberately. If there was any unusual noise, it wouldn't carry through the vacant unit to the third one where the house mother was."

"That means," said Spiotto, "that he probably has been watching the place. He might be a resident of the neighborhood, he might be a hobo who got off a train"—he pointed to the railroad tracks only five minutes' walk across a field—"or a bum who hangs around the taverns and happened to notice this place."

He suggested that some of the detectives begin their canvass at the city limits, 100th and Torrence Avenue, and that others concentrate on taverns and rooming houses in the area.

Armed with Miss Amurao's description of the killer, the detectives started out.

Inside the town house, Detectives Carlisle, Wallenda and others methodically checked the bedrooms. Each was in a state of wild disarray. Some of this could have been caused by last-minute struggles by the girl victims. But most of it undoubtedly had been caused by the killer as he ransacked drawers and searched every place where he thought he was likely to find money. Examination of the purses belonging to the nine nurses showed there was no money in any of them. Between them, Miss Amurao and her roommate had $31 and that was missing. How much was taken from the other purses was not known and probably never will be.

Detectives Carlisle and Wallenda had watched the pathologists as they removed the bindings from the wrists of each of the slain girls.

"The way he tied those girls up he had to know how to tie knots," Carlisle told Chief Spiotto. "They were good, square knots. Nobody could open them and he had their hands tied behind them the right way, with the front of the wrists against each other and the palms facing the sides."

"That's the way we handcuff prisoners," Wallenda added. "If you tie the hands with the palms straight down, they can work them around and twist their fingers enough to get at the rope."

"Not the way this guy did it," said Carlisle. "He must have been arrested in his time. A convict, probably. And he surely has been around rope."

"A seaman, maybe," Spiotto suggested.

Down the street, just across the next intersection to the east, less than half a block from the murder scene, was the hiring hall of a seaman's union. It would be a place for the canvassing detectives to ask a few questions.

One team of those detectives — Eugene Ivano, Edward A. Wielosinski, Edward A. Boyle and John T. Mitchell — already had picked up a lead that seemed worth following. At a filling station at 100th and Torrence, near the Indiana line, they had described the killer to the owner.

Yes, he told the detectives, a man who matched that description had come to the station Tuesday afternoon, carrying a brown plaid flight bag and a small brown overnight case. He explained that he had gone to Indiana when he heard of a job opening, but it had been filled.

The talkative young man, who spoke in a soft voice with a southern accent, said he now was looking for a place to stay. He said he had slept on the beach Sunday night and had stayed in a rooming house Monday night. But his room was taken when he got back from Indiana.

He asked permission to leave his bags at the filling station and the owner readily agreed. The young man showed up the next morning, Wednesday, claimed his bags and said he was going to check in at the Ship Yard Inn.

The detectives hurried to the Ship Yard Inn, whose clientele is mostly transients and seamen. The clerk said a man matching the description had checked in and paid $9 for a week's rent. Then he had made a call to a sister who lived in Chicago.

For some reason, unknown to the hotel personnel, the man had checked out Thursday, taking his bags. They had no idea where he had gone. He had used a name, but the detectives were reasonably sure it was fictitious.

Nevertheless, it was called in by radio to the Criminal Records section at central headquarters, where recently installed electronic devices make it possible to check out a record in moments. Word came back that there was no record for that name.

It was agreed among the detectives that the man might have gone back to the rooming house or that he might be in some tavern in the area. A radio call went out to the other canvassing teams to meet the first group.

The other teams were Lieutenant William Mc-Carthy, Detectives Carl R. Edenfield, Peter S. Vale-saresand, Joseph M. Dawson; Sergeant Victor A. Vrdyolak, Detectives William McHugh, Thomas Doyle and Arthur Robinson; Sergeant Michael E. Cleary, Detectives Thomas Kelleher, John Griffin and Joseph Nolan; Detectives James Madison, Robert R. Reynolds, James McDonough and William Tolliver.

They all went into a huddle to consider what the first team had discovered. It was agreed that a canvass of rooming houses and barrooms should be productive, so while the first group went on to the seamen's hiring hall near the nurses' town house, Lieutenant McCarthy led the group of 15 detectives on the canvass and the original four officers started for the hiring hall.

Before they went into the hall, they checked with Deputy Chief Spiotto, who told them of the square knots used by the killer to tie up the girls. The hiring hall seemed the logical place to look next.

Meanwhile, the surviving nurse had been escorted to South Chicago Community in a state of shock. She was heavily guarded in the convoy that took her. Two rooms had been made available, one for Miss Amurao and one for the police. She was put to bed and given heavy sedation, while a uniformed policeman took a seat in front of her door. Others waited in the room next door and detectives prowled the floors of the 300-bed hospital.

Detectives also were assigned to check the hospital's 600 employees, any one of whom could have known about the town house arrangement for student nurses and one of whom might have had some reason for invading the nurses' residence. Checking of employees began, but it had to be handled carefully. The hospital's routine must not be disrupted more than it already had been by the tragic news that now had most of the nurses, especially the students, in a state of nervous tension.

In other parts of Chicago, people were looking for a tall man who wanted to go to New Orleans. At the Delta Airlines ticket office in the Loop, a man was making reservations for New Orleans when the clerk noticed bloodstains on his shirt.

When he saw her staring at the stains, he fled. But police quickly nabbed him at nearby State and Madison Streets. He was questioned and satisfied the officers that he had not been near the murder scene. He also satisfactorily accounted for the bloodstain on his shirt. He said he panicked when he realized that he was the same general size as the killer, that he was going to New Orleans and that he had blood on his shirt.

He was cleared and released.

At the union hiring hall, the detectives made inquiries. They were told that a man matching the description had come in Monday and asked about a job as a seaman, saying he would like to get on a ship for New Orleans.

The only opening was on an ore boat operating out of Indiana Harbor. He went to see about that, but was too late. He returned to the union hall Tuesday and Wednesday. There was nothing for him, but he had made an application and it was kept on file. It showed that he had worked on Great Lakes ore ships as a laborer, but that he was learning to be a seaman.

His name was Richard F. Speck and clipped to his application was a passport-type photo of the kind produced by a 25-cent coin machine. Nevertheless, it was a good picture.

The union official, William O'Neill, said that Speck had come again Wednesday, but there still was nothing. He had left the phone number of his sister, who could be called if a job opening occurred.

Questioning others, the detectives were told that Speck had strolled over to Luella Park, directly behind the town houses, and loafed during the afternoon. The witnesses said it was not unusual for one or more of the student nurses to sunbathe in the yard behind the town houses. One speculated that this could have attracted Speck to the park, where he would have a good view of the girls if they did appear to sunbathe.

Since then, nobody had seen Speck.

Excited and believing they might be on the trail of the killer, the detectives reported to Deputy Chief Spiotto and Commander Flanagan. Both agreed it was a good lead. But the detectives were instructed that nothing was to be mentioned about it yet.

Plans for trapping Speck were carefully made. Spiotto ordered additional copies of the picture made so that one would be available to each of the 20 detectives assigned to this phase of the investigation. Then Spiotto checked the files at central headquarters; there was nothing on Speck.

But union officials said a more complete dossier, including fingerprints, could be obtained from the

National Maritime Commission in Washington. Spiotto took this up with Marlin W. Johnson, special agent in charge of the FBI office in Chicago.

"How's the fastest and best way to get that record?" the deputy chief asked.

Marlin said he would send a special agent to Washington by plane to pick up the dossier and prints. However, there was an airline strike on and the earliest reservation the agent could get was Friday morning, with a return Friday evening.

Meanwhile, at the hiring hall, a detective phoned Speck's sister and posing as a union official, told her to have her brother come to the hall as soon as she could get in touch with him.

At 3:10 that afternoon, a man phoned and identified himself as Richard Speck. The detective, still posing as a union official, told him there was a job for him and asked how soon he could get to the hall. Speck said he would be there within the hour.

Commander Flanagan was notified and the long wait for the goods began.

On a widespread front, other phases of the investigation were going on. The crime lab technicians had found more than 100 fingerprints and all but 36 had been matched up with those of the nine nurses. The remainder, some fragmentary, could not be identified.

Director Dragel and his men impatiently awaited Friday evening and the prints of Richard Speck from Washington. But they had much other work. From the town house, they had taken more than 125 items of possible evidence, in addition to bloodstained night garments removed from the slain girls, as well as many bloodsoaked uniforms, apparently stained when they were tossed out of closets and drawers by the ransacking killer.

At the Cook County morgue, relatives made tearful identifications of six of the student nurses. Friends had identified the Filipino girls. Then the pathologists had made their postmortem examinations and made their preliminary report:

Evidence indicated that none of the girls had been raped or sexually molested. The girls had died in this manner:

Miss Davy had been strangled. Miss Farris had died of stab wounds, as had Miss Jordan and Miss Gargullo. Miss Matusek had been strangled. Miss Farris, Miss Wilkening, Miss Schmale and Miss Pasion all had been stabbed and strangled.

Preliminary examination also indicated, the pathologists said, that none of the girls had been drugged. However, tissue tests would be made to determine this more definitely.

Scrapings were taken from under the fingernails of each of the victims. These would be examined by crime lab technicians to determine if any of the girls scratched the killer. This seemed unlikely, however, since all were bound.

When he talked to reporters after the eight murders, Dr. Toman called it "the crime of the century." He said it was the worst mass murder in Chicago since the St. Valentine's Day Massacre. On February 14, 1929, seven members of the Bugs Moran gang were lined up against the wall inside a garage on North Clark Street and shot to death. The massacre was attributed to the Al Capone gang, though this was never proved in court.

Commander Flanagan, haggard from the worry of the investigation and the fear that the killer, still at large, might strike again, was asked to comment for TV cameras. "What kind of a human being would do a thing like this? He's a sub-animal. I don't know who he is or where he is or how soon we'll get him. *But get him we will!*"

About 250 miles downstate, a truck driver reported that he had given a ride to a tall, blond young man who was hitchhiking his way to Louisiana. Roadblocks were set up by the state police and the young man was soon picked up.

But he was able to prove that he had not been in Chicago at the time the student nurses were murdered and he was released.

At the union hall, an hour passed and Richard Speck didn't show up. The detectives stayed there until the hall closed and he still had not put in an appearance. It was improbable that he would.

But the detectives under Lieutenant McCarthy had better luck. They found the rooming house where Speck had rented a room on Monday night. He had returned on Tuesday and the room was rented. But he had come back Tuesday night and had been permitted to sleep on a couch in the living room.

He hadn't been back for a room, but the manager said that he had spent a lot of time at a nearby tavern. The detectives went there and picked up Speck's trail. Armed with the pictures, they learned he had been at several taverns.

Finally, they came to one where he had been that day. He had left, but a man who had worked with him on an ore boat and who had drunk with him was found. He said Speck had tried to get him to go up on the north side where there was "some action," but refused.

He said this happened shortly after Speck had made two telephone calls. He thought one was to his sister; he didn't know what the other was. They had parted when Speck had taken a cab. Fortunately, he recalled the cab.

The detectives began the long, tedious search for the cabbie.

Even though this was the most spectacular case in their history, the Chicago police could not give it their undivided attention. For as night fell, the rioting flared again on the west side. Despite the presence of more than 1,000 cops, vandalism spread.

Scores of display windows were broken and looters invaded the stores, carting away nearly everything that wasn't nailed down. Gangs of young hoodlums, some armed with rocks, some with guns, attacked the police and frustrated them in their attempts to halt the vandalism and restore order.

In some sections, fires were started and as firemen fought the blazes the hoodlum gangs pelted them with rocks. It was not until the police moved in with riot guns that the firemen were able to bring the fires under control.

It was a wild, chaotic night for the Chicago police. Even with Plan 3 in operation with all police officers assigned to 12-hour shifts and many working around the clock, the force of some 12,000 officers was not enough.

Early Friday, Mayor Daley asked Governor Otto

Kerner for help. The governor promptly sent out a call for 3,000 National Guardsmen to report to the turbulent west side. Almost immediately, units began to mobilize and trucks rolled toward Chicago.

Friday was destined to be an eventful, unforgettable day for the Chicago police. Early that morning, the detectives under Lieutenant McCarthy—none had slept and all 20 had worked through the night—found the cabbie who had picked up Richard Speck. He said he had taken Speck to the 1300 block of North Sedgwick Street. He hadn't gone to any particular address and had been put out on the street with his bags. The fare was $5.90.

Since this was a neighborhood whose residents were predominantly Negro, Lieutenant McCarthy hoped that Speck's presence would have been noticed by someone. Commander Flanagan was notified of the latest development and Lieutenant McCarthy and his 19 men sped to the north side.

The 1200 block of North Sedgwick did not offer much hope. On the west side is a parking lot, on the east side a high school. But there were apartment buildings in both the 1100 and 1300 blocks. It was a tedious job, but Lieutenant McCarthy split the group and they began canvassing both blocks.

About that time, an FBI special agent left for Washington to pick up the dossier on Richard Speck.

Also about that time, Deputy Chief Spiotto was notified that Corazon Amurao had slept through the night, that she had awakened refreshed and that she could be questioned. Spiotto contacted Flanagan, Otis Rathel, a police artist assigned to the crime lab, and Detective Joseph Gonzales, who speaks Spanish and is attached to the crime lab.

Before he left central headquarters, Spiotto had picked up 180 mug shots of men in their twenties who had been suspected of crimes against women or who had served time and been released. Each matched the general description given by the survivor. Included in these 180 mug shots was one of Richard Speck, a copy of the picture obtained from the union hiring official.

Spiotto confined his questioning of Miss Amurao to the man's appearance. The girl was remarkably perceptive and was able to describe the killer's features as Rathel made quick strokes with his pencil. He determined the size of the face in the sketch by comparison with his own face—by asking if the face was larger or smaller than his, if it was longer or shorter, wider or narrower.

The facial expression was important, he told her. She said he looked like a man who wouldn't harm anybody; she said he had a very gentle appearance.

When the first sketch had been completed, Miss Amurao said the eyes looked too mean and she had him soften their expression. Then she suggested other changes. He used an eraser to wipe out the part to be changed, then drew it again. One change was in the mouth. Another was in the hair. She was vague about the color of what appeared to be a long crewcut, but with the help of Detective Gonzales, she conveyed the impression that the hair could best be described as "dishwater blond," a shade of light brown.

Finally, the sketch was completed and Miss Amurao said it looked like the killer. Rathel left and took the sketch to central headquarters, where Superintendent Wilson ordered it reproduced in 40,000 copies of the daily Police Bulletin. Of these, 20,000 would be for use of police officers in the Chicago area, the others would be distributed to law enforcement agencies throughout the country.

Other copies were made for immediate distribution to newspapers, wire services, television stations and networks.

After the artist had left, Deputy Chief Spiotto produced the mug shots and Miss Amurao began studying them.

On Sedgwick Street, meanwhile, Lieutenant McCarthy's detectives struck pay dirt in the first building they canvassed in the 1100 block. A woman living on the 12th floor of a highrise apartment building said she had been looking out the window with binoculars when she saw a cab stop in the 1300 block late Thursday afternoon. A tall, blond young man with two bags got out, paid the cabbie and the taxi left.

She watched as the young man strolled back to Division Street, which is 1200 north, then turned east. She was able to see him until he turned south in Dearborn Street. And, she told the officers, a tattoo "Born to Raise Hell" was plainly visible on his arm.

With this lead, the detectives began canvassing southward on Dearborn Street, where there are many small hotels and rooming houses and on Clark Street, which has many small hotels as well as an abundance of barrooms. This is the section that is best known as Chicago's vice strip.

Using the police sketch the detectives began asking

74

for Speck. In a tavern on North Clark Street, they encountered a man suspected of being a narcotics pusher. When they told him they were not looking for him on a narcotics charge, he seemed so relieved that he eagerly looked at the picture.

"Sure, I seen that guy in here, but he didn't stay long. I think he was looking for broads."

The man said he believed Speck had gone on to the next tavern. The detectives went there and encountered two more men with records of narcotics arrests. Both agreed that he had stayed there for some time, drinking and dancing and finally left with a prostitute they knew only as Mary.

But Mary wasn't there. She might be in any of the taverns along the street of she might be in a room in some hotel with a customer.

The detectives decided to try the Clark Street hotels.

At the hospital, Miss Amurao continued to look at mug shots, discarding one after another. She looked at 177 and there were only three left. Then Deputy Chief Spiotto slipped the three in front of her. Without hesitation, she pointed to the picture in the center.

It was the photo of Richard Speck.

"This is similar," she said. "Everything except the hair."

In the picture the hair was long. Miss Amurao remembered it as a long crewcut. But she was positive in her identification.

Deputy Chief Spiotto left and hurried to central headquarters, where he huddled with Superintendent Wilson, Chief of Detectives Kreuzer and Com-

75

mander Flanagan.

The resemblance between the picture of Speck and Rathel's drawing was remarkable. Already, phones at central headquarters and in numerous other police stations in Chicago were jangling. Many people thought they recognized the man in the sketch, which had been shown on TV and was now appearing in the afternoon papers.

All these calls were carefully checked out. But they didn't lead to Richard Speck.

The top brass debated whether to reveal the identity of the wanted man and decided against it for the time being. They would wait for the FBI agent to return from Washington. He was due back at seven o'clock.

The canvassing detectives came to a hotel on North Clark Street where the picture of Speck was recognized. He had come in Thursday evening with a prostitute known as Mary. The girl had left about midnight, Speck about 3 a.m. He apparently had a sleeping room somewhere else.

So the detectives started looking again, for Speck and for the girl named Mary. They finally found her and she cooperated. She admitted having gone to the hotel with Speck, said she had left about midnight, after paying her $3. She didn't know where he lived, but she thought it was at another place, because he'd had to register when they entered the hotel where she had entertained him.

The detectives kept inquiring and they found a habitué of a saloon with a four o'clock closing license who said he had seen the man in the picture. He had shown up a little after 3 a.m., and had left with a 40-

year-old Negro prostitute, whose price was $5. He didn't know where they had gone.

The weary detectives kept trying.

On the west side, the National Guard arrived in force. There were a few incidents of looting, but the presence of the armed men, whose orders were to shoot to kill if anyone shot at them, had its effect. Most of the troublemakers stayed under cover.

The FBI special agent phoned from Washington to say that he had Speck's dossier. It showed that he was an ex-convict, that he had been in trouble with the law when he was 18 and that he had a long record in Dallas, Texas. He was a native of Monmouth, Illinois. The agent said he expected to arrive on schedule.

But long before that time, the Chicago police were checking on the man who now had become their prime suspect. Records in Dallas showed that Speck had been convicted of forgery in 1963 and had been sent to prison for three years. He had been released on parole in January, 1965, and in a few months was in trouble again.

He had put a knife to the neck of a young woman as she parked her car late one night in the garage behind her home. She had screamed and a man living across the alley had shouted at Speck. He fled but was caught. He still had the weapon, a carving knife with a blade more than 17 inches long. He admitted threatening the woman and was convicted on a charge of aggravated assault. He was sentenced to serve 490 days in the county jail in Dallas.

However, he was sent back to the state prison at Huntsville as a parole violator, on June 16, 1965.

But he was released again 16 days later and didn't bother to return to serve his county jail sentence, though he did return to Dallas briefly for a visit to the home of his mother.

He held many laboring-type jobs, though none of them for very long. He wandered about the country and worked on ore boats on the Great Lakes. He had been married, but his wife had divorced him. He went back to Dallas for a visit in March, 1966, but soon left.

Next he showed up in Monmouth, Illinois, where he was born and attended the first grade. After the death of his father, his mother moved to Dallas and took him with her. He attended Dallas schools through the ninth grade.

An older brother had remained in Monmouth, where he has become a respected citizen. Dick Speck went to visit his brother, who got him a job as an apprentice carpenter and arranged for a place for him to live. But he didn't live there long, moving instead into a Monmouth hotel.

His principal pastime appeared to be hanging around Monmouth taverns where, according to his drinking companions, he was known as a woman chaser.

"He bragged about all the women he could get, but he never got a date with one," said one man. "He'd stare at a girl and then tell me: 'I'd like to meet her.' Girls would talk to him, dance with him, but he never got a date with one."

The last week he was in Monmouth was eventful. On April 10th, Mrs. Mary Pierce, a divorcee who was a barmaid at a tavern where Speck drank, disappeared. Three days later, her nude, beaten body was found in a hogpen on a lot behind the tavern.

Five days later, a 65-year-old woman was raped and robbed. Police Chief Harold Tinder wanted to question Speck, but when he went to the hotel, Speck had left suddenly. Chief Tinder said he still wanted to question Speck about the Monmouth rape and murder.

Maritime records showed that Speck had gone to work on a Great Lakes ore boat shortly afterward. He had been fired from one job and had obtained another. While at work on this boat on May 3rd, Speck had become violently sick and had been rushed to St. Joseph Hospital in Hancock, Michigan.

He had an appendix that was about to rupture and quick surgery saved his life. During his recuperation he became acquainted with and dated one of the nurses. When he was well enough, he left and took another ore boat job. The nurse said he wrote her many letters from Sault Sainte Marie and Chicago.

A month later, he came to visit her and she noticed a change. "He was still gentle, but he had a hatred in him," she said. Once, she said, he told her about two people in Texas he didn't like and if he ever got the chance, he would kill them.

She said she had last seen him on June 27th. "For some reason, I thought of him when I heard about the girls," she said. "Then I felt bad for even thinking it."

The records showed that Speck had been fired from his job on the ore boat when it was at Indiana Harbor on July 2nd. Only a short distance away that same day, three girls who had gone to the Indiana Dunes Park for an outing mysteriously disappeared. They were in swimsuits and left behind were their purses, their personal belongings and a car belonging to one of them. A week-long widespread search failed to turn up the missing girls. They are still missing.

In Benton Harbor, Michigan, less than 50 miles away, four females were murdered. They were of four generations: One was seven, one was 19, another was 37, the other was 60. One was found in an abandoned building in February, 1966. The others all were found on the same day in April, their bodies within 200 feet of each other. Some had been strangled, one had been slashed from breastbone to pelvis, another had been decapitated.

The killer is still at large, but when the Benton Harbor police learned of the murders of the eight girls, they suspected that the same man could be responsible.

By the time the Chicago police had learned all this, it was decided to set the entire department to looking for the fugitive. That was after the FBI agent had returned and handed the dossier on Richard Speck to Crime Lab Director Dan Dragel.

Dragel immediately assigned Lieutenant Emil G. Giese and Sergeant Hugh Granahan to begin their comparisons — Speck's prints against the unidentified prints found at the town house where the eight girls were slain. Dragel told them to notify him if they learned anything.

Meanwhile, the order to look for Speck was received at the Chicago Avenue police station. Somebody recalled a report that had been turned in that morning, as the result of a call from a small hotel on Dearborn Street. A prostitute had left a man's room about seven that morning and had stopped at the desk. She had told the manager the man she had been with had a gun. The manager reported this to the Chicago Avenue police station and two patrolmen were sent to the man's room.

He gave his name as Richard Speck and readily produced a .22-caliber revolver and six cartridges. He said the gun was not his, that it belonged to the woman who had just left. The officers took the gun and ammunition, which were inventoried at the station about nine o'clock Friday morning.

At the time, they had not heard the name Speck and they didn't connect it with the slaughter of the eight nurses. Now they did. Lieutenant McCarthy and his men, still canvassing the area—they were only a short distance from the hotel—were notified.

They immediately surrounded the hotel and one detective went in. The manager said Speck was registered there and his rent had been paid up for a week. But he had left about 30 minutes before, carrying a bundle and saying casually that he was going out to a laundromat.

The hotel was staked out and hours passed. Speck didn't return. His room was searched and the clothing Miss Amurao had described—a black jacket, black pants and a T-shirt—were there. They were on hangers and they had been freshly laundered.

The stakeout was maintained through the night and continued Saturday morning. But Speck did not appear.

Meanwhile, the Philippine consul in Chicago had visited Miss Amurao and she had cleared up a point that had puzzled investigators ever since the eight bodies were found: Why hadn't the girls screamed? Why hadn't they ganged up on him and tried to fight him off?

Miss Amurao said that after the first girl had been led from the room—to be killed, as it later developed—the eight who remained had discussed this. The three Filipino girls wanted to scream and fight. But the American girls didn't.

"Maybe if we are quiet and calm, he will be quiet and calm," Miss Amurao quoted one of the American girls.

"But they were wrong," she said. "They were too trusting." Then she added: "But the other girls said they were sure that he would not harm anyone. They said: 'We more or less have to trust him. If we keep quiet, maybe he won't do something crazy.' "

Miss Amurao hadn't agreed with this and after the second girl had been led away, she rolled under the bunk bed and hid, saving her own life.

The fingerprint technicians worked until early morning and they found four prints that matched those of Speck on at least 12 points—the legal requirement. When they were sure, Director Dragel was notified. That was about 4:30 a.m. Saturday.

Dragel contacted Commander Flanagan who was out on the street, directing the manhunt. He hadn't slept since the crime broke and he was haggard and weary, but his spirit was undaunted.

As soon as he had the news, he called Lieutenant Griese and said: "You boys have done it again!

Great work."

Some of the identified prints had come from the door to the bedroom where the girls had been held captive. Dragel and some of his men immediately drove to the town house, which had been sealed and guarded by the police. The door was removed and preserved as evidence.

During that Saturday morning, there was a lot of discussion among the top brass as to whether the identity of the suspect should be publicly disclosed. They all had in mind recent Supreme Court decisions about publicity and its effect on a fair trial.

Finally, when Speck hadn't returned to his room by early afternoon and it became clear that he didn't intend to, Superintendent Wilson decided to ask the help of the public. At 2:40 p.m., he went before the television network cameras and announced that Richard Speck had been identified by the police as the killer. He said the police had enough evidence to convict him and that the survivor had identified his picture.

In the dossier brought from Washington was the information that there were tattoos on both of Speck's arms. The outstanding one was an inscription on the left arm: BORN TO RAISE HELL.

Then Superintendent Wilson held up a picture of Speck. He said he was sure this was the right man.

The picture was published in all Chicago papers and in newspapers throughout the country. But hours passed and there was no trace of Richard Speck. Had he left the city or the state?

U.S. Attorney Edward Hanrahan went before a federal judge and obtained a fugitive warrant on the theory that the suspect had left the state. This provided federal jurisdiction and the FBI immediately entered the case.

Even so, Speck might have escaped attention had it not been for the publicity given the hunt for him. A young man in a skid row hotel on West Madison Street apparently attempted suicide by cutting a vein on his left arm and on his right wrist. This happens so often in skid row hotels that it has become routine. Two patrolmen took the man to County Hospital, where he was wheeled to the trauma ward to be treated by Dr. Smith, a resident. Only a short time before, Dr. Smith had read of the identification of Speck and the search for him. He had noted the photograph and had read about the tattoos.

Now, as he looked down at his new patient, he thought the face was familiar. He looked at the right arm and saw a tattoo. But the left arm was covered with blood.

"Bring me a copy of a newspaper," he told Nurse Kathy O'Connor.

While she was away, he moistened a finger and rubbed some of the blood away. The letter "B" emerged. Then, Dr. Smith rubbed off more blood and a whole tattoo — Born To Raise Hell — was visible.

Nurse O'Connor returned with the paper and they compared the picture with the face of the patient, who had been listed as B. Brian, the name of the skid row hotel-register.

"What's your name?" Dr. Smith asked.

"Richard," the man replied and as Dr. Smith waited: "Richard Speck." Then, after a pause: "Are you going to get the $10,000 reward?"

84

Dr. Smith didn't answer this and he didn't question Speck further. "Get the police," he told nurse O'Connor.

There was a policeman in the hospital and he made the arrest. Then headquarters was notified.

From that moment on, the authorities literally walked on eggs to be sure they didn't violate any of the guidelines laid down by the Supreme Court's June decision about interrogation of prisoners.

Speck was heavily guarded and as soon as he had been given emergency treatment, he was moved to the Bridewell Hospital adjacent to the county jail. It was then early Sunday morning. Prosecutor Ward planned to take Speck into court on Monday morning on a charge of murdering one girl.

But doctors at the hospital said Speck was too weak and the hearing was postponed. Nevertheless, the murder warrant was issued. Miss Amurao was taken to the hospital and remained outside for 2½ hours, but she wasn't permitted to see Speck. She was returned to South Chicago Hospital under heavy guard.

Later, doctors said Speck had suffered a minor heart attack and it might be three weeks before he could appear in court. Meanwhile, as his condition improved, Miss Amurao was taken into his room. She left after five minutes and said: "That is the man."

At the request of Speck's relatives, Public Defender Gerald Getty was appointed to defend him. Getty has hinted that he will enter an insanity plea.

As this is written, Richard Speck is still in the closely guarded Bridewell Hospital and further legal action against him is pending. Meanwhile, the Chicago police have been widely acclaimed for the heads-up police work.

Homicide Commander Frank Flanagan and a lot of his buddies who had worked 72 hours without rest finally got a good night's sleep. So did thousands of jittery residents of Jeffrey Manor.

JUAN GONZALES
"HOLIDAY HORROR ON A FERRY BOAT"
by Don Unatin

It was all over. The international naval armada had weighed anchor. The tall ships had sailed well past Gravesend Bay on the first leg of their long journey home.

All the V.I.P.'s who had represented such a security nightmare to federal and local lawmen had returned to the world scene for new rounds of wheeling and dealing.

Department of Sanitation bulldozers had worked through the night removing the last vestiges of trash left behind by more than six million tourists.

Sidewalk vendors had folded their stands and were busy licking their wounds over a souvenir business which had never really gotten off the ground.

Those who had been charged with maintaining law and order could breathe a collective sigh of relief.

All of the visions of terrorist activity, of the potential for thousands of possibly fatal boating accidents, for rip-offs, muggings and shootings on the streets, had proved nothing more than a worrisome non-happening that had not occurred.

The reverse had been true.

One high police official who'd been assigned to the four-day celebration of the rededication of the Statue of Liberty in New York Harbor was to report that the mood of the city and the orderliness of the crowds had been little short of amazing.

"Everybody was in a good humor. There were very few incidents. I guess maybe it was the sea of blue uniforms and the awesomeness of the event itself which kept things cool. The police and the public were getting along beautifully," he said.

There had been a couple of scrapes. Police radio bands had crackled throughout July 4th evening with reports of small boats having gone aground on the shoals of the Hudson and East Rivers.

There had been an alert on McDougall Street in Greenwich Village for "shots fired." Shortly afterward had come the reassuring words of the dispatcher to mobile units, "Slow it down, perps are in custody."

There had been an ugly fireworks accident in Queens which had called for Police Emergency Units and EMS ambulances.

But, by and large, the celebration had been as smooth as it could have been.

And now it was Monday, July 7th.

A city which was somewhat groggy from the mind-boggling display of tons of fireworks, marching bands numbering hundreds of musicians, thousands of tap dancers, symphony concerts, show biz celebrities and all the other attractions which had taken over the Big Apple for Miss Liberty's rededication was reluctantly returning to the work-a-day world.

Monday, July 7th, promised to be a scorcher. By 8 a.m. you could already cut the humidity with a knife. The Weather Bureau had predicted a temperature close to 100 degrees.

A brassy sun, which gave every evidence that the meteorologists would be right, was climbing the eastern sky.

In its berth at the southern tip of Manhattan, the huge passenger Staten Island ferry boat, *Samuel I. Newhouse,* was taking on its consignment of from 400 to 500 early travelers for the junket to St. George, Staten Island, some 25 minutes away.

Those traveling at that early hour were typical of the people one might expect to board the ferry at that time on a business day.

There were a number of night workers who had spent the weekend on security jobs in Manhattan's skyscrapers.

There were a number of people on personal business — visiting the ill, calling on relatives, that sort of thing.

There were professionals — lawyers scheduled for appearances in Richmond County Supreme Court.

And there were even some vacationers who wanted to get a last look or snap a last picture of the "Lady By The Sea," before flying out Monday afternoon.

At 8:35 a.m., the *Samuel I. Newhouse*'s powerful engines began throbbing. The vessel inched away from its pier and pointed its prow southeastward.

The 400 to 500 aboard the ferry settled in for the best sea voyage in the world that can be bought for a quarter.

Some began reading morning newspapers and paperback books. Others lined the rails in anticipation of passing Liberty Island and the glamorous "new girl in town." Some opened attache cases and went about putting their files in order for conferences which lay ahead. Some closed their eyes—remembering the hectic weekend fondly, or just relaxing in the cooling harbor breeze.

At 8:45 a.m. the *Samuel I. Newhouse* was approximately two-fifths through its journey. The ferry had just passed the Statue of Liberty. The steady hum of its engine and the high-pitched cries of circling sea gulls broke through the morning quiet.

Whatever else the passengers and crew aboard had on their minds, they were paying no attention to the stocky middle-aged man who sat alone on the ship's middle deck.

Even if the man's dress might have seemed slightly bizarre—he was wearing jeans and a sweatshirt—there wasn't that much which might be termed unusual about this part of his attire. However, he had donned a pair of metal-spiked leather wristbands.

The man was also carrying an oddly shaped, two-foot-long object which had been wrapped in newspapers. Upon boarding the ferry, he had taken his position on the saloon deck and had slipped the newspaper-wrapped package under his seat.

Now he pulled the package out. As he undid the wrappings, he began chanting in a monotone. Some said his words were, "Viva Islam! Viva Salaam!"

Others were not quite so sure. They contended that the man's speech was a meaningless gibberish.

But there was no mistaking what his package contained. It was a two-foot-long ceremonial sword which can be purchased easily in any number of martial arts stores in the sleazier districts of the city.

Anybody with from $20 to $50 burning in his pocket can claim the item for his own. The one stipulation is that the ceremonial sword must be sold with its metal edges still blunt. But that's not to stop a person with ideas of his own from using a common file to hone the blade razor-sharp.

As the chanting man pulled the ceremonial blade from its scabbard, there was no doubt that he had done just such a job of honing.

Now the middle-aged man in the sweatshirt and jeans was on his feet. He was screaming at the top of his voice, "Freedom for all!" He was also shouting hysterically in Spanish.

Worst of all, he was now chasing whatever passengers happened to be before him from the middle deck to the top deck. The burnished blade of his weapon glinted in the morning light as he hacked and stabbed away at anybody in his path.

The panic and bedlam of the next few minutes can best be described in the actual words of those who watched fragmented sections of the bloody action and lived to tell of it.

A young man employed by the City of New York was enjoying the cooling July harbor breeze when he first noticed the berserk assailant.

The city worker said, "I saw him plunge the sword into a deckhand. The crewman put his hand to his

91

side. I thought it must be some sort of a joke. I didn't want any part of the byplay, so I got up and walked away.

"But this was no joke. The guy moved to another man and stuck him. Now I could see blood flowing. Now passengers were running and screaming as the guy moved to the upper deck."

A 34-year-old Manhattan man was sitting in the non-smoking section of the top deck. He saw the mad swordsman approaching. The witness recalled "I saw five or six passengers drop to the deck and scramble to get out of the way. I thought maybe it was a terrorist operation. The guy really got going. He was stabbing people lying on the deck. I jumped up on top of a seat. The guy looked right at me. Then, for no reason I know, he just turned and ran away."

One middle-aged couple were making the most of the last hours of their visit to the historic festivities surrounding the reopening of the Statue of Liberty. They were standing at the ferry boat's promenade deck railing, taking a long look at Miss Liberty. The wife was scanning the harbor with a pair of field glasses. The husband was concentrating on the view of the statue itself.

Remembered the wife, "We were looking at the Statue of Liberty, and he came out with a large, what do you call it, sabre. He was very wild and he just attacked several of us.

"I saw him out of the corner of my eye. I didn't realize what was happening. Suddenly he moved past. He slashed a man who was standing nearby. Then he stabbed my husband in the back.

"Next, he turned toward me. I felt something hit me hard in the stomach, but there was no pain. I was bewildered and unsure of what had actually happened to me. I helped my husband and the other wounded man to seats. I tore up some plastic bags I'd been carrying to make a makeshift tourniquet for the other man's arm."

A teenage high school student from New Dorp, Staten Island, who was returning home with her aunt from a Manhattan visit, recalled, "I heard a lot of screaming and people running. And I turned around and my aunt said: 'Get down on the floor. There's a guy swinging a sword.'

"Then he was hitting this woman with it. And then he swung it on the side, and he hit me in the back. Then I went down. All I remember was some man coming, and I was down."

A 32-year-old woman who was seated on the promenade deck facing the statue noted that she had first heard the screams of fellow passengers and had jumped up herself. She'd seen a group of panic-stricken voyagers running toward her. Right behind them was the disheveled and incoherent assailant who was brandishing his blood-dripping sword.

"I started to run," said the woman, "and that's when I got struck for the first time.

"Then I fell by the seats, and that's when I got struck for the second time. Then an elderly woman fell on top of me. And I could feel the third blow strike her rather than me.

"She (the woman who was pinning the younger woman under her weight) was lying there in a pool of blood with her eyes open."

93

A Manhattan lawyer who was due in court in Staten Island to argue a case related how he, too, had been passing the time gazing at the statue.

"I heard a commotion and sensed some kind of movement," he said.

"I thought it might be kids messing around inside. Then people were running from the front of the boat to the back of the boat. On the left, where I sat, was a girl with her aunt. On the right was a lady who got stabbed in the breast and head. The lady who died, I think, was sitting two seats from me."

"At the beginning, I saw the man and thought he was some nut hitting people with a stick. Then, when I saw the blood on the woman's chest, I realized this was no stick.

"I heard somebody yelling something like, 'Get down! Get down!' So I got down.

"Then I felt something hot on my foot. It turned out it was someone's hot coffee.

"After the crowd passed, I felt a weight on top of me. It was the dead lady. There were people all around me. I was covered with blood. Everybody was covered.

"Suddenly I heard the crack of what was clearly a gun."

There never will be any way to determine how many lives were saved by the single report of a snub-nosed .38-caliber weapon. But there will never be any doubts as to the heroism of the owner of that Smith & Wesson gun.

For 24 years, Edward Del Pino had been a cop of the New York force. During those years, the veteran officer had never fired his gun on a duty tour. This despite the fact that he'd worked the infamous Bowery—where he'd seen plenty of danger and ugliness—as well as having been assigned to quieter Staten Island precincts.

Five years ago, Del Pino had retired from the N.Y.P.D. On the morning of the *Samuel I. Newhouse* massacre, the stocky and husky former cop was returning to his Staten Island home from his night job as a security guard.

Like many of his fellow passengers, Del Pino was enjoying the harbor view of the statue when the commotion broke out.

Later, he would say, "The job, the instincts you develop, take over."

At the moment that the pandemonium was swirling around him, Del Pino saw the assailant rise from a bench, raise the sword over his head and plunge it into somebody out of Del Pino's view.

"All I wanted to do was stop the sword," Del Pino was to recall. "He looked up at me. I saw him raise the sword again."

Those who had been close by had heard the heroic former officer shout, "Drop it!"

Referring to this moment, Del Pino estimated that the distance between him and the maniac had been about 20 feet. "The gun came out automatically," Del Pino added, referring to the Smith & Wesson.

"I knew I couldn't fire low because of the people in the seats, but I didn't really have time to take aim. The thought was to get a shot off just to stop him."

The intrepid lawman's shot did not hit the assailant. However, it did cause the marauder to stop his stabbing motions and dive under a bench. Once the swordsman had heard Del Pino's rasped warning, "Drop the sword!" the authority ringing in the three words left no doubt — even in his befuddled mind — of the retired cop's own intentions.

From his hiding place under the bench, the madman shoved the martial arts weapon in the general direction of the man covering him.

Now Del Pino clearly had the upper hand. Brandishing his pistol, the hero of the *Samuel I. Newhouse* tragedy ordered his captive to lie face down across a bench. Del Pino placed his gun against his prisoner's head.

"Don't move or you're dead!" he warned.

Now with the assailant totally immobilized, the ferry crew radioed ahead to the St. George terminal, requesting intensive police backup.

Meanwhile, those aboard the vessel began to take inventory of the carnage suffered.

Dead were Jordan Walker, 61, of Park Hill, Staten Island and Mrs. Rose M. Cammarota, 71, of Riverside Drive, Manhattan.

Nine others who had been wounded in the melee would be rushed to either St. Vincent's Hospital or Bayley Seton Hospital, both of which are situated on Staten Island.

As the stricken boat touched the pilings of its St. George pier, hundreds of cops, including members of the highly regarded S.W.A.T. units, waited to swarm aboard. All units were under the personal command of First Deputy Police Commissioner Richard Condon.

As the cops moved in, the swordsman once more became so violent that he had to be carried off the boat in a plastic body bag.

Now began the arduous duty of sorting out the details of the horrendous events of the last half hour.

The suspect in the two killings and nine woundings was identified immediately as Juan J. Gonzalez, a homeless and allegedly deranged drifter. Police reported Gonzalez had a history of mental instability. As a matter of fact, he had been admitted to Presbyterian Hospital on the evening of Thursday, July 3rd, for observation.

Police blotters showed that cops had been called to the Fort Washington Men's Shelter at 216 Fort Washington Avenue on Manhattan's Upper West Side. The call had gone out because Gonzalez had become unmanageable after hearing an inner voice that he reported told him, "God wants you to kill!"

Officers on the scene had been forced to subdue the deranged man and handcuff him in preparation for his transfer to the hospital.

For two days, Gonzalez had been held for evaluation and treatment.

On July 4th, the day that the Liberty Celebration was getting into high gear, Gonzalez signed a form to be admitted to a hospital voluntarily. He was not admitted to Presbyterian, which had a vacant bed available in its psychiatric section. (The hospital had taken this action because another patient was due to enter the mental unit on Monday. The bed was being reserved for this patient's arrival.)

Perhaps doctors at Presbyterian felt reassured by the fact that on Saturday, July 5th, they had been told by Gonzalez that he was no longer hearing the inner voices which had urged him to kill shelter

97

mates in the names of Jesus and God.

When they strongly suggested that Gonzalez check himself into Harlem Hospital for further psychiatric evaluation and treatment, he told them he would comply.

However, the suspected killer's medical records show that there is nothing to indicate he had gone to Harlem Hospital. For its part, the hospital says it never saw the patient.

Back on the streets by Sunday July 6th, Gonzalez is said to have made his way to a Times Square store which features martial arts paraphernalia. There he is alleged to have made the purchase of the ceremonial sword which was to claim two lives and wound nine other victims.

Throughout Sunday, Gonzalez was seen riding several Staten Island ferries. His behavior had become hostile and aggressive as he had tried to stone other passengers. But he had not gone so far as to attack them with the sword.

Then, on this suffocating July Monday morning, the furies pent up within him had exploded. He had struck.

Now with the alleged slayer under lock and key, police began the sad task of informing next of kin of the dead and sorting out the details of what had brought the participants in the summer tragedy to the same spot at exactly the same time.

For each, the road to the ferry slip at the Battery had been long and twisted.

Gonzalez had first come to the attention of American authorities back in 1977. That was when the Cuban and seven of his countrymen had made good their escape from the Communist Caribbean island in a makeshift 20-foot-long boat. They had been intercepted by the United States Coast Guard and taken to a refugee center.

Gonzalez was given refugee status, which allowed him to work in the United States as if he were a citizen. The Immigration and Naturalization Service had waived its rules on the required "Green Card."

He'd applied for permanent residency and had expressed a desire to become a United States citizen. But he had never shown up for an interview. It is alleged that the refugee had a criminal record in his native Cuba, where he had worked as a farmer.

Less than a year after his arrival in New York City, Gonzalez had been in trouble with the law there. According to police records, he was picked up as a street-corner three-card monte dealer 11 times.

Those who had been his neighbors in the Bronx knew there was a time bomb of violence ticking away within him.

Said one, "Sure, I know Juan Gonzalez. He's a mental.

"He complained he heard voices and kids walking around upstairs," the man recalled. The informant also noted that the apartment above the one Gonzalez had occupied at the time had been vacant. He reported that he had taken the troubled Cuban to inspect the empty flat. Despite what he had seen with his own eyes, Gonzalez had insisted that the noises were continuing. At one point, he had drawn a .38-caliber pistol.

"He was violence-prone," the man who had attempted to allay Gonzalez's phobias said.

Another neighbor commented, "The guy (Gonzalez) wasn't normal . . . Just on his face, on his look, you knew he wasn't good."

The violence within him had not been spotted at the shelter for the homeless where Gonzalez had lodged in recent months. Most guards and residents rather remembered him as a quiet and withdrawn person who kept to himself.

One guard said of Gonzalez, "He was a real quiet man, a calm, subtle person who frequently went out for long, solitary walks.

"He seemed to have a lot on his mind," the guard commented.

"He would carry it within himself, never tell anyone."

Frequent searches of Gonzalez and his quarters by shelter security personnel had never uncovered any weapons.

Said a guard, "He was never violent, never a problem."

The big change had come in the Cuban refugee on July 3rd. It was then that he began intimidating other shelter dwellers; a call went out to the Wadsworth Avenue station. It took two police officers to subdue and handcuff the distraught man for transportation to Presbyterian Hospital.

If Gonzalez had been violence-prone, there had been nothing but gentleness and good will in the personalities of the two people he allegedly had slain aboard the *Samuel I. Newhouse*.

Rose Cammarota, who had been on her way from her apartment in the International Ladies Garment Workers Union Co-op Village on Manhattan's lower

East Side to visit a friend in a Staten Island nursing home, was described as an "angel" by friends and relatives.

Although Mrs. Cammarota's life had been marked by great personal tragedy, her desire to help others had never flagged.

"She was a saint," noted one grieving relative. "She was so wonderful to everybody. She was an angel. She had every qualification to be a saint."

Others reported that the slain woman had always had a kind, loving word for everybody she met. She'd been a dedicated volunteer worker at St. Mary's Catholic Church. Intensely patriotic, one of her last acts had been to drape a huge American flag across the terrace of her apartment in tribute to the four-day Liberty celebration.

In the last year, Mrs. Cammarota had suffered twin tragedies. First, her husband had died during the summer of 1985 following a series of strokes. Then her son had plunged to his death from a terrace of her apartment dismantling Christmas decorations which had been placed there for the Yule holidays.

Recalled one lifelong friend, "She and her family ran a popular grocery store on Grand Street until 20 years ago when they sold it."

Jordan Walker, the other person to have his life snuffed out by the voices that allegedly spoke to Juan Gonzalez, left behind memories which matched those of Mrs. Cammarota. The 61-year-old man who had worked as a guard at the WABC-TV studios on the West Side was eulogized by a grieving relative in these terms:

"Everybody in the neighborhood knew him as 'Papa,' and he tried his best to guide the kids and point them in the right direction.

"He didn't like what was going on in the neighborhood—drugs, crack, things like that. The kids who came here, he tried to teach them the right thing."

Edward Del Pino, whose quick and heroic actions had saved the lives of an unestimated number of other potential victims, is a man of self-effacing modesty.

He summed up his feelings by saying, "I responded the way any cop would have. Once a cop, always a cop."

Instead of accepting unstinted praise for what he had done, Del Pino was troubled by the fact that he had not been able to act faster to subdue the alleged killer.

He said he was a little angry with himself for not having ended the mayhem sooner. "What really gets me is I didn't get to the others in time."

The retired officer's desire to be of service to others goes way back to his childhood. Both of his parents were deaf. As he was growing up in the Fordham section of the Bronx, he studied sign language and became the "eyes and ears" of his mother and father.

During his career in the police department, he worked for six years out of the 5th Precinct (mostly in the Bowery) and 18 years in the 120th Precinct in Northern Staten Island. He earned two commendations over that period.

Of the day when he was first called upon to fire a

shot to save innocent lives, Del Pino said, "In my 24 years as a cop, I've seen everything from people hit by cars to slit throats to bums dying from alcohol poisoning.

"But I've never seen something like this happen in front of me. All I could see was red, red because she (the dead woman) was covered with blood. It was just horrible."

As this is being written, an investigation still continues as to whether hospital psychiatric procedures in admitting and retaining potentially dangerous patients are adequate.

The probe is being spurred on by comments from New York City Mayor Edward Koch. Said Koch, "Someone comes into a hospital and tells of hearing voices commanding him to kill. Such a person should not be able to walk out 48 hours later. That definitely doesn't make much sense to me."

Further legal action is now pending against the suspect, Juan Gonzalez, who at this time has the constitutional right to be considered innocent unless and until proved otherwise in a court of law.

WAYNE NANCE
"THE SERIAL KILLER SNUFFED TWO MORE!"
by Franklyn Sharpe

Eight months after the murders of Michael and Teresa Shook, Ravalli County Sheriff Dale Dye in Hamilton, Montana, did not have a suspect or any leads in the slayings, despite hundreds of hours of investigation.

Nevertheless, for his untiring effort, Dye had received high praise for his expertise in conducting it. One of the accolades came from Dr. Ronald Rivers, chief medical examiner at the state laboratory in Missoula.

In a letter to Ravalli County Commissioners, he stated that Sheriff Dye and Sergeant Jay Printz had done an outstanding job in videotaping the crime scene that was extremely helpful in trying to reconstruct the events that had taken place.

At eight o'clock on Friday morning, December 13, 1985, a friend of Michael and Teresa Shook stopped by their rural two-story home outside of Hamilton.

He was dropping off his son whom Teresa cared for during the day.

It was cold with snow on the ground in the Bitterroot Valley, but he did not notice that there was no smoke coming from the chimney of the Shook house. However, when he rapped repeatedly on the front door, there was no response from inside.

The friend thought it was strange because the Shooks had three children, two of them pre-school age, and it wasn't likely that Teresa would be going anywhere at that time of the morning and particularly because she hadn't called him if something had come up.

He went around to the back door and found it unlocked. As soon as he entered, he smelled the acrid odor of smoke. He went into the living room and saw Mike Shook, in his nightclothes, sprawled on his back. A glance told him that Mike hadn't been overcome by the smoke which seemed to come from under the stairs to the bedrooms on the second floor.

Blood spilled from an ugly wound in Mike's chest, staining his nightclothes and forming a pool on the floor. He obviously was dead.

The friend shouted Teresa's name and ran up the stairs.

Teresa, in her nightclothes, was on the bed. There was the same ugly wound in her chest that had spilled blood. The friend stopped only long enough in the smoke-filled room to determine that she was not breathing. He raced to the adjoining rooms of the children.

The two boys, seven and four years old, and their two-year-old sister, were in their beds. They did not appear to have been wounded, but were unconscious from smoke inhalation.

He snatched up the children and hurriedly took them outside and administered first aid. Satisfied that they were breathing, he called the sheriff's office and asked for an ambulance and officers to come to the house.

The medics determined that Mike and Teresa Shook were dead. The children were whisked off to the Daly Memorial Hospital in Hamilton. They were given primary care there and then flown to the Porter Memorial Hospital in Denver, Colorado, to receive additional treatment.

The first officers on the scene determined that a fire had been set to crumpled magazines and some furniture in the stairwell. No flammable liquids had been added so that it smouldered and filled the rooms with smoke but had not burst into flames. Officers extinguished the smouldering fire.

Sheriff Dye with Sgt. Printz and Detective Scott Leete arrived on the scene. They went inside the house, careful not to touch anything, only long enough to determine that the victims each had died from a single stab wound in their chests.

Dye ordered the house and grounds around it sealed until Printz could direct crime scene experts to make a videotape and collect any possible physical evidence.

Mike Shook, 34, had been a popular teacher of history and government at Stevensville High School for seven years. He and his 32-year-old wife had the home built where they lived with their two sons and a daughter.

After a brief examination inside the house, Printz reported to Dye, "Whoever killed them intended to burn the kids alive. It's a miracle that the place didn't burn down, but apparently he closed the door to the area under the stairs and it didn't get enough oxygen to start flaming."

Dye gritted his teeth at the thought of the three children being burned alive as they slept while their parents were dead from stab wounds.

"What kind of a monster would do a thing like that?" Printz questioned.

"I don't know," Dye replied. "But I swear if it's the last thing I do, we'll find him."

As the crime scene examination continued, the investigators began to formulate a theory on what had taken place. They reasoned the Shook family had been in their beds. Mike had heard something either inside or outside the house and went downstairs to investigate.

The killer had either been in the living room or Mike had let him in and the killer, without warning, had thrust the knife into Mike's chest. There was no evidence of a struggle.

The murderer had then gone upstairs, the detectives surmised. Teresa might not have been awakened by Mike when he went downstairs. She possibly had been sleeping when the killer plunged the knife into her chest.

The probers' theory had no explanation for why the murderer hadn't continued his bloody slaughter by killing the children, but it was definite that he planned they should die.

If the fire under the stairwell erupted, it would

have burned out the escape route for the youngsters in their bedrooms and they would have perished in the fire.

Residents of Bitterroot Valley were first shocked by the news of the murder of the popular teacher and his wife and then angered and fearful. There was a rush at hardware stores for deadbolts and ammunition and talk of a madman killer on the loose.

Dye attempted to calm their fears by stating that he felt the slayings of Mike and Teresa Shook was not a random case. He said police thought the killer knew his victims, but was unable to explain the reasons for such a conclusion.

Relatives and friends of the slain couple were adamant that they had no known enemies and had never been threatened.

What Dye refrained from saying publicly was that in examining the crime scene sleuths had found that the only articles taken from the house were a ceramic elk and a custom hunting knife with a carved handle. The killer had passed up the usual loot taken by a burglar such as jewelry, cameras, radios and a television set.

Sheriff Dye was certain the killer hadn't come to the house for those articles, but was at a loss to explain why they had been taken and other things more valuable had been left untouched.

"But someday those two pieces are going to solve the case for us," Dye told Printz. "The killer wouldn't have taken them unless he wanted them and the chances are good that he's going to keep them. When we find them, we'll know we've got our man."

Dye issued strict orders that no mention should be

made that the ceramic elk and hunting knife had been taken by the killer.

"We don't want him to know that we know he's got them," Dye said, "or he might get rid of them."

Meanwhile, word came from the hospital in Denver that the Shook children had recovered from the smoke inhalation. Physicians said it was fortunate that the friend of the Shooks had come to the house at the time he did and gave them artificial respiration. It was almost certain that if they had remained in the house for even a short time longer they would have succumbed to smoke inhalation.

With no witnesses and little physical evidence, the investigators concentrated their efforts on attempting to learn what motivated the slaying.

An ugly rumor circulated in the valley that the murders were the work of a demonic cult when it was learned that Teresa Shook embraced the "Eckanar" philosophy.

Dye attempted to squash the rumor by saying that he had taken a crash course in Eckanar and found it only to be a thought process described as self-discipline and personal responsibility. It was in no way connected with any demonic rites or ritual, he added.

After several weeks passed and the fears of the residents of Bitterroot Valley subsided, their thoughts turned to the welfare of the Shook children. In addition to donations being received at a bank, they decided to hold an auction to raise money.

Items given to be auctioned off were generous. They ranged from beer signs and bird cages to kayaks, registered quarter horses and a log cabin. The bidding was spirited and generous. The auction raised $21,343.50 that was put into a trust fund for the youngsters.

The Shook murder remained the prime case for the Ravalli County Sheriff's Office.

Dye scanned every report of criminal activities in the state looking for something that might be related to the crime or a mention of a custom hunting knife or ceramic elk.

Twice, he went to Ravalli County attorney Robert Brown with requests for search warrants and once to county attorney Robert Deschamps in Missoula. The searches were made but without finding the evidence that Dye was looking for.

As months passed without any suspect taken into custody, the initial shock of the Shook murders diminished and eventually it was no longer the prime thing to talk about and mention of it disappeared from the news media.

The case, however, was not out of the minds of Sheriff Dye and his staff. They continued to check every possible source for a lead to the motive for the slayings.

On Thursday, September 4, 1986, more than nine months after the murder of the Shooks, a couple returned to their home in Missoula, some 60 miles north of Hamilton, shortly after midnight from visiting with friends.

As they drove up to their house, they noticed an unfamiliar truck with a camper top parked nearby. The man went over to inspect it and looked inside.

"There's a guy in it asleep," he told his wife. "Maybe he had too much to drink and passed out."

110

The couple went inside their home. The woman asked her husband, "Will you take out the garbage? We might forget it in the morning."

The man took out the trash and was confronted by a stranger in the yard. The stranger said he had noticed the lights on in the house. He said he had lost something and asked if he could borrow a flashlight.

The man said he had a flashlight and would go into the house to get it. The stranger followed him in. Suddenly, he struck the man in the head with a club, knocking him unconscious.

His wife heard the commotion and came out to the kitchen to investigate. She was confronted by the stranger holding a pistol.

She recognized the man as a driver who delivered furniture for the store she managed.

"What are you doing here?" she demanded.

"You just do what I tell you or I'm going to have to kill you and your old man," he said. He handed her some rope he had brought in with him and directed her to tie up her husband's feet and hands.

With no other choice but to comply, she followed the order. The gunman tested the knots.

Threatening the woman with the pistol, he ordered her into a bedroom. He forced her to lie on the bed and tied her hand and foot and fastened her to a bedpost.

"Why are you doing this?" the woman asked.

The gunman told her, "I've done something real bad and I need money to get out of town."

"Why didn't you just ask for it?" she questioned.

"Fat chance you would have given it to me," he responded.

111

The gunman left the bedroom with the woman tied to the bed. She could hear him dragging her unconscious husband and the bumping sound as he was dragged to the basement.

The gunman tied her husband to a post in the basement. The husband regained consciousness and demanded, "What in hell are you doing?"

The answer came with the gunman drawing a hunting knife which he then plunged into the man's chest. As the man slumped with blood gushing from his chest, the gunman, apparently satisfied that his victim was dead, returned to the bedroom.

In the meantime, the woman had managed to free one hand and was attempting to reach the telephone to dial the 9-1-1 emergency number.

"Don't be stupid," the gunman warned her. "You try anything and you'll be dead."

"What did you do to my husband?" the woman demanded.

"Forget about your old man," the gunman told her. "We've got a little business to take care of right here."

The woman was aware of the meaning of the gunman's words. She reasoned that he planned to rape her and once finished with that most likely would kill her because she recognized him and could identify him.

The gunman appeared to be in no hurry to carry out whatever he had in mind, however.

Meanwhile in the basement, the man, although seriously wounded by the stab wound, had managed to remain conscious and struggled to untie his hands, feet and the rope that bound him to the post.

He had a rifle in the basement. It was a small caliber but high-powered weapon. Unfortunately, he had only one cartridge for the gun. He had neglected to buy additional ammunition after using it last.

He came up the stairs with the rifle loaded with the single cartridge.

The gunman in the bedroom apparently had been alerted by some sound as the man came out of the basement. The gunman left the bedroom and confronted the man with the rifle in the living room.

"Drop your gun," the man holding the rifle ordered.

The response was a shot from the pistol that missed its mark and lodged in the ceiling.

The man with the rifle fired his weapon. The slug hit the gunman in his right side but did not fell him. He lunged forward with the rifle, grasping it by the barrel, and used the butt as a club. The stock broke as it hit the gunman on the shoulder.

The gunman shot again, this time striking the man in the leg with the slug.

Bleeding profusely from the stab wound in his chest, the man grappled with the gunman and they fell to the floor. They wrestled for control of the pistol and rolled into the bedroom.

The assailant managed to get off two more shots, both missing the victim they were intended for.

The man who had been stabbed managed to get control of the pistol and he shot his assailant in the head.

The struggle was over.

The man managed to untie his wife from her bondage before dropping unconscious from his chest wound and the struggle.

She called 9-1-1 requesting an ambulance and medics.

When they arrived, they found the men unconscious, but alive. The woman, except for the traumatic experience, was unharmed. Both men were rushed to the hospital.

Captain Larry Weatherman, chief of detectives for the Missoula police, was notified of the shooting. He interviewed the woman who told him that she had recognized the man who had assaulted her husband and tied her up on the bed.

She identified him as Wayne Nance, a 30-year-old independent truck driver who delivered furniture from the store she managed.

"I know he would have raped me and killed me if my husband hadn't managed to somehow escape from being tied up in the basement," she said.

Questioned more about the details of what had taken place, she recalled that Nance had told her he had done something real bad and needed money to leave town.

Weatherman couldn't recall any recent major crime cases in Missoula. He directed that a teletype be sent out to all police agencies with the details of what had taken place in Missoula and with Nance's name.

A check at the hospital revealed that Nance had died from the bullet wound to his head. The man he had stabbed was in serious condition from the chest wound but would survive.

Weatherman called in attorney Deschamps later in the morning. "I'll be damned," Weatherman said.

"He really did do it."

He was not referring to the case that had just taken place. It was a case that had taken place 12 years earlier.

"You remember the Donna Pounds case?" Weatherman asked.

It was a rhetorical question. Of course Deschamps recalled the Pounds case. He had just been elected country attorney at the time and had held the post since that time. Deschamps had a close association with the investigators and at one time had taken the evidence they had collected to a grand jury but they had failed to return an indictment.

The Pounds case had started when a local minister returned to his home at six o'clock in the evening and found his 39-year-old wife and mother of three children in the basement of the house.

Donna Pounds had been bound hands-and-feet with her mouth taped and shot five times with a .22-caliber pistol. The weapon was found near her body.

A postmortem determined that she had been sexually assaulted before being slain.

The investigators determined that the weapon used to kill the woman was one that had been in the house. They were unable to raise fingerprints and little other physical evidence.

There were no signs of forced entry, indicating that the victim possibly knew the person who had killed her and had let him into the house.

Weatherman was one of the detectives who had investigated the case at the time. The one lead they managed to turn up came from a witness who recalled having seen a young man carrying a black bag leaving the area at about the time the murder had taken place.

Checking out all persons known to the Pounds family, their attention became focused upon Wayne Nance. He was an 18-year-old high school student at the time and a friend of the victim's son.

Persons who knew Nance described him as being a loner and a weirdo. He was into satanic worship and at one time had branded himself with a satanic symbol by heating a hot wire from a clothes hanger and burning his skin and flesh.

Teachers told police that Nance had a talent for art, but that his drawings were often of fantasy bloody monsters with two heads. The monsters were depicted as having big claws and big fangs dripping blood. Persons he drew had daggers stuck in their backs dripping blood.

It was said that Nance would recite from memory the entire "Jabberwocky" by Lewis Carroll with lines that went "Beware of Jabberwocky, my son! The jaws that bite, the claws that catch!"

Schoolmates told sleuths that Nance bragged of having skinned cats alive and mutilated other animals.

The detectives learned that Nance had not attended classes on the day the Pounds murder took place. He claimed he had been out looking for Indian artifacts as a project for a class he was taking. Detectives determined he had actually taken that class the year before.

A search warrant was issued for the home where Nance lived. Officers found a black bag with .22-caliber ammunition in it that was similar to the one described by the witness who had seen a young man carrying a black bag near the Pounds home on the day of the murder.

They also impounded rope from the house that was similar to the rope used to tie up Donna Pounds before she was shot to death.

Forensic pathologists determined that the victim had been most likely kneeling and begging for her life when slain.

After more than a month of investigation, Deschamps had taken the evidence collected to a grand jury. They failed to indict Nance or anyone else for the crime.

The victim's husband moved from Missoula to Dayton, Washington, following the slaying. Thereafter, he died of a heart attack.

Persons who knew the Pounds family said it was a double murder. They said he had died of a broken heart from the grief over his wife's murder.

"Damn!" Deschamps said as he and Weatherman discussed the Donna Pounds case. "If we could have nailed him then, none of this would have happened."

"This, and who knows what," Weatherman said. "That was 12 years ago and I doubt if he's been a good boy since then. I'm going to start checking out files on all major cases."

When the news media was informed of Wayne Nance's death and the details surrounding it, one of the detectives was quoted as saying, "It's like Christmas for us. The good guys finally won."

When the teletype of Nance was received in the Ravalli County Sheriff's Office, Sheriff Dye called in Sgt. Printz and Det. Leete.

"I think we've found our man for the Shook murders," Dye said. He pointed out that Nance had used a knife to assault his victim and had not used his gun until confronted by the victim with a rifle.

"It fits the pattern," Dye stated.

However, there was one problem. During the months of investigation in which the lawmen had questioned just about everyone who had known the Shooks, the name of Wayne Nance had not been mentioned.

"I'm going to Missoula," Dye said. "You guys start checking on the name Nance and what connection he could have had to the Shooks. It says here he drove a truck for a furniture company up in Missoula. I felt from the beginning the Shook murders were a random thing, so there has to be some connection somewhere."

Sheriff Dye drove up to Missoula and met with Captain Weatherman. He said he was checking to see if Nance could have killed the Shooks in Hamilton.

"It's possible," Weatherman told him. "We've got him pegged for a murder that took place here 12 years ago and I'm almost sure we're going to find others."

Dye asked if in a search of Nance's property they had located a ceramic elk and a custom hunting knife.

"I don't know," Weatherman replied. "We've got a truckload of stuff we took out of the house where he was living. The guy had a fascination for knives and daggers. We've got about a dozen of them, including a yard-long carved sword, that are being examined at the lab."

"I know what I'm looking for," Dye said. He related how the hunting knife with a carved handle and the ceramic elk had been taken from the Shook home while the killer had passed up more valuable things.

"Do you have any idea of why he would choose the Shook family and set fire to the house with the intent to kill their three children?" Dye asked. "It's bugged me for nine months and I haven't found an answer."

"If Nance killed them, you may never get an answer," Weatherman answered.

Weatherman said he felt sure Nance had gone to the home in Missoula with the intent to kill his victims, not to rob them as he had said before he had been slain.

"The woman knew him," Weatherman said. "She could identify him, so there was no way he could have left without killing both of them.

"If he had been looking for someone to rob, he would have picked on a stranger or somehow disguised his features."

The puzzling thing, however, was that the victims knew Nance only casually.

"She told me that he had never made any advances toward her, nor had there been any trouble with his work at the store," Weatherman said. "It seems to me that he just got it into his head to kill somebody and chose them for the victims."

"I don't know what reason he could have had for killing the Shooks," Dye said. "And about the only thing we've got is if we can locate that ceramic elk and knife taken from their home."

"Let's check with the lab boys and see what they've got," Weatherman suggested.

When they reached the lab, one of the technicians approached Weatherman. He handed them a small photo with two head shots of a woman that apparently had been taken in a coin-operated booth.

Weatherman studied the not-too-clear photo of a woman who appeared to be in her early 20s. He shook his head and passed the photo to Dye. He stared at it but said he could not recognize it as anyone he knew.

The technician said that it must have meant something to Nance. He used adhesive tape to attach it to a piece of cardboard and had tacked it on his wall.

"I'll get some copies made and have it shown around town," Weatherman said.

Dye asked about the ceramic elk and the custom hunting knife.

"I don't know about the knife," the technician said. "We collected a whole bunch of knives, daggers and ceremonial swords at his place. We can check and see, but I think I saw a ceramic elk at his place. We didn't take it because it didn't seem to be involved."

Sheriff Dye looked over the collection of weapons that had been taken from the Nance home. After examining them, he selected one of the shiny knives and said, "This looks like the one that was described to me. Can I take it? I've got a witness in Hamilton who can identify it, if it is the right one."

Weatherman gave Dye permission. Dye then asked if they could go to Nance's house to see if the ceramic elk was there.

Weatherman said the search warrant was still in effect and that he would go with Dye to the house.

On the way, Weatherman told Dye about the Donna Pounds murder and that Nance had been a prime suspect for the killing at the time but that they had not turned up enough evidence or witnesses to have a grand jury indict him.

"We're checking through the files on another case that has had us puzzled for a long time," Weatherman said. "But what we know about Nance right now, I think maybe he will do for it."

He explained that two years after the Donna Pounds murder, a Missoula special education teacher, Vern Kvale, had been bound with tape, sexually assaulted and stabbed to death. The case hadn't been connected to the Pounds murder because she had been shot to death and the teacher had been stabbed to death.

"It looks like this guy Nance may have been a serial killer," Dye said.

"It's beginning to look that way," Captain Weatherman agreed. "We don't want to close the books on all of our unsolved cases because the guy is dead, but we're sure going to do a lot of checking to see if he could have been involved."

When they reached Nance's home, Dye was elated when he spotted a ceramic elk on a shelf. "That's it!" he exclaimed. "I'm sure of it now."

Dye signed for the ceramic elk and hunting knife and hurried back to Hamilton. Printz and Leete were waiting for him.

"We've got a link to that guy Nance and the

Shooks," Sgt. Printz announced.

"Yes?" Dye queried.

Printz explained they had checked with relatives of the Shooks and learned that they had purchased a number of pieces of furniture from the store in Missoula in November. A check with the store revealed that Nance had made the delivery.

"As far as we can learn, it was his only contact with the Shooks," Printz said. "There wasn't any trouble with him. He delivered the stuff on November 30th and they were killed on December 13th. If he did it, I don't know what the motive could have been."

"From what I've been able to find out he didn't need a motive," Dye said. "He just killed to be killing."

Dye told them he had located the ceramic elk and the hunting knife.

"If we get them identified as having been taken from the Shook home at the time they were slain, it looks like we're finally going to wrap this one up," Dye said.

Meanwhile, a development was taking place in Missoula.

One of the lab technicians reported to Captain Weatherman that they had found several long hairs that had been caught in a hinge in the camper top of Nance's truck.

The truck and camper had been found parked near the home of the couple who was assaulted.

"A woman's hair?" Weatherman asked.

The technician nodded and smiled.

"What more have you got?" Weatherman asked,

anticipating that the technician had not told him all that was known.

The technician related that they had put the hairs under a microscope and found that they had been dyed several times. The hairs had originally been a natural light brown, then dyed blond with a final dye of auburn.

"Under a microscope it is sort of like layers of paint," the technician explained.

"The body that was found on Christmas Eve of 1984," Weatherman said. "That's the one thing we knew about the woman."

"You guessed it," the technician said. "Right after I checked out those hairs, it hit me, too."

He said that a microscopic comparison of the hairs showed they were identical.

The case they were referring to was the nude body of a young woman who had been found buried in a shallow grave near Deer Creek, about 20 miles out of Missoula.

The corpse was badly decomposed. Forensic pathologists stated that the victim, in her early 20s, most likely had been slain sometime during the previous summer or fall. The remains had decomposed to the point that it was impossible to determine the cause of death. They had speculated that she had either been strangled or stabbed to death.

Investigators had tried to learn the victim's identity. She had been buried nude so there were no clothes to help with the identification. The lab crew had examined her hair and determined that it had been dyed several times.

No one answering the meager description had

been reported missing in the Missoula area. Information on the murder had been sent to the National Crime Information Center and distributed to law enforcement agencies throughout the country along with a chart of her teeth, but there had been no response.

The photo found in Nance's home provided a clue to her identity. Officers exhibiting the photo located witnesses who recalled having seen the woman.

In September of 1984, Nance had been working part-time in the evenings as a bouncer at a bar. A young woman had come into the place. She said she was just hitchhiking around the country and had no place to stay.

Nance had taken her to his home where she lived with him for several weeks. Persons who had known Nance recalled her as being a very friendly and attractive young woman, but knew her only by the name of "Robin" and from things she had said assumed that she might have been originally from Texas.

When the girl presumably had left, Nance told acquaintances that she had decided to travel to somewhere else and he had given her money for bus fare to Seattle. Others recalled that Nance had said he didn't know where she was headed. She had just walked out, went to a truck stop and caught a ride with a long-haul driver.

No one questioned that anything might have happened to her.

"She most likely was the girl that was found in the grave at Deer Creek," Weatherman said. "And if she was a drifter, it explains why she hadn't been reported missing anywhere and she may just have assumed the name of Robin."

Weatherman said it was doubtful that a positive case could be made with just the photo and the hair, but he had no doubt from the information they had been able to gather that Wayne Nance had killed her.

"Officially, with Nance dead, I don't think we can close the case," Weatherman said. "But as far as I am concerned, it's a closed book."

Copies of the photo of the young woman and the information known about her were sent to Texas authorities. They were requested to check their missing person files for anyone who might have been the victim.

It was not the only case that the Missoula detectives were examining for a possible link to Wayne Nance.

In March of 1980, a group having a picnic on Beavertail Hill outside Missoula found a shallow grave with the decomposing corpse of a girl in it. The body was nude and there was nothing to identify the victim.

Pathologists determined that she had been in her teens and likely been dead for several months. There were indications that she might have been bound with rope and sexually assaulted before being stabbed to death.

Detectives learned that a teenage girl, who was not known locally, had been seen around town. They put out a bulletin with a chart of her teeth and it was determined that she had been a runaway from Seattle, Washington.

The investigators had questioned a number of persons who were known to have been with the girl, but were unable to uncover evidence to point to a suspect.

Nance had not been a suspect at the time and had not been questioned. However, in light of what they now knew about Nance, probers would attempt to see if possibly she had been with him.

Meanwhile, in Hamilton, Sheriff Dye located several witnesses who could positively state that the ceramic elk and hunting knife found in Nance's home were the items taken from the Shook home on the night they were slain.

Dye and County Attorney Brown called a press conference in which they announced that with the evidence that had been discovered they were classifying the Shook case as solved and naming Nance as the killer. The case was now closed.

Dye recounted the similarity of the Shooks' murder with the assault that had taken place on the couple in Missoula. Coupled with finding the ceramic elk and the hunting knife, he said it was conclusive that Nance had killed them.

Questioned as to the motive for the murders, Dye was unable to supply a reason.

He said the only contact that they had been able to establish between Nance and the Shooks was when Nance had delivered furniture to the Shook home.

A relative of the Shooks had been present at the time. He recalled that the deliveryman had been very helpful in helping carry in the furniture. Teresa Shook had given him some coffee and cookies and everything had been completely friendly. The youngsters had been in the house at the time, so Nance knew that she had children.

Dye said he had no idea what prompted Nance to return to the home three weeks later to kill the victims.

"He's dead, so we can't ask him," Dye said. "But from all of the evidence we have, we feel certain that he killed them."

Brown agreed with the conclusions of Dye. He said it would have been nice if they had found some motive for the senseless slaying, but if Nance was a serial killer as the investigators were beginning to believe, it would not have required a motive for him to kill.

"Why he killed the Shooks we don't know and very possibly will never know," Brown said. "It was a horrible tragedy that he just happened to pick them to satisfy some need he had to kill someone."

A coroner's inquest into the death of Nance was held in Missoula.

The panel heard testimony from the surviving couple whom Nance assaulted.

The man related that Nance had shown little emotion when he stabbed him in the chest. He said he was positive that Nance had left thinking he was dead and would have assaulted and killed his wife if he had not been able to free himself from his bonds.

The woman testified that she had known Nance only casually as someone who made deliveries from the store. There had been no social contact and he had not been at their home previously. She said she had no idea why Nance had selected her and her husband as the target for his assault.

The jury returned a verdict finding that the death of Nance was a justifiable homicide.

Following the hearing, Weatherman and Missoula County attorney Deschamps held a press conference in which they stated that Nance was being considered a serial killer.

"We knew that he was a strange young man and considered by acquaintances of being something of a weirdo," Deschamps said. "Unfortunately, we could never get enough evidence to persuade a grand jury to indict him."

"We could probably clear our files of unsolved murder cases by naming Nance as a suspect," Weatherman said. "But that isn't the way we operate. Until we have positive proof that he killed the persons, they will remain in our active file."

Weatherman said the investigations would continue in the Kvale murder and other unsolved cases to either positively link Nance to the slayings or to clear him.

"What I'm saying is that while we're pretty much convinced Nance was a serial killer, we don't want to clear our books of all our unsolved crimes until we are positive," Weatherman said.

Information on Nance and the murders he was suspected of having committed was sent to the National Crime Information Center and forwarded to the FBI.

Agent Brent Warberg, a specialist on serial killings, contacted Weatherman. He said he was coming to Missoula for additional information on Nance to be given to the forensic psychologist with the Bureau's Behavioral Science Division for a personality profile.

Experts in the Behavioral Science department compare the modus operandi of major crime cases and criminal. It has proven fruitful in numerous cases to suggest the type of person who might have committed a crime.

Warberg said that the information on Nance was typical of serial killers. Most serial killers present two distinct personalities. One is that of a perfectly natural person who is seldom suspected by relatives or friends of being capable of committing a murder. The other is a carefully concealed and cunning killer who most often select victims at random and kills without motive to satisfy an unnatural desire to spill blood.

Except for the Donna Pounds case, Nance had not been considered a suspect in any of the other murders in Montana. Outwardly, he appeared to be a friendly, hard-working truck driver. His daily contact with others had been perfectly normal and he had managed to conceal his interest in satanism, his fantasies concerning monsters or love of knives.

Warberg summed it up by saying, "Most often a serial killer will kill casually and in ways that defy comprehension. They are often known to be friendly and generous community members. It is the reason they are so difficult to identify and why they can continue with their killings."

Warberg has said that he will work with local officers to try to determine the whereabouts of Wayne Nance over the past 12 years in and out of the state of Montana. A check will be made on unsolved murders and the report of missing persons to determine if Nance may have been in the area at the time.

Warberg said since Nance is dead, the investigation would not be for the normal purpose of prosecution, but to provide more information to the Behavioral Science department in preparing profiles on other serial killings.

It must be noted, however, that while authorities have said their files are closed on murders after the death of Nance, he was not charged with any crimes at the time of his death.

MICHAEL WAYNE JOHNSON:
"STOP THE MADMAN'S MURDER MISSION!"

by Barry Benedict

Wright City, MO.
September 24, 1986

"You bet we are scared. I got a shotgun, a hunting rifle and two pistols. They're all loaded and I ain't afraid to use them. Anyone coming up that walk that I don't know or ain't a cop is taking a chance."

The Missouri farmer was scared down to the mud on his boots. And he had every right to be. Fear had infiltrated the rural hamlet of Wright city in northeast Missouri like a fatal virus.

Everyone was heavily armed and no one ventured out unless absolutely necessary. It had been that way since a madman on a self-appointed death mission invaded their community Monday evening, September 22, 1986.

In a little over an hour, he gunned down a motorist, wounded a cop, assaulted three women and stole two cars.

These crimes were added to a string of murders, kidnappings and robberies that crossed two state lines and was called the largest Midwest crime wave since Dillinger and Ma Barker. The man who eluded police would have felt right at home in this Rogue's gallery of twisted killers.

The tri-state manhunt began after Indianapolis police received a report of a shooting in northeast Indianapolis. The dispatcher logged the time at 8:17 Monday morning, September 22, 1986. "He is laying in the street," the caller said. "I think he is dead."

Police officers and medics sped to a home on East Pleasant Run Parkway. They found a man in a suit lying dead by the curb, his chest and face covered with blood. The victim was Thomas E. Gahl, a 39-year-old federal probation officer. A medic draped the body with a white sheet.

Witnesses told investigators Officer Gahl had gone to the home on Pleasant Run at 8 a.m. and knocked loudly on the front door. There was no answer, but Gahl continued knocking.

"He knew someone was home," said the next-door neighbor. "I got the impression he wasn't going to leave until someone answered."

A few minutes later, the neighbor heard a scream, followed by a gunshot. "I ran to the window and saw this guy standing over the fellow in the suit," the witness said. "The guy on the ground was screaming, 'Don't do it, don't do it.' That's when the guy shot him again."

A woman across the street saw the whole thing and told officers the shooting was unprovoked. "The man was running away, when the gunshot spun him around. He didn't have a chance. It was just terrible."

A motorcyclist was driving by and heard the three shots and saw a man with long hair and thick beard run back into the house.

"He came out a few seconds later and climbed into a gray Ford pickup truck," the witness continued. "He was carrying a gun and looked like he had changed clothes."

The suspected gunman was Michael Wayne Jackson, 41, an ex-con from Ponotoc, Mississippi. Witnesses said Jackson had lived in the neighborhood for less than a month. Investigators learned the house had been abandoned and was without electricity or running water. Kittens and rabbits ran wild through the house, dodging trash, clothing, canned goods and personal papers. In one room, a headless Santa Claus doll stood next to a legless chair. Mattresses on the floor served as bedding and furniture.

Investigators radioed descriptions of Jackson and the gray pickup to headquarters. By then there had been two abductions and another shooting.

At 8:32 a.m., police received a call about a shooting at a market on South Meridian Street. When lawmen arrived, the owner, J. B. Hall, lay sprawled behind the counter, half his face blown away with a shotgun.

Two minutes earlier, the unmarried, popular grocer had been chatting with a regular customer. A deliveryman arrived with bread and began stacking the shelves.

Suddenly, a man with a full beard appeared in the store waving a shotgun. He ran to the counter and yelled, "Where the hell is the deliveryman?"

"We didn't say anything," J.B.'s friend told police. "The guy stuck the shotgun under J.B.'s nose and told him to forget the bread man and empty the till."

Hall reached for the money but wasn't fast enough. "J.B. said, 'All right, all right,' and gave him the money," the witness said. "Then the gun went off."

The blast caught Hall in the left side of the throat, spun him around and dropped him behind the counter. He was dead when medics arrived.

Witnesses outside the store saw the man with the beard jump into the bread truck and drive away. Police issued an APB on the vehicle which was last seen headed north on South Meridian.

At 8:54 a.m., police got a call from the bread truck driver that sent them racing to the Indianapolis International Airport. "He stuck a gun in my face and told me to drive," the driver said. "I did what he said."

As lawmen combed the airport parking lot, detectives searched the gray Ford pickup Jackson left behind at the market. Inside they found a partially empty box of shotgun shells, a straw hat, a blue jacket and what appeared to be an Indiana map. The evidence indicated to detectives that Jackson was preparing a series of holdups.

However, it didn't tell them where Jackson was or where he might hit next. Sleuths learned soon enough when they talked to a man who dropped his boss off at the airport Holiday Inn at 9 o'clock, six minutes after Jackson cut loose the truck driver.

"I went inside to make a call then went back to my

car," the man said. "I no sooner started it, than the passenger door swings open and there is a guy with a 12-gauge shotgun. He said, 'Get out! Get the hell out!' I put my hands up and said, 'I'm out! I'm out!' He got in and drove away."

The vehicle sped from the airport and stopped 11 minutes later in front of a home on the 7100 block of Carlsen Avenue, where a 27-year-old woman was headed for Wishard Memorial Hospital, where she worked as a paramedic.

By the time police interviewed her, however, she was a patient recovering from a broken leg.

"He walked up to me with a big gun and said he needed my car," she told detectives. She gave him the keys and expected him to drive away. Instead, he grabbed her elbow and pushed her into the car next to him.

She said they filled up at a gas station, left without paying, then headed north toward Clinton County.

The woman was a hostage for 75 terrifying minutes before she decided to escape. She saw her opportunity when the gunman slowed for a stop sign in Frankfort, Indiana.

"I opened the passenger door and rolled out," she said. "I hurt my arm when I hit the pavement." Pain ran up her spine when the rear wheel ran over her right leg. It snapped the bone, but she still managed to get away.

The woman's screams attracted residents who came to her aid. She was taken to Clinton County Hospital, where her leg was set in a cast and she was treated for the shoulder injury and shock.

Her description of the kidnapper fit Michael Wayne Jackson to a T. "I thought he was crazy," she told police. "I kept glancing at him because I knew I would need a good description. He had a big, bushy beard, kind of like singer Kenny Rogers. He had silver paint on his face and pants. He was nice and polite and was really desperate."

Police found the woman's Ford Escort abandoned at the Stewart Manor Mobile Home Park on the north edge of Frankfort, where Jackson abducted a 27-year-old woman and her young son and forced her to drive her 1982 beige Mercury.

The woman told Frankfort police that they drove out of town for 12 to 13 miles, whereupon she and her son were released.

"I told him to please let us go because my child had been burned in a cooking accident and was due for a burn treatment at Riley Hospital for Children in Indianapolis. He said okay but took my wedding ring and all my cash."

Jackson did not say where he was headed or what his plans were. Police figured he might head for Illinois, or double back to Indianapolis, or head south. The map left behind at Jackson's house indicated he might head to Springfield, Missouri, where he had been jailed prior to his April, 1985 parole.

"He is a hard guy to predict," an Indianapolis lawman noted. "He is wacko and extremely violent. There is no telling what he might do."

The renegade fugitive was certainly twisted and sick. Medication would help, but he didn't always take it. Jackson was also addicted to drugs—cocaine, amphetamines, and heroin. One condition of his parole was to use only drugs that had been prescribed for him. But Jackson marched to his own drummer.

It had not always been that way, however. As a young boy growing upon a farm in Mississippi, Jackson hated violence and often got sick at the bloody sight of his mother slaughtering chickens.

"Mike loved almost everything in his own way," recalled a relative. "He liked everything to be free. He thought nothing should be confined."

The gentle, animal-loving boy grew into a raging, violent paranoid. In 1962, he was arrested with two other youths for robbing a cab driver in Indianapolis. Over the next two decades, he was in and out of prison in Indiana, Tennessee, and Missouri, serving time for rape, sodomy, kidnapping, auto theft, battery and assault, shoplifting and firearms violations. His criminal jacket showed 35 arrests.

Jackson was also diagnosed as a violence-prone paranoid schizophrenic and had been institutionalized on several occasions.

"He did all right and was a pretty good old boy as long as he was on his medication," another relative remarked. "When he didn't, he got in trouble." Jackson didn't like the drugs. He complained they made him woozy and lazy. Besides, he didn't need them, he said, because drugs were for crazy people and he wasn't crazy.

Doctors said the reaction was not unusual for psychotic patients. And Jackson was severely psychotic.

Sometimes the sickness showed a bizarre sense of humor. While waiting trial on federal firearm charges last year, Jackson gave defense attorneys a list of possible character witnesses, naming several

137

celebrities who he said would attest to his character.

Another time, while incarcerated in Indianapolis, Jackson sent a threatening letter to President Ronald Reagan, with the return address Ted Kennedy, Marion County Jail.

A more ominous note was received by relatives in the spring of 1985, when the then inmate said he planned to murder people and make them fear him because he had a score to settle.

Jackson was married in 1964, but divorced five years later while in prison. He and his ex-wife married again in 1971, but divorced a year later. He had two daughters he saw only three times.

When not in prison, mental institutions or awaiting trial, Jackson worked as a laborer, carpenter and welder. He had a habit of threatening his bosses and fellow workers when things didn't go right, which explained why he had a hard time holding a job. He was unemployed when his crime spree began.

Reading through his file, lawmen wondered how Michael Wayne Jackson ever got paroled. On March 1, 1985 the ex-con was arrested by Indianapolis police for shoplifting and outstanding warrants. A week later, federal agents searched Jackson's pickup truck and found a 12-gauge homemade shotgun and four Molotov cocktails.

While Jackson was being held in jail, a family member wrote four letters to the sheriff's office warning them of Jackson's violent nature and enclosed a note from a psychiatrist that read, "Jackson needs psychiatric help and confinement" in a state institution.

Jackson pleaded guilty to the possession of the

shotgun and homemade bombs and was confined at the Medical Center for Federal Prisoners in Springfield, Missouri. A three-person panel of mental health experts determined he was a dangerously sick man and needed confinement and therapy. A federal prosecutor sought a court order that allowed the prison hospital to keep Jackson beyond the terms of his sentence.

Despite the warnings, Jackson was paroled in April, 1986. A staff psychiatrist agreed the inmate was extremely and dangerously sick, but noted, "The patient has made rapid improvement and is well enough for parole, providing he take the antipsychotic drug, Mellaril."

Shortly after his parole, police received word from one of Jackson's relatives, saying that he was not taking his medicine and was acting strangely.

The relative said she thought he was back to taking illegal drugs. "He would be abusive and would just sit here and giggle," she said. "You could tell by the look in his eyes."

The relative later told a reporter, "I don't know why it keeps going on repeating itself all the time, people like Mike being turned loose on innocent people. He has been a living dead person for a long time."

Probation Officer Tom Gahl had gone to Jackson's home to collect a urine sample to make sure the parolee was taking his medications and not using illegal drugs, as he had a history of it.

It was a routine call; now he was dead, and the person police called the most dangerous man alive was loose.

Law enforcement agencies in a ten-state area were alerted to be on the lookout for Jackson. He was last seen driving the beige 1982 Mercury he took from the mobile home in Clinton County and was to be considered armed and extremely dangerous.

News reports blanketed Indiana and sent citizens rushing to their telephones. One told Indianapolis police: "He's back in his house and hiding in the basement."

A SWAT team searched the home but found no evidence the fugitive had returned.

Lawmen kept an eye on Jackson's relatives and the Midtown Community Mental Health Center in Indianapolis, which had given medication and psychiatric counseling to Jackson while he was on parole.

The next sighting, however, came from O'Fallon, Missouri, 40 miles north of St. Louis. Normally a quiet town, police received reports at 9:15 p.m. that a man with a beard had stolen at least three cars and assaulted two women. He was seen heading north toward Wright City driving a 1970 Cadillac Seville.

Wright City Patrolman Roland E. Clemonds had Monday night off. But he was bored sitting around the house and went into town to join Police Chief William D. Burgess in patrolling this town of 1,200.

A normal Monday evening, their main duties might have been chasing the town's teenagers from the back lot of a gas station.

At 9 o'clock, they received a report that a Cadillac Seville stolen from O'Fallon had been spotted on I-70 and might be headed for Wright City.

The two lawmen parked at a church where they could watch for the car on the interstate. The chief figured it was a false sighting, or the car would be caught up the highway, but what the heck, it never hurt to be safe.

The two had no sooner taken their position, when a gold-colored Cadillac raced down the off ramp leading into town.

"That's it," Clemonds said excitedly.

The chief couldn't believe it either.

The Cadillac stopped abruptly about 15 feet from them, so the driver faced the passenger side of the cruiser. Clemonds stepped from the car, raised his revolver and identified himself. The driver replied by pointing the barrel of a shotgun at him.

"Duck, Chief!" Clemonds yelled. "He's gonna shoot."

The first blast sprayed the car with shotgun pellets, several of which hit Clemonds in the head, knocking him down. Before he fell, he pumped off a slug at the car, hitting the driver's side door.

The driver put his foot on the accelerator and the Cadillac roared away from the parking lot, tires smoking.

Chief Burgess leveled his revolver and pumped four slugs at the fleeing car. He then looked at his only patrol officer on the ground, holding his forehead.

"I'll be all right," Clemonds said. "Get Jackson."

The chief roared off after the Cadillac while Clemonds lay bleeding on the street. A bunch of teenagers who had seen the whole thing circled Clemonds to protect him until help arrived.

The patrolman was taken to the hospital where he was treated for a wound above the right eye. It wasn't serious and he was back on duty in a couple of hours.

Meanwhile, Chief Burgess pursued the Cadillac, followed by other lawmen who learned of the shooting. They found it two miles northeast of Wright City, after Jackson tried to crash through a fence to get back on the Interstate.

In the trunk was a 26-year-old O'Fallon man. He said he had been waxing the Cadillac near his apartment when a man with a beard stuck a shotgun under his nose and ordered him to drive to the Interstate.

The driver said he was so nervous that he could not find it immediately and the gunman ordered him to pull over and get into the trunk.

The man was taken to a local hospital and treated for minor injuries suffered when Jackson crashed the car through the fence.

Not so fortunate was Earl Dallas Finn, a 47-year-old motorist found dead in his car at 6:48 p.m. in St. Peter, Missouri, just east of O'Fallon.

Missouri State Highway patrol officers initially thought Finn had died in a car accident and learned later that he had been killed with a shotgun. Police speculated Finn had been shot because the automobile he was driving resembled an unmarked police car.

Missouri State Police searched the wooded area off Interstate 70 near the abandoned Cadillac but found no sign of Jackson.

The lawmen noticed a bullet hole in the driver's side door about waist high, and bloodstains on the seat. Jackson had either been hit by the bullet or injured when the car crashed. Either way, he was wounded.

Jackson was also still armed. The shotgun that wounded the patrol officer and sprayed the police cruiser was not in the car. Nor were any other weapons. A wounded, psychotic killer was on the run with nothing to lose. Police could not think of a more deadly animal.

Jackson was also aided by a torrential rainstorm that drenched Missouri and southern Illinois, reducing visibility to almost nothing. Lawmen decided to wait until daybreak to renew the search for the madman.

Meanwhile, the peaceful community of Wright City became an armed camp. Missouri State Highway Patrol officers, looking more like soldiers in their combat gear, set up roadblocks and manned every major intersection leading in and out of town.

"This has got to be the safest little community in America," Police Chief Burgess said, eyeing the lawmen who had made Wright City an armed fortress.

The SWAT officers, dressed in bullet-proof vests, searched the woods south of town but found no sign of Jackson. The search expanded to nearby homes and barns, but without success.

Officials also searched freight trains carrying coal and grain, and watched the interstate and highway. The search had focused national attention on this town of 1,200. Dozens of media people, hundreds of lawmen and curiosity seekers, flooded the town. "It's the busiest I've seen the downtown since the last street dance," chuckled one observer.

Restaurants and stores did turn-away business, but

143

the rest of the local economy had come to a halt. Merchants complained that business was off 30 to 50 percent.

Mail wasn't being delivered to rural residents and 60 to 65 percent of the town's 380 students stayed home.

"It's irritating how one person can do this to a town," one resident complained.

Lawmen weren't having much luck either. Tracking dogs were brought in, but heavy rains had apparently washed away the scent. Helicopter pilots and ground searchers had also been unable to pick up Jackson's trace.

Rumors were as thick as the summer foliage. One had it that Jackson was dead and his bones were discovered buried in a pit. Another one said Jackson was hiding out with relatives on the south side of town. Police checked it out and learned a family named Jackson lived there but was no relation to the fugitive.

Still another rumor had it that Jackson had checked himself into a mental health facility in Dallas. That, too, proved to be untrue. Like the others, it, too, was erroneous.

The manhunt continued through the end of the week. Searing 90-degree heat replaced the rains and took a toll on the searchers. On Saturday, 15 members of the Missouri Highway Patrol Special Emergency Response Team were given the day off.

"We had no choice," explained Lieutenant Roy Foss. "They've been hitting it pretty hard and it would have been easy for them to get tired and hurt."

144

Other troopers took their place but had little luck. Abandoned homes and barns were searched several times but without success.

That weekend, specially trained tracking dogs on loan from the Kansas Department of Corrections were brought to Wright City. One was trained to follow cold trails, one to follow hot ones and the third to find bodies.

The dogs sniffed and yelped and went every which way, but caught only fleas. Their trainer said the heavy rains, followed by the heat, had likely ruined the scent.

Then at 5:30 on Sunday afternoon, a man called to report the burglary of his trailer.

Police investigators went to the trailer, located three miles south of town, and less than a mile from where Jackson ditched the Cadillac.

Inside the trailer, they found an open can of soup, half a sandwich, several disposable razors and a broken mirror.

The hair matched the texture and color of Jackson's beard. It appeared the fugitive had broken into the trailer for food and a chance to clean himself up.

Sergeant Jim Lee of the Missouri Highway Patrol radioed the information to headquarters. Tracking dogs were brought to the trailer and presented with clothing taken from the Cadillac.

The dogs jumped and yelped and started back toward town. At 1 a.m., the dogs had followed a path back through the center of Wright City and to a three-story, white-frame house on East North Second Street, a block from city hall. The flak-jacketed officers thought of rushing the building, then decided it was too dangerous at dark and decided to wait for daylight.

Daytime, nighttime—it didn't matter. The house was empty. Troopers learned that when they burst through the doors at 6:15 a.m.

Troopers grumbled about the heat and went back to work. The search had entered its second week and Wright City was getting grumpy.

"The troopers won't let me go back to my house," complained a man who lived south of Wright City. "They've searched my place two times now. You think they would have caught him by now."

Residents complained about the inconvenience, but no one wanted the police to leave. "It's spooky," said one. "We keep the doors locked and don't go out. It is like a whole army out there, not just one man."

Police were certain Jackson hadn't escaped because there were no other reports of shootings or cars being stolen. What they didn't know was if he was still alive or dead.

"We have had several reports of vultures circling," Highway Patrol Sergeant Lee told newsmen. "We've checked them out but they weren't anything."

The search continued into Thursday. At 6:35, officers went through a farmhouse off Route H, about 1½ miles south of the highway rest area where Jackson ditched the Cadillac nine days earlier. They had searched the property twice before and found nothing. This time, however, lawmen found a blue raincoat, identical to the one Jackson was last seen wearing.

The officers radioed their findings to police head-

146

quarters, then continued the search to the barn. Moments later, shots rang out.

Over 100 FBI agents, state troopers and sheriff's deputies rushed to the scene. Floodlights were set up to illuminate the barn, while a helicopter equipped with a searchlight hovered overhead.

Residents were not allowed on Route H. Reporters were stopped and threatened with arrest as they tried to cross railroad tracks, about one-fourth of a mile south of the outer road.

Word that Jackson was trapped inside the barn spread to the city. Some 200 residents piled into cars and formed instant parking lots at the roadblocks. They turned on radios and cracked beers and watched from a distance as police tried to talk Jackson into giving himself up.

"Come on, Mike," boomed an officer over a loudspeaker. "We don't want to hurt you. Mike, I know you're hungry. You want to end this also. You can help all of us."

After 30 minutes and no response, eight tear gas canisters were fired into the barn at intervals of 30 to 45 seconds. The gas also failed to get a response, but police did not appear worried or in a hurry.

"We have been here a week and a half," one lawman noted. "There's no reason in getting in a hurry now."

An hour later, after repeated requests for Jackson to give himself up, SWAT officers rushed the barn. They kicked in the doors ready to empty their automatic weapons into the man suspected of a three-state reign of terror.

Instead, they found Michael Wayne Jackson's

crumpled body on the floor of the abandoned barn, with half his face blown away from his own shotgun.

"We are pleased to bring peace and quiet back to Wright City," announced Hal Helterhoff, head of the FBI office in St. Louis. "You always get very pleased when you can bring a menace to society to final justice."

Jackson, still bearded and wearing the same clothes he had on when last seen, was positively identified by fingerprints. He was barefoot at the time he was found, apparently trying to dry his shoes and indicating he recently had been in the rain.

"He hadn't been in there that long," one Missouri Highway Patrol officer noted. "That barn had been checked and rechecked numerous times. There were a of cars patrolling all the time, so he couldn't stay in one place very long."

JOHN LIST
"17-YEAR TRACK OF THE FAMILY SLAYER!"
by Bill Ryder

It all began with a routine call. Before it was to end some 18 years later, it took on the unbelievably grotesque proportions of a "Nightmare on Elm Street" horror scenario. Its bloodstained history would leave at least three American communities in a state of benumbed shock. For those living in the well-to-do community of Westfield, New Jersey, things would never be quite the same again.

It was early in November 1971 that a series of notes and telephone calls were put through to teachers in the Westfield school system and to local tradesmen.

The message was, with a few minor variations, primarily the same: Please excuse the three children of local residents Alma and John List from classes until further notice. Please suspend mail and newspaper deliveries to 431 Hillside Avenue until further notice.

According to the then 45-year-old Joseph List, he, his wife and three youngsters would be away from their 18-room, $500,000 Victorian mansion for an indeterminate period of time. In placing the messages, List was said to have variously mentioned a protracted vacation and the need to care for an ailing relative who was said to be residing in North Carolina.

List was a highly respected accountant. He had served in such worthy capacities as a Sunday School teacher in the Lutheran church where his family worshipped. There was no reason to suspect that anything sinister could touch the man, let alone be instituted by him.

The devoted husband and father possessed other impeccable credentials. He was reputed to hold an M.B.A. degree from the University of Michigan. He had been a successful insurance salesman before entering the field of accounting and was (in 1971) a former vice president of a local bank.

He and his family completely fit into the respectable, conservative, affluent suburban town that was Westfield in the early 1970s.

A month passed before anyone felt that something was amiss in the List household. Neighbors began reporting that the lights which had been left on at the Hillside Avenue address—a seemingly standard practice of suburbanites wishing to discourage housebreakers and vandals—were beginning to wink out.

In the ensuing days, concern grew. The neighbors contacted the Westfield police, asking them to check the List premises to determine if everything there was in order.

It was on a cold, foggy, drab December 7, 1971, that a detail under the command of Westfield Police Chief James Moran entered the sprawling turn-of-the-century mansion.

Some 18 years later, Moran would say, "It's something I remember like yesterday. I walked into that house and saw that one kid was shot with nine bullets in him, just savagely.

"You don't forget something like that."

It was more than the numbing chill of the interior (the heat had been turned off to slow the decomposition of the bodies) that caused those who accompanied Moran on his tour of horror to shiver as if attacked by some nameless, malignant ague.

One of those who had been there at the moment of the grisly discoveries would write nearly two decades later, "The ballroom of the List mansion was one of the most beautiful rooms I'd ever seen. But on its hardwood floors was a scene more horrible than any I'd ever seen or imagined."

The man would go on to tell of how four bodies, rotted and blackening in the putrification of decomposition, had been discovered.

"I've never forgotten that sight," the man would continue.

"The smell struck me and the Westfield police officers I accompanied as soon as we entered. The bodies were those of List's wife and three children, all neatly laid out in a row on sleeping bags. Only later did we find the corpse of his mother upstairs.

"I remember one of the police officers telling me that the woman had been crammed into a bedroom

151

closet and that they'd had to break her legs to re-move her."

As the nauseated searchers continued their probe of the mansion-now-turned-charnel-house, they came upon one obscene discovery after another. In-cluded were bunches of blood-soaked paper toweling which had been stuffed into paper bags in the kitchen. The walls had been hastily washed in an at-tempt to eradicate the gory stains which besmirched the house's walls and woodwork. The attempt had failed.

Propped on the dining room table was a letter (al-legedly written by John List) reputedly explaining why and how he had killed his family.

Caught in the maelstrom of violence which had wiped out three generations of Lists had been Alma List, the missing accountant's 85-year-old mother, Helen List, 45, John's wife; his 16-year-old daughter, Patricia; and his two sons, John Jr., 15, and Fred-erick, 12.

One theory had it that the murders had occurred on November 9th, two days before List himself had disappeared.

The chronology espoused by those investigating the savage bloodletting had it that List allegedly be-gan the carnage after his three children had left for school on the fatal morning. First to be shot to death had been the missing man's wife. Then, allegedly, John murdered his aged mother.

According to police speculation, there had been a temporary respite in the mortal proceedings. The al-leged killer had awaited the return of the teenage children from their classes. It was thought that Patricia had been the first to enter the house and had been cut down by a single bullet when she did. John Jr. had been the next arrival. Because he had probably put up a valiant but futile struggle, the 15-year-old had been made the target of nine bullets. Twelve-year-old Frederick had been the last to come home and the last to die.

Police have never revealed the full contents of the five-page confessional letter allegedly written by List and addressed to the pastor of the Redeemer Lutheran Church in Westfield. However, local lawmen have reported that the note describes how the shootings had been carried out and the reasons behind them in graphic detail.

It was believed that the accountant had been in severe financial straits. This theory was shored up by information developed that he had taken out two mortgages on his home and that he had been dipping into his mother's savings account, estimated at $200,000.

There were also reports that John Sr. had been failing in a financial consultant business he'd set up.

Possibly compounding the missing man's animosity towards his next of kin, according to those with inside information of the contents of the "confessional letter," was List's sense of having lost control over the women of his family. He was said to have felt that his wife and daughter had been going down the wrong path and that his sons would not have understood their father's reasons for having slain Helen and Patricia.

At this point in the probe, local police only had these shreds of evidence to go on . . .

Five people had been coldbloodedly shot to death at the Hillside Avenue address.

Bullets recovered from the decomposed bodies indicated that a .22-caliber rifle and a 9 mm pistol had been used in the executions.

The condition of the bodies and the continuing absence of John List led probers to believe that the slayings had taken place on November 9th at the latest and that the corpses had remained undetected until December 7th.

The sequence of the murders had been determined by the fact that while the bodies of Alma and Helen List had been dressed in indoor clothing, the three teenagers' cadavers had been stretched out still garbed in their overcoats. The rationale was that the children had been intercepted as they arrived home.

No sight of John List Sr. had been reported since November 9th.

The enigma surrounding the missing bespectacled man's whereabouts thickened on December 9th when his car was discovered in a parking lot at Kennedy Airport, just two days after police had first entered the Hillside Avenue home.

Now an APB was issued on the balding executive and churchman. Everything that was known about his earlier life was disseminated in hopes that it would produce leads. Included in the dossier was List's earlier service in the armed forces. It was learned that the erstwhile Westfield financial expert had entered the Army as a private during World War II. Later, during the Korean War, he served as a reservist. He'd left the Army as a first lieutenant.

But there was nothing in these facts which would

keep List's trail from turning ice-cold. Both the police, who wanted to bring him in on the indictments for five counts of murder which had been lodged against him in absentia, and the FBI, which was tracing him for having unlawfully fled to avoid prosecution for murder, were stymied.

It was obvious that the fugitive had made excellent use of his month-long head start over his pursuers.

The fact that he had abandoned his car at Kennedy added to the confusion. Lawmen had to wrestle with other possibilities.

Perhaps List himself had become a victim. The area around Kennedy Airport has long been known as a mob dumping ground.

If List was still alive, he could be just about anywhere on earth. Flights from Kennedy not only stretched over the furthest reaches of the United States, but the airport served as the point of departure for all overseas flights from the New York City area.

There were numerous sightings, not only from the 50 states, but from Europe and South America, as well. None panned out.

The simple truth was that if John List Jr. resembled anybody at all, that person was "Everyman." Outside of a jagged scar that had been left behind his ear by an earlier mastoidectomy, John List had few if any other distinguishing physical characteristics. Although his fingerprints were on file in Washington, as are those of all persons who have served in the Armed Forces, they would prove of little value unless List was apprehended on some other charge. As long as he kept his nose clean, he could probably go about his new business in complete anonymity.

As the search remained stalled, the Hillside Avenue home came to be thought of more as a haunted house than a mansion. It became a magnet to teenagers who drove by and dared each other to walk around the grounds and peer through the windows.

The macabre hijinks surrounding the property ended suddenly in 1972 when the house mysteriously burned to the ground.

The months slipped into years. Still there was little hope that John List would ever surface. People talked of the quintuple shootings which had wiped out the List family as they talked about the other "great unsolved crimes of history." The common thought was that the slayings would go down alongside the "Jack The Ripper" murders as a prime example of somebody getting away with murder. However, Chief Moran, as well as Frank Marranca, head of the homicide division of the Union County (New Jersey) Prosecutor's office, John C. McGinley, agent in charge of the Newark Office of the FBI, and scores of other lawmen throughout the country, felt somewhat differently.

Moran, for example, retired as Westfield Chief of Police in 1986. But he continued his quest. Three years after his retirement, he was still tracking down leads. He never gave up the "wanted" flyer which contained List's picture and pertinent facts concerning the fugitive.

Never mind that FBI agents from 23 offices had at one time or another gone out on wild-goose chases which had led nowhere. Never mind that there was nobody who could say with certainty that John List,

Sr., was still alive.

Then, early in 1989, Marranca had an idea. It concerned the Fox Network weekly program, "America's Most Wanted."

Although most lawmen had expressed early dislike for the weekly show which graphically stressed sensational unsolved cases and urged civilians to contact the producers with possible leads, the enthusiastic public response had not gone unnoticed. In recent months editors and executives of "America's Most Wanted" were able to boast that the show had been responsible for eliciting information which had led to the arrest of 48 prime suspects in 48 major crimes.

Playing a hunch, the Union County Prosecutor's homicide division head contacted program representatives, asking them to do an item on the List case.

The talented sculptor worked from the only photos which were currently available of the fugitive. He improvised such details as a receding hairline and the wrinkles which would have accrued over an 18-year span.

Later Ms. Roberts would say of the project, "The bust was an experiment. Our show hinges on the indelible image of the human face. In this case, all we had was precious few photographs almost twenty years old. This crime was the most notorious in New Jersey history."

Now all systems were go for the cooperative venture. On Sunday evening, May 21, 1989, the List story was beamed to viewers on 125 of the Fox Television Network's stations.

Minutes after the List portion of the telecast was aired Fox switchboards were deluged with tips. Over

300 callers came forward with their views as to List's current identity and where he might be located.

To FBI agents, at least 200 of the leads held promise of being "substantive." One, in particular, stood out.

This was the one which was to send three federal agents from their Richmond, Virginia headquarters to nearby suburban Midlothian, Virginia home of 63-year-old Robert P. Clark.

There the G-Men showed Clark's wife a number of pictures they had of List. At first the thunderstruck middle-aged-woman refused to believe that the man she had wed in 1985 could be the John List, Sr.

Later, Agent McGinley of the Newark, New Jersey FBI office would say of the interview with Mrs. Clark, "She reacted with disbelief and shock when the agents showed her the pictures of List. But she was very cooperative and helpful in resolving questions about his identity. She brought out wedding pictures which showed a man who still resembled the pictures of List that were circulated after the murders."

Once she had been convinced of Clark's alleged other identity, his wife provided two Norfolk-based agents with the one item they felt they needed to complete the puzzle. This was the name and Richmond address of Clark's current employer.

A short time later, two agents were walking through the doors of one of the biggest accounting firms in the Richmond area. The third agent had stayed behind with Clark's visibly shaken wife.

At the firm's reception desk, the agents asked for Clark's employers and were told by the receptionist that the executives were out of town. They then inquired as to whether Clark was in.

The receptionist led the G-Men to a small office where the 63-year-old suspect was seated at his desk.

Reportedly the agents asked the suspect, "Are you John List?"

They claim that Clark denied he was the man they sought. However, the receptionist who had watched the dramatic climax of the 18-year search being played out would report, "He (Clark) didn't seem surprised to see them (the FBI agents). He didn't say anything, other than he wasn't John List.

"They took him into custody and when they led him out, he turned his head and glanced at me and gave me this strange look. He looked full of anger."

An attorney who works in the office building and who viewed the arrest, said, "He didn't offer any resistance and he didn't look surprised."

The man who had over the course of 18 years apparently built an entire new life was taken in handcuffs to the Richmond FBI field office and fingerprinted. According to the FBI, Clark's prints were a perfect match for those of John List Jr. which had been in their files.

An official FBI statement noted, "Although he would not admit to his identity, List was positively identified by his fingerprints."

For retired Chief Moran, June 1, 1989, was a banner day. Said the former head of the Westfield Police Force, "That's the best thing that ever happened to me. How can a guy murder five people and walk away?

"That's what bothered me these many years."

The sense of vindication for the effort he'd put into the almost two-decade-long search was apparent as the triumphant Moran added, "We knew he had to be somewhere."

The suspect, who was described as "very calm and self-contained," was taken before United States Magistrate David G. Lowe in Richmond for a preliminary hearing. He was ordered held at the Henrico County Jail pending extradition hearings to bring him back to New Jersey to face further court proceedings.

As List was led from the courtroom, clad in a white sport shirt and slacks and with his manacled wrists attached to a chain which encircled his waist, he glared balefully through his thick-lensed eyeglasses.

With List securely in custody, authorities turned to piecing together his comings and goings over the past 18 years.

They claimed that while he had changed his name to Robert P. Clark, he had made no effort to alter his appearance or embark on a new vocation.

At the time of his arrest, List was earning $24,000 a year from his employers. He had been handling corporate work and clients' personal finances, including preparation of income tax returns.

He had posed as the upright citizen he had once been in New Jersey.

List had not run afoul of the law since having fled to Denver, Colorado, in 1972.

Those who had known him in Denver, where he'd remained until 1988, described List as a quiet churchgoing accountant who impressed neighbors, pastors and acquaintances as respectable and altogether average.

Some referred to him as "an American John Doe" who lived in a modest home, worked steadily and spent his free time puttering around his garden and watching television.

Generally, the feeling about List was that he had always been friendly, generously doing odd jobs for neighbors, trading videotapes and books. But he had remained tight-lipped about his past. Acquaintances stressed that his life in the Denver area had centered around home, work and church, and that he seemed, if anything, like the antithesis of evil.

Said one woman, "I don't know what a guy who's killed five people is supposed to look like, but he was not that person."

Added a man who had been a Clark neighbor in Midlothian, "He worked hard in his yard, went to work every day, went to church every Sunday—the guy was so average. You talk about an average neighborhood, this is it. This just doesn't happen in my neighborhood."

A Denver pastor commented, "He was well-liked. He had gained the respect of the parish. There was nothing to cause us to be suspicious of his demeanor or his credibility. Somehow, some way, he was able to stabilize himself here."

The clergyman attributed the Clarks' move from Denver to the Richmond area to the fact that Clark's wife reportedly had relatives living in Virginia. He said he had recently received a letter from Clark (List) which gave no indication that anything was wrong.

One co-worker at the Richmond accounting firm

called Clark "a nice fellow, almost too nice to be true. He even had a fraternal Order of Police sticker on his car."

With irony, a woman co-worker stated, "I would hold him up to my husband as a model because I heard him talk to his wife on the phone—he would say how much he loved her."

The pastor of the Lutheran Church the Clarks had joined after they had moved into the Midlothian bedroom community, 15 miles from Richmond, noted, "The congregation is stunned. I think we are all trying to reserve judgment. They have been kind to people. They have been faithful church members."

One Richmond friend seemed to sum up the feelings of many when he stated, "I only know Bobby Clark. I don't know John List. But even if it's all true, this is not a man with a history of murder, but a man with murder in his history. It was one day after all these many years."

The friend stressed Clark's abhorrence of violence, saying, "He didn't even like football because he said it was just men out there battering their heads together, instead of using their brains. Clark liked baseball, the *National Geographic,* Walter Cronkite and documentaries.

"He is deeply religious. If he goes into a McDonald's for a hamburger, the man is going to bow his head and say grace to God."

Piecing together the events of Clark's (List's) life since 1972, sources close to the situation said that a resume he prepared for a position after moving to Richmond in 1988, listed a business in Wheatridge, Colorado, under the name of R.C. Miller. They said no such R.C. Miller is currently in business there, nor is there any evidence that it ever existed.

In 1973, a close friend from that time places Clark as working as a night cook at a Holiday Inn in Golden, Colorado.

Clark's name first appeared in a Denver telephone directory in 1974. He continued working as a restaurant and hotel cook. By 1977, Clark was seeking employment in accounting.

Noted one executive who interviewed him at that time, "He was an introvert galore, if there is such a thing. He spoke slowly, softly, almost under his breath."

The man recollects that Clark's clothes at the interview were ill-matched. "He was living hand-to-mouth, doing bookkeeping work," the man holds. "I had the impression he was barely eking out enough of a living to buy weenies and a room somewhere. He was living meagerly and said he needed a full-time job."

An employer for whom Clark had worked in 1977 recalled that he had found him a little strange. He cited Clark's penchant for eating a solitary luncheon in his automobile while listening to classical programs on his car radio. Said the man, "We kind of liked him and felt sorry for him.

"I remember talking to him a few times about marriage, because I was having marital problems at the time. He said he'd been through that before and knew what I meant. I'd tell him I wasn't going to get into that kind of a mess again, and he said he wasn't going to, either. He insinuated that it had been a bad experience."

The year 1977, had been a good one for Clark. His salary rose to $400 a week and he met his future second wife at a Lutheran Church function.

However, there were apparent discrepancies in stories he allegedly told friends concerning his past familial relationships.

One friend said, "When asked about his family, he would make some reference to Minnesota or Michigan. He would say that he had been married before but that his wife had been terminally ill and took years to die and that he took care of her. Her illness left astronomical bills, he'd tell me. We all made assumptions, such as the fact that he didn't have any children, since his wife had been so sick."

However, later in Richmond, another friend quoted him as having confided that his wife had been an alcoholic and a spendthrift who had died of cancer, and that he had a daughter who was "somewhat uncontrollable."

At a news conference held after Clark's arrest, his second wife reported that he had told her that his first wife was "a very sick, sickly lady."

During the same news conference, Mrs. Clark corroborated a neighbor's report that the woman had shown her a tabloid edition in 1985 which carried John List's photograph accompanied by a story of the Westfield murders.

Said Mrs. Clark, "I dismissed it because I felt it was not true. It still is not true."

The neighbor's fears for Mrs. Clark were rekindled when she watched "America's Most Wanted" on May 21st, long after the Clarks had moved to Virginia. She revealed that she had instructed her son-in-law to call the program's telephone number which had been flashed across the screen to give the operator the Clarks' address and telephone number in Virginia.

It was also revealed that the Clarks had been beset by financial troubles since having made the Virginia move.

In her interview with the *Richmond News Leader,* Mrs. Clark was quoted as saying, "I find it impossible to believe my husband is a killer.

"I hope somehow this is not true, and if it is, he was so stressed out that something snapped.

"I am devoted to him. I hope that somehow, God will see us through."

For the people who suffered through 18 years of the malaise which gripped Westfield, New Jersey, between the gun deaths of the five family members of John List Jr. and the arrest of Robert P. Clark in Richmond, Virginia, on June 1, 1989, the sense of relief at the possibility that at long last the case has been broken, is great.

However there are those who still mourn the dead.

This was shown shortly after Clark was taken into custody when somebody left a small card amidst the five graves which marked the final resting place of Alma, Helen, Patricia, John Jr. and Frederick List.

The message was simple. It read, "Now at last you can rest in peace."

As this is being written, Robert P. Clark, identified by the FBI as John List Sr. — is awaiting further court action on the five counts of murder and one federal count of unlawful escape to avoid prosecution for murder.

Under the United States Constitution he has the right to be presumed innocent of these charges until and unless proved otherwise under due process of law.

TEOFILO MEDINA
"FOUR EXECUTIONS BY THE RAMPAGING PSYCHO!"
by Turk Ryder

Sadistic midgets. Jesus Christ. Voices from the grave. Worms and snakes.

He couldn't take it anymore. Standing up, he screamed. "Aaaiiieee!!!"

His fingers gripped the bottom of the five-foot-long table. With a violent jerk, he flipped it over on its top.

The attorney turned, startled. A juror gasped. The judge ordered, "Subdue him!"

A court marshall leaped over the gate and tackled the screaming man who saw midgets and Jesus. They went down on the floor. Another bailiff joined the fracas.

The judge told the jury to leave the courtroom until order had been restored. Turning to the marshalls, he ordered, "Put him in shackles."

The defense attorney, gaining composure, took his client aside. "Teo, what's going on?"

Teo, looking baffled, shook his head. "I don't know why," he said, pointing to his head. "I don't know why."

The prosecutor thought he knew why. He believed the violent outburst was not the reaction of a man crazed by cryptic voices and sadistic midgets, but a carefully orchestrated act to avoid standing trial. Avoid it at all costs. And he had good reason to.

Four people were dead, a woman raped, and a man threatened with death in a midnight reign of terror that left hardened lawmen shaking their heads in disgust.

It began on the gritty streets of Santa Ana, California, in the shadow of the courthouse where the man visited by Jesus fought to avoid the death sentence.

The date: Thursday evening, October 18, 1984. At 7:30 p.m. Horacio Ariza, 23, left his Santa Ana home and headed for the gas station on North Bristol Street to begin the graveyard shift.

Working the night shift alone, in a high-crime area, was not the gravy train. But Horacio didn't mind. He was happy to have a job. Besides, he had other plans.

Handsome, dark-haired Horacio grew up in the Canal Zone, Panama, where his mom, a career Marine, was stationed.

From her, he received love and affection and learned the value of discipline and hard work. In school, he did well, showed a flair for athletics, was popular with classmates and displayed a burning desire to succeed. That desire did not diminish when, as a high school sophomore, he returned to live with

168

his father in the City of Orange, California. After graduation, he gave some thought to taking classes at the local junior college and maybe getting a civil service job. To support himself, he worked afternoons part-time at a dry cleaning business, and fulltime evenings at the gas station.

He missed his mom, and wrote her often. "They were very close," said Horacio's girlfriend. "He was close to everyone in his family."

In a letter, he learned that his mom was finishing up her tour of duty and was returning to California. Horacio was excited by the good news, and as he arrived at the station to begin another night of the graveyard shift, he thought of how he looked forward to seeing her.

Fifteen miles east of Santa Ana, in Corona, 18-year-old Craig Martin had finished dinner and was getting ready to work at the gas station on East Sixth Street.

Craig took the job to earn money for classes in police sciences at Chaffey Community College. The sandy-haired teenager wanted to be a cop, and he could barely wait to get through classes to go to the academy.

Craig didn't mind the work, or the fact that he worked alone. He once joked that he wasn't afraid of being robbed because he was "bulletproof." The threat of robbery was a fact of life for anyone working the night shift, and he had discussed the danger with his father, who had once held the same job. The two agreed that heroics were pointless; better to give them the money than lose your life for a few bucks.

It was just another Thursday evening for Craig

Martin and Horacio Ariza, and much of Orange and Riverside Counties, when a motorist pulled into the gas station on North Bristol Street where Horacio was the attendant. He went to the mini-mart to pay in advance but found no one behind the counter. He went back to the pumps, found no one there, then returned to the counter to see if the attendant, perhaps in the storeroom, had returned.

He hadn't and the confused motorist was just about to leave, when he noticed the cash register drawer was open. Then he looked behind the counter.

Horacio Ariza lay on the floor unconscious, blood pouring from a bullet wound in his head. The 23-year-old clerk was rushed by ambulance to the University of California's Irvine Medical Center. He had been shot twice in the head at point-blank range with a small-caliber weapon that had left burned gunpowder embedded in his skin. A police officer rode in the ambulance with him but Horacio Ariza never regained consciousness, and was never able to tell who shot him.

"He's in very critical condition," the emergency room physician said. "There isn't a whole lot we can do."

Five days later, Horacio was dead.

The shooting was investigated by Santa Ana police detectives headed by Sergeant John McCallum under the supervision of Lieutenant Earl Porter.

Computerized receipts indicated the shooting likely occurred between 11:30 and midnight. The weapon was a .22- or .25-caliber pistol, such as the type used for target practice or gopher shooting. The clerk had been shot from behind the counter at almost point-blank range — execution-style slaying.

The motive, police believed, was robbery, but they were puzzled about why Horacio was shot. Employees at the station were instructed in case of a holdup, to comply with the robber's demands and to avoid provoking him or doing anything that might lead to violence.

Relatives told police Horacio was "brave but no dummy" and would have followed company policy. He would not have jeopardized himself for a few dollars. There was no indication of a struggle or anything else to indicate a motive for the gunman to pull the trigger.

The only conclusion was that Horacio had been killed so there would be no witness to identify the gunman.

On Friday morning, detectives learned of a second shooting at a gas station, which sent them scurrying to Corona, in Riverside County.

Craig Martin was halfway through his shift when a man stormed into the gas station and demanded the money from the till. Martin gave it to him; as he had discussed with his father, there was no reason to play hero.

Corona police estimated the robber made off with $200 in cash. But instead of fleeing, he raised his weapon and fired one slug into the teenager's head.

His body was discovered at 1:13 Friday morning by a customer wanting gas.

Corona police investigators Sergeant Roger Brabant and Detective Dale Stewart met with the Santa Ana sleuths. There were many similarities indicating

171

the same person or persons were responsible for the shootings of Horacio Ariza and Craig Martin.

The victims were both graveyard shift attendants working alone at stations owned or operated by the same company. Both were shot within two hours of each other, execution-style with a small-caliber weapon. There was no evidence the two had resisted or tried to flee, or done anything other than follow the gunman's orders.

"This was a brutal, senseless crime," Detective Stewart snarled. "There was no reason for this boy to die."

Like other clerks working the graveyard shift, Douglas Metal, 23, knew there were risks. He worked the night shift at a store on Garden Grove Boulevard in Garden Grove. But he figured chances were slight he would get robbed, and besides, he didn't figure he would be doing it much longer.

Metal wanted to be a professional musician. He taught himself to play guitar, later mastered keyboards and drums. Tall, thin, with long blond hair, he looked the part of a rock star.

"Music was everything to him," said a friend. "That was his life."

His bedroom was cluttered with musical and stereo equipment and the walls were lined with rock music posters and momentos, such as a circular he distributed nine years earlier when he formed his first "little garage band."

The circular read: "Drummer, 14 years old, would like to form rock group. I have not had any group experience, but would like to start anyway. I'm looking for a lead guitarist and/or bass guitarist. I've been playing on my own for three years mostly with records. I can play all kinds of rock and hope you can too!!! I have had a few lessons. If interested call me."

Metal had been in several bands since then, many he formed himself. But clubs didn't pay unknowns very much, and he took a part-time job at the all-night store. He worked between eight and 12 hours a week at the dairy, helping to stock shelves on weekends and minding the store when the owner had errands to run.

Then in March 1984, Metal told the owner that he wanted to work more hours. The owner quickly agreed. "Douglas was a hard worker and very reliable," the owner recalled with a touch of sadness.

The job paid the bills and gave Douglas time to practice and go to auditions. He hoped the club business would improve so he could make a living with his band and play full time. There had been some offers and other signs of encouragement that made Douglas Metal feel that day was close at hand when he went to the store Saturday evening, November 4th, to begin his shift.

At 2:15 Sunday morning the young clerk was found dead behind the counter, shot twice in the head. Like Horacio Ariza and Craig Martin, Douglas Metal had been gunned down execution-style with a small-caliber pistol.

Victor Rea, 20, was a Renaissance man. He drew. He sculpted. He threw pottery. He designed clothing and jewelry and made many of his own clothes.

But his main interest was photography. He started out with a cheap little camera and a beginning course at a local high school. Within two years, he was a professional-caliber fashion photographer.

"Victor's mind was always running," according to a relative. "He was always playing with ideas for clothes or drawings or photographs. He never sat around and did nothing. He'd always get out a piece of paper and start drawing. He always had a new idea."

Victor wanted a career as a fashion photographer. He enrolled at the Fashion Institute of Design and Merchandising in Santa Ana. Instructors who saw his work said he had the eye and the drive to turn his dream into reality.

To pay tuition he took a $6-an-hour job at the all-night gas station on Newhope Street in Santa Ana.

He liked the money, didn't mind the work, but was troubled by the job. "These places get robbed all the time," he told a relative. "I don't want to die over a few dollars. I will have to find something else."

Rea was thinking of giving his two-weeks' notice and finding other work when he began the midnight shift Sunday, November 2nd. Two hours later, Rea was found sprawled behind the counter, shot to death with two bullets in his head.

Investigators with the Corona, Garden Grove and Santa Ana police departments and the Orange and Riverside sheriff's offices met to compare notes.

Ballistics compared bullets and bullet fragments and was certain the same weapon was used to shoot all four victims. In addition, fingerprint technicians had raised a few prints that were good enough for identification, if and when a suspect was caught.

Witnesses placed a late model, pea-green sedan at

two of the crime scenes at about the times the hold-ups occurred. The detectives theorized the killer probably had an arrest jacket, and feared being returned to jail or prison if caught on a long stretch.

"A first-timer would get probation for a stop and rob," Garden Grove Detective Sergeant Bill Dalton noted. "And a second offender wouldn't get much worse. It looks like we have a career criminal on our hands. Someone who would kill rather than go back behind bars."

Detectives searched reports for other crimes that might have been committed by the same person. They also made a request to the Sacramento Police Department for names of convicted robbers and other violent criminals who had recently been paroled to Orange or Riverside Counties.

The detectives had barely made a dent in the paperwork when Doug McCallum left home Wednesday, November 30th to work the day shift at his Santa Ana market. The 45-year-old owner of the mom-and-pop store had read about the slayings of the clerks and was concerned.

His store was located on West McFadden Avenue and had already been robbed three times and now with another robber loose on the streets, he was starting to wonder if all the work was worth it. McCallum was married and had three teenage children. Who was going to support them if he was gone?

The thought went through his mind as he arrived at the store shortly after 9 a.m. to put in another day of work selling groceries and last-minute purchases to neighborhood customers.

At 10 a.m., a tall, heavyset man in his late 30s or

early 40s entered the store. He walked to the counter and asked McCallum if he stocked a peach-flavored drink.

McCallum said he didn't.

Suddenly, the man pulled a pistol from inside his coat and stuck it in McCallum's face. "This is a holdup," he shouted.

McCallum had been through this three times before. But instead of opening the till, the 45-year-old grocer leaped over the counter and ran into the street screaming for help.

A 24-year-old Sunset Beach woman wearing a cowboy hat and sitting in her pickup with her boyfriend, heard the screams and saw the fleeing grocer.

"It's a holdup," she said. A man then ran out the door, jamming what looked like a pistol in his pocket, and jumped into a green Maverick parked beside the store.

The witness tried to block the robber's escape. She drove after him, chased him through Santa Ana at speeds up to 100 miles an hour. A licensed chauffeur who had recently spent a month enrolled in a police academy, the pretty brunette had no trouble keeping up. She honked her horn to attract attention, while her boyfriend hung out the window with a stick pointed toward the Maverick so that the fleeing burglar would think they had a gun.

The chase took them into neighboring Anaheim, where the green Maverick turned off onto a side street and stopped. The driver leaped from his car and fired twice at the pickup, missing both times.

He then jumped back into the Maverick and sped off. The woman managed to write down the license plate number before the robber left.

Police ran a check on the Maverick and learned that the vehicle was registered to a woman in Lake Elsinore, California. Probers went to her house but she wasn't there, nor was the car.

Residents told sleuths the woman shared the small, tidy home with a man called Teo. "We don't see a lot of him," one said. "He spends most of his time in the house."

Police checked utility and telephone company bills but they were in the woman's name. The post office knew who received mail at the house, but it was closed and police didn't want to wait until morning.

"If the guy is an ex-con, he's probably on parole," offered one detective. "Feed the address through the Sacramento computers and see if you get a name."

The address was entered into the crime computer in Sacramento. Minutes later, detectives had an answer. Teofilo Medina, an ex-con on parole for rape had been living at the home in Lake Elsinore.

In trouble for 20 years, Medina had been paroled from prison in Arizona on October 20th.

Detectives took Medina's mugshot from the files and showed it to Doug McCallum. "That's the guy," the store owner said. "That's the guy who stuck the gun in my face."

Police placed stakeouts at the home in Lake Elsinore and on residences in Santa Ana and Anaheim where Medina had relatives.

At 7:30 Thursday evening, November 30th, a tall, heavyset man with dark hair and glasses arrived at the home in Lake Elsinore and went inside.

He was arrested minutes later, taken to the substation in Lake Elsinore and questioned. Afterwards, he was booked into the Orange County Jail in lieu of $100,000 bail.

Investigators then obtained search warrants for Medina's house and recovered a .22-caliber pistol stolen from a Santa Ana pawnshop October 13th. Medina's fingerprints were on the weapon, which was later linked to two of the three Orange County murders.

When asked about the weapon, the 6-foot-3, 230-pound suspect shrugged and declined to talk. Detectives weren't surprised. "The guy has been in trouble before," one said. "Hell, he has been in trouble almost his whole life."

It began in 1961 when Medina, then 18, was arrested on suspicion of unlawful possession of a weapon. There was no court disposition in that case, but the same year he was arrested for theft and was sentenced to two years probation.

Medina was arrested again in 1967 for statutory rape and child molestation. The charges, however, were reduced to contributing to the delinquency of a minor and a three-year probated sentence when the 12-year-old girl turned out to be Medina's girlfriend. That same year, Medina and another man crashed a fraternity party. Several college students told the men to go and were badly beaten. "They called me a dirty name," Medina told police when arrested. He was sentenced to nine months in jail.

The next year, he emptied a shotgun into a crowded Santa Ana restaurant. Miraculously, no one was injured, but he was convicted of firing into an inhabited building and was sentenced to one to five years.

In 1974, less than a year after his release from San Quentin, Medina beat up a fellow employee while working as a clerk at a store in Ahaheim. He was sentenced to 12 days in jail.

Three years later, he kidnapped a 19-year-old barmaid, took her to a motel and raped her. Medina claimed it wasn't rape and that she was begging for it, but no one believed him.

He was sentenced to seven years in the Arizona penitentiary, before being paroled on August 24, 1984. While in prison, he was shot and wounded by a prison guard during a fight with a reputed leader of a white supremacist prison gang.

"Medina has had a great deal of exposure to law enforcement," an Orange County probation officer wrote in a 1968 report. "The older he gets the worse the crimes become."

On Wednesday, November 14, 1984, he was charged with four counts of murder and robbery in connection with the slayings of the four clerks.

Two days later, rape was added to the list of charges after a woman said she recognized Medina in a newspaper photo as the man who had assaulted her on October 20th.

The victim was a waitress who was kidnapped after she left work, forced into the motel where she was living and raped repeatedly.

The rape charge was eventually dropped in March 1985, when the victim failed to appear as a witness at Medina's preliminary hearing before Judge James Gray. The judge also ruled that Medina couldn't be tried for the murder of Craig Martin because it occurred in Riverside County.

At the hearing, a firearms expert with the State Department of Justice testified that bullet fragments in the bodies of all four victims were fired from a .22-caliber handgun that was seized from Medina's home after his arrest.

Medina, dressed in an orange jail-issued jumpsuit, appeared solemn during the two-day hearing, talking with his attorney and doodling on a notepad.

He was ordered to jail and held without bond. In February, 1985, he was seriously wounded when he was stabbed 28 to 30 times by another inmate. He recovered but complained about health problems and hallucinations.

He was briefly institutionalized, then returned to jail. In April, 1986, several days before his trial was scheduled to begin, Medina slashed his forehead, chest and arms with a razor blade he snuck into his cell.

He was placed in an isolation cell and ordered to undergo psychiatric examination. "I saw Jesus," he told a doctor. "He came into my room — twice."

Medina said he didn't remember killing anyone, but thought it was possible, because he thought he was a warlock and was under orders from Satan.

In July, 1986, the defendant was ordered to appear at a competency hearing to determine if he was mentally and physically capable of standing trial.

At the trial, Deputy D. A. Bryan Brown told jurors Medina might be faking his bizarre behavior to avoid going to trial. The psychiatric director at the Orange County Jail then testified that Medina's uncooperative and destructive behavior usually occurred before he was to appear in court.

Medina didn't like what he heard. While in a holding cell outside the courtroom, he banged his fists against a wall and screamed, "They might as well shoot me," after learning a photographer was in the courtroom.

Then, during the psychiatrist's testimony, he leaped from his chair and flipped the defense table upside down. Medina was wrestled to the ground, slapped into handcuffs and shackles and ordered to remain quiet. Medina responded by shouting incomprehensibly.

Jurors were shocked by the erratic behavior, but didn't believe Medina was insane, taking just 90 minutes to vote the defendant was mentally competent to stand trial.

Medina roared his disapproval, kicked over a chair and charged the holding cell. This time it took five marshalls to subdue the hulking, babbling suspect.

The murder trial began in September, 1986, before Judge James Turner. Prosecutor Bryan Brown told jurors the crime spree began October 17, 1984, when Medina stole a small .22-caliber pistol from a Santa Ana pawnshop. He then purchased hollow-point bullets for the weapon, which are designed to kill, not wound.

"He didn't want any witnesses," the prosecutor said. "These were cold, calculated crimes committed by a cold, calculating killer and coward. He's the biggest coward you've ever seen."

Heavily medicated, Teofila Medina sat quietly through the month-long trial. He remained calm and relaxed Friday afternoon, October 17, 1986, when jurors found him guilty of three counts of murder.

They also found that Medina committed the murders during robberies and burglaries and that he committed multiple murders — findings that could bring the death sentence.

Medina appeared at a competency hearing November 6th to convince a jury he was insane and should undergo psychiatric therapy and institutionalization.

Taking the witness stand, he told jurors about nocturnal visits he received from his dead mother, Jesus Christ and the Virgin Mary. "I first saw Jesus ten years ago when he came to my home in Santa Ana," he said. "He made me a high priest. It was like being chosen, like a birthright when you are born."

Medina said he spoke to Jesus through a 12-inch wooden cross fixed to his bed. A second time, he talked to him while confined to a bed in a mental hospital. "A warm yellow glow — like a big ball of light — came to me. Jesus was kneeling in a robe and sandals. The light felt so good it filled me inside."

But there were bad visits, too, like when the Devil spoke to him from beneath the floorboards of his home. And, while in prison, he was attacked by sadistic midgets.

"They were about this tall," Medina said, spreading his hands about a foot apart. "They snuck up on me when I was asleep and grabbed my buns.

"I woke up and saw them scurrying away. They had these long tails, like lizards. I was so angry I could have killed whoever was responsible for those midgets."

One juror broke out in a smile. Others leaned forward to hear more about the midgets. None, however, believed him.

"We didn't think he was incompetent," said the jury foreman. "We were satisfied that he knew exactly what he was doing."

Jurors then voted that Medina should die in the gas chamber for his crimes. The vote came on Wednesday, December 3, 1986, after just one ballot.

Defense attorneys expected as much. "The biggest fact was four apparently cold-blooded murders," said attorney James Stone. "I don't know how you can overcome something like that. And when you tie that in with twenty-five years of violence, you have some pretty strong aggravating factors for the prosecution."

One juror said she had been somewhat sympathetic toward Medina when the trial started in July. "But I didn't have any sympathy for him by the time we got to the penalty phase. I think we're all real comfortable about our decision. We're just glad that it's all over."

By state law, Medina's death sentence has been automatically appealed to the State Supreme Court. Until a ruling is handed down, Teofilo Medina will reside on San Quentin's Death Row.

EDITOR'S NOTE:

Doug McCallum is not the real name of the person so named in the foregoing story. A fictitious name has been used because there is no reason for public interest in the identity of this person.

PATRICK SHERRILL
"A MANIAC'S RAGE CLAIMED 15 LIVES!"

by Bill Ryder

The time is 7:05 a.m., Wednesday, August 20, 1986. He is wearing his full postal worker's uniform and is carrying his mailbag as he moves through the employee entrance of the Edmond, Oklahoma post office.

There are two major differences between his appearance today and the usual. The mail pouch is somewhat heavier than normal since it is weighted down by two .45-caliber automatic pistols and a .22-caliber pistol. Over his shoulder are slung bandoliers of ammunition.

7:06 a.m. He extracts two weapons from the mailbag and enters a glass cubicle in the center of the post office's sorting room. Without uttering a word, he opens fire. Richard Esser, 38, of Bethany, Oklahoma, and Mike Rockne, 33, of Edmond, grandson of the late famed Knute Rockne, who won immortality as the coach of Notre Dame's juggernaut gridiron teams of a half century ago, fall to the floor, mortally wounded.

7:07 a.m. The sound of gunfire causes sorting room postal workers to panic. They flee the cubicle, screaming in terror. Brandishing two guns, he follows them.

7:08 a.m. Five women postal workers huddle together before him. They are in one of the three sorting alcoves. He opens fire once more. Patricia Gabbard, 47, Oklahoma City; Patricia Chambers, 41, Wellston; Judy Denney, 39, Edmond; Joanna Gragert Hamilton, 30, Moore and Patti Welch, 27, Oklahoma City, die.

7:10 a.m. He systematically begins checking the other two sorting alcoves. Finding the first empty, he enters the second. Huddled there are four co-workers. The killer's guns bark once more. Thomas Shader, Jr., 31, Bethany; Patty Husband, 49, Oklahoma City, and Betty Jarred, 34, Oklahoma City, are killed. The fourth worker in the cubicle is critically wounded. He will survive by playing dead.

7:11 a.m. The killer returns to the main sorting area in search of new victims. He finds nobody there.

7:12 a.m. Kenneth Morey, 49, of Guthrie, apparently unaware of the massacre, walks into the area. He is carrying an armload of newspapers. He is shot and killed. His death probably saves the lives of three others who manage to rush past the madman-executioner and lock themselves inside a vault.

7:13 a.m. William Miller, 30, of Piedmont, attempts to get out of the line of fire by crawling under a table. The slayer spots him and fires at pointblank range. Miller is dead.

An instant later, the berserk man spies Lee Phillips, 42, of Choctaw, in the lunchroom. Phillips is pouring himself a cup of coffee and opening a box of chocolate doughnuts. The killer fires. Phillips dies.

7:14 a.m. Now that the killer is in the lunchroom, postal workers from the sorting room dash for freedom to the parking lot. The madman follows them, guns still in hand. He opens fire once more. Jerry Pyle, 51, of Edmond, staggers and falls. He is the 14th person to die under the hail of bullets.

7:15 a.m. The killer returns inside the post office. He moves past the corpses and enters the superintendent's office. There will be no more sounds of gunfire until an hour and 15 minutes later. Only then will the full extent of what has happened on this hot August morning in the city of Edmond, Oklahoma become known.

As the alarms go out and the S.W.A.T. teams of the Edmond, Oklahoma Police Department converge on the scene of mass carnage, the extent of the tragedy and its impact on this community of 50,000 mostly middle-class residents is yet to be learned. Only when they have will it be recognized that here in Edmond, situated just 18 miles from Oklahoma City, one of the great mass killings of the century has occurred.

First Edmond police units arrive shortly after 7 a.m. As a command post is set up around the post office, heavily armed lawmen, wearing flak jackets and bullet-proof vests, take up strategic positions.

An ominous silence from inside the post office

greets them. Hurriedly, they confer with surviving postal workers in order to get a grasp on what has happened thus far and what their next move should be.

From the government employees they learn that the gunman is, in fact, a co-worker. He is identified as Patrick Henry Sherrill, 44, a part-time letter carrier who had worked on and off at the post office for about a year and a half.

Later, there will be time to sift out the details, to determine what caused Sherrill to undertake his savage rampage. For now, the safety of the community in general and those who may be still trapped inside the federal property is paramount.

The lawmen develop a strategy. On the theory that some of the hostages inside the building may still be alive, they decide to sweat it out. Attempts are made to reach Sherrill by telephone. The ringing instrument inside the post office goes unanswered.

The tension mounts. The cloak of silence is more unnerving than would be an artillery barrage. Concern continues to grow over the condition of those injured inside the one-story building and their probable urgent need for medical attention.

At 8:30, guns drawn, fingers on triggers, the officers make their move. As they enter the post office, they hear two shots go off. Then there are no further sounds. The cops do not return the fire. The grotesque sprawled bodies which they discover all around them give clear evidence that the violence is over.

Patrick Henry Sherrill is among the dead from a self-inflicted head wound. The grisly business of identifying and removing the dead and rushing the wounded to nearby Mercy Health Center and Edmond Memorial Hospital gets under way even as shaken police try to come to grips with their own sense of horror at what had happened.

Talking of what he had found inside, with typical professional understatement, Edmond Police Lieutenant Mike Woolridge says, "There was a lot of blood in there. With 15 people, you're going to have a lot of blood."

From the fragmentary accounts as given by shocked survivors, a true picture of the 10 minutes of unmitigated horror begins to take form.

One veteran of 18 years in the postal service who had helped train Sherrill, said that when the shooting started, nobody knew what was going on. But when he looked up toward the supervisor's desk, he saw two bodies lying on the floor.

"That's when I leaped over the counter and out the front door. All I could think of was getting out of there. There were several who didn't," he says.

Another man describes how he lay among a pile of bodies, playing dead, as Sherrill stalked a hallway in the building. He can't give an explanation for Sherrill's rampage or why the berserk gunman wanted to destroy him.

He says, "I tried to be nice to him. But he just responded to everything in a weird way."

A 32-year-old co-worker tells how he survived by hurling himself to the floor as the shooting began.

"I saw one of my friends hit the ground and I saw another run by with a bullet hole in his side — blood coming out his back.

"Sherrill just started shooting people. He shot the supervisor almost at point blank range. He shot one of my best friends, point blank. And then he just turned around and started spraying the room.

"I knew him. I didn't know him well. Nobody did. I don't think he was a loner. He just didn't know how to carry mail. He just couldn't get a handle on it. They chewed him out yesterday," the man states.

A young woman who managed to hide from the furious onslaught reports, "I heard the screams of the dying. I heard someone holler, 'This is for real, get down!' "

A letter carrier says, "I just happened to turn around and saw two of my carriers go down.

"Someone yelled that a man had a gun and everyone started running. Some of them got trapped in some of the rooms. The gunman was just pointing and shooting. When he sent the third shot in my direction, that's when I got out. Many of the workers ran to safety out the front of the building."

One woman tells of what went on when Sherrill tried to gain entrance to a vault while she and two fellow workers hid there.

"Outside, I heard their supervisor yelling, 'No, Pat, no!'

"He came back twice, trying to get in the vault. He started breathing hard. I heard people yelling and moaning. I stayed there (in the vault) until I knew the police were there," she recalls.

One courier tells of seeing "people coming out of every door they could come out of."

Some of the escapees were half-dragging, half-carrying the wounded with them. He believes Sherrill had locked the employees' back doors before he had begun shooting.

One thought the whole thing was a prank when it began. "Then I heard the moans and groans and it got real quiet; then I heard someone yell, 'He's got a gun!' I knew then he was going to waste everybody he could."

The survivor tells of having saved his own life by having ducked under a pile of mail sorting cases. In all, he heard 12 to 15 shots being fired before he was able to make good his own escape by running out a loading door.

For the relatives left behind in the senseless slaughter there was pain to match the death agony of their loved ones.

They were taken to temporary headquarters set up in the Edmond City Hall to await the lengthy process of forensic identification of the victims.

One couple tells of having heard about the shooting over the radio at 7:45 a.m. while eating breakfast. They drove 30 miles to Edmond to learn the fate of their daughter, a 30-year-old postal worker.

When they arrived at the City Council chambers where others had assembled, they were told their daughter had been killed.

"Everyone was in shock," the bereaved mother says. "Some were crying. Some were in disbelief. Some of them were just hopeful that, you know, it wasn't theirs."

The woman says she had no such illusions. "I knew before I reached Edmond that my daughter was dead," she relates. "We're Christians, and I just felt the Lord tell me she was one of them."

For the Reverend Richard Huggins of the Emmanuel Southern Baptist Church, who is among those charged with caring for the bereaved, the stress is unbelievable.

He cannot forget the one family who began rejoicing when their relative's name failed to show up on early casualty lists. A few minutes later, it turned out that the relative's name had been spelled incorrectly in the confusion. The person had been one of those who had been killed.

"It was a terrible, terrible scene," the clergyman said.

There is literally nobody in Edmond who has not been touched in some way by the mass murders. The sense of loss is codified by Mayor pro tem Randel Shadid, a 38-year-old lawyer.

Comments Shadid, "This town is small enough that if you didn't know someone killed, chances are you knew someone in their families. You always think something like this can't happen in a town like this, but of course it can. There are a lot of nuts everywhere these days."

Edmond District Attorney Bob Macy does his best to keep his sense of outrage at the senseless killing under control. It is a difficult task.

The district attorney states, "The slayings are the worst in Oklahoma's history.

"You look at the carnage and you look at the dead people and you become so angry, you would like to walk through and shoot him. He apparently tried to eliminate everybody in the building."

However, the lawman is aware of his responsibilities as Edmond's prosecuting attorney.

"What makes a man do something like that?" Macy asks. "God only knows. That's what we're trying to find out."

Lieutenant Woolridge of the Edmond Police Department takes a similar tack. He reports, "We're looking for reasons why all this rage would suddenly explode.

"We know the killing is done, but we want to know why. We're talking to his neighbors, his friends, anybody who might shed some light."

First answers to whys and wherefores of Sherrill's rampage tend to be overly simplistic.

The police are told that Sherrill had apparently received unfavorable performance ratings from his supervisors and was in fear of losing his job. On the day before the killings, he telephoned union officials twice, demanding that he be transferred to Oklahoma City.

Union officials in Edmond confirm that there has been increasing friction between rank and file postal workers and their supervisor. This, they contend, results from a postal service realignment. They argue that the realignment has caused extraordinary pressure, even harassment of employees, to increase productivity.

Although the union spokesmen are as appalled by the 15 deaths at the Edmond post office as are the rest of the townspeople, they are not totally surprised by them. They said Sherrill had been sharply reprimanded on the day before he coldly shot down 14 co-workers. They also claim that Sherrill had been threatened with dismissal by his superiors on that day.

"A few of us were talking about it some weeks ago and someone said that one of these days someone is going to go off the nut and shoot somebody," says Bob Bearden, the local union's recording secretary. "This is not an isolated incident. There have been other confrontations. Most people can let off steam and then walk away. This time it was taken to the ultimate."

In Washington, D.C., Vincent R. Sombrotto, president of the National Association of Letter Carriers, claims that his union has received an unusually high number of complaints about management in the Oklahoma City area, including the Edmond facility.

According to Sombrotto, the complaints involved allegations of verbal abuse, including threats of discipline and dismissal. Sombrotto says he has received these reports from local union officials.

There is an immediate rejoinder from Bob Becker, director of news and public affairs for the United States Postal Service in Washington. Becker refuses to comment on postal labor-management relations, but adds that Sombrotto's remarks "border on the disgraceful."

"We have been in contact with Mr. Sombrotto all day long," Becker states. "It's obvious he doesn't have all the facts. I think that statements like that in the time of terrible tragedy are irresponsible at best."

Co-workers' views of the dead killer are less cut-and-dried. They paint a picture of a federal employee who earned approximately $13,000 a year based on his hourly pay of $9.35, as being a person in deep emotional trouble with or without the on-the-job stress.

Says one postal worker, "He (Sherrill) was never happy, not with himself, not with his fellow workers, not with the world."

A neighbor who lives close to Sherrill's home goes even further in describing his oddball behavior. She says, "Sherrill was sick in the head—he should have been put away long ago.

"He was always angry at something, like he didn't know what he was angry about.

"At night he would go out on his bicycle and scoot up and down the street, just in a rage, all sweaty."

Calling the dead mass killer, "tall, weird and ugly," she cites an incident which took place about two months before the shootings. She says the 44-year-old man sneaked into her garage and threatened to hurt her 11-year-old son. She charges the boy was forced to defend himself with a fire axe to keep Sherrill from making good on his threat.

"Why was he so angry at my boy? Heaven knows. We're black and he didn't like blacks. He didn't like much of anything."

It is learned that Sherrill had been living the life of a recluse since the death of his mother several years ago.

There had been strange aberrations in Sherrill's behavior and they had been growing in intensity.

The mass killer's bizarre actions in recent years had made him the subject of widespread ridicule. The deterioration in his mental state seemed to begin with his return from a two-year Marine Corps stint in 1966.

Says one young man who grew up in Edmond, "Whenever you'd see him when he first came home he'd always be in those Army fatigues.

"At first he (Sherrill) was pretty nice to us kids. He even played ball with us once in a while.

"But he always was a loner and the boys began to develop nicknames for him. We had two names for him, 'Fat Pat' and 'Crazy Pat.' "

The adolescent derision of Sherrill had been triggered by the ex-Marine's Peeping Tom activities in the community.

"We caught him right up at the windows peeping. He'd be seen in this neighborhood walking around at all hours of the night, walking across lawns," said another Edmond resident.

"And in the daytime, he'd stand and look at you, just stare at you and not say a word."

A woman who lives close to the Sherrill home calls him "a very strange person." She recalls, "He stayed to himself and he wasn't neighborly or friendly. I never saw him smile.

"All of the kids made fun of him. They called him 'Crazy Pat.'

"Once he grabbed one of the kids who was sitting on a car and tossed him onto a lawn.

"He (Sherrill) said they were teasing him. Those were the only words I had with him. I told him to leave."

There were a number of similar incidents where adults moved to block Sherrill from carrying out assaults on teasing youths.

One person who was acquainted with Sherrill over the course of 15 years tells of his trigger temper.

"Once I was joking with him about something and he reaches behind him and yanks out a pistol the size of my arm."

Others recall how the troubled man had grieved over his mother's death. The mother had willed him her house, but he had seemed unable to care for it.

Some say he had once tried to love a little white boxer puppy he had been given as a gift. However, he was annoyed by the dog's persistent barking. The sources contend the dog disappeared one night. They are convinced that Sherrill killed it.

There is some confusion concerning his attitudes toward women. Some say his Peeping Tom activities were sexually inspired. Others contend they weren't, citing his habits of spying into windows of living rooms where residents would neither be dressing, undressing, or carrying out any marital activities.

Says one woman, "He used to whistle at me and thump his legs like he really was hot for me."

However, nobody can remember Sherrill's ever having had a girlfriend.

Notes one co-worker, "Women were nothing but pictures in a dirty magazine to him."

A young woman lawyer who first met Sherrill professionally following his mother's death paints a different picture of him.

Speaking of his habit of visiting her office after she had completed her legal services for him, the attorney says, "He just seemed to want to keep in touch. He never sought a date or any kind of sexual relationship.

"It was more a brother-sister kind of relationship—not even that," she comments. "I'd just got out of law school. He said he was proud I was making it. He'd say he was just in the neighborhood and he thought he would drop by to make sure I was all right.

"He always walked into my office with a smile, to cheer me up. He never talked about friends, and I just had the impression he was extremely lonely. I do a lot of work with juveniles, and he had that look in his eyes, the kind I have seen in a lonely, abandoned child, left by his parents."

The last time she saw Sherrill he had seemed excited. He told her that he had an opportunity for a job that would take him abroad for two years.

The watershed of Sherrill's emotional problems seems to have been his two-year Marine career.

Those who knew him as a schoolboy remember him as having been quiet and shy, but dedicated. He had gone out for his high school teams. A strong, stocky youngster of limited natural athletic abilities, he had nevertheless earned varsity letters in three sports. They say he never quite reached star status in any one of them.

On his discharge from the Marines, Sherrill had a new passion—guns. Imbued with militaristic fervor, the ex-serviceman had earned a service reputation as an expert marksman. To further his prowess, he joined the Oklahoma Air National Guard. He earned the unit's good conduct medal and a 100 percent drill attendance badge.

More important, he became the captain of a pistol team, having once traveled by plane to London to take part in an international pistol competition.

The Air National Guard association was to play a

key role in the bloody climax of his life. It was from the unit's armory that Sherrill requisitioned the three weapons which were responsible for 15 deaths, including his own.

The erratic postman had been scheduled to participate in a national marksmanship competition scheduled for August 31st at Little Rock, Arkansas.

Says Major General Bob Morgan, adjutant general of the Oklahoma National Guard, "There had been no reports, including medical, that would have precluded him from serving in the Guard or from being a member of the marksmanship program."

According to Morgan, Sherrill was issued 200 rounds of .45-caliber ammunition the Saturday before the massacre. This ammo was to be used in a National Rifle Association-sponsored contest at Arcadia, near Edmond. In addition, on the Sunday before the killings, Sherrill drew another 300 rounds to be used in the National Guard competition.

"The entire membership of the Oklahoma National Guard, composed of 12,000 members . . . deeply regret this incident and wish to express their sympathy to the families of the victims," says Morgan.

While there is some doubt as to whether the bullets issued to Sherrill were the actual ones used in the killings, the .45-caliber pistols had been drawn by him from National Guard supplies.

While Sherrill's bizarre behavior had alienated neighbors and co-workers in Edmond, his conduct while on Air National Guard duty had remained exemplary to the very end.

Other Guardsmen attest to that. Morgan says of

the dead man, "He was a quiet person, but he served the military well."

Things military seemed to be the one thing in his life which gave him a sense of self-worth. In his Post-Marine Corps days, Sherrill had created a fiction that he had served in Vietnam. Official records prove that his duty tour was spent within the confines of the United States.

Some say the troubled man had developed a massive inferiority complex because of his premature baldness. Even his interest in ham radio transmission could not bring him out of his shell. Unlike most amateur radio operators, Sherrill never developed any lasting friendships with fellow hobbyists.

Police, who now enter the home of the recluse, get a harrowing insight into the life-style of the crazed dead man.

Edmond Police Lieutenant Ron Clavin reports that Sherrill actually prepared for the massacre by taking target practice at his leisure. Sherrill had set up an in-house shooting range running from the far end of the hallway to a bedroom, where he had mounted small targets. The targets were ripped with dead-center hits, Clavin says.

An inventory of the mass killer's personal effects includes:

A silencer, two air pistols, an air rifle and boxes of ammunition.

Piles of paramilitary and sexually explicit magazines.

Neatly pressed military fatigues.

A Russian map, a Russian language book and about 20 copies of a Soviet magazine.

Says Clavin, "The front room was filled with stacks of books and clothing—it was a like a maze, all through the living room area."

The living room also contained Sherrill's computer and a number of discs. District Attorney Macy says he hopes that one of the computer discs may contain a suicide note from Sherrill. (At this writing, no such note has been discovered.)

The hallway leading from the living room houses a desk covered with elaborate ham radio and CB equipment.

Clavin reports that there is only one chair, that being placed in front of the desk. He says, "There was nothing in the house for a visitor to sit on."

The grimmest discovery of all is a pan containing the remains of some scrambled eggs. This could have been Patrick Sherrill's last meal before he embarked on the murder/suicide expedition that was to bring unrelenting horror to Edmond.

For the people of Edmond, torn by their singular and collective grief, the grim tasks of burying the dead must be given top priority. However, there is time to remember, as well.

The suddenness of their bereavement is etched in the cryptic words of a co-worker of the fallen Paul Michael Rockne.

He says, "I heard what sounded like a firecracker while Mike was sitting at my desk. It sounded like one of those party favors that goes 'pop'—and Mike hit the ground face first.

"I thought it was a big joke at first. I said, 'Mike, you can get up now. You really fooled me.'

"But when I saw the puddle of blood forming under his neck. I knew it was no gag."

Rockne is mourned by associates as "warm, outgoing, and a friend to everyone."

Says one relative, "If anyone could have talked him (Sherrill) out of using a gun, (Rockne) would have been it."

One woman postal worker thinks of the slain 30-year-old Bill Miller.

"I'll never forget," the stunned postal employee says. "He (Miller) heard me say yesterday that I had a craving for chocolate chip cookies.

"This morning he brought some chocolate chip cookies his wife had made."

The agony of the moment when the shooting erupted is etched in her memory. The woman and three or four others in her immediate vicinity ran for the door.

"Bill had gotten out of his crouched position and looked up at me like a lost little puppy," she says.

"I assumed . . . he'd be right with us but he didn't do it. I don't know if he froze or what."

Relatives, who had been elated when Rick Esser had been appointed a supervisor only two months before, see things in a different light on the morning of the massacre. (Esser had been one of the people Sherrill reported to.)

"It seemed so wonderful at the time," says a relative. "But now it's a tragedy. (Esser, himself, had been a letter carrier for six years.)

"Rick was concerned about this man, Sherrill," the relative continues. "They had some talks. Sherrill was having some problems. But Rick didn't know it was serious."

In the realm of horror that he perpetrated, it is difficult to believe that the crazed killer was capable of an act of humanity.

And yet there is evidence that he was.

This comes from a 21-year-old woman who was a co-worker. She related how Sherrill tried to make sure she would not be in the post office when he claimed his revenge on the others.

"I considered him a real squirrel, but I was nice to him," she reports.

A letter carrier had warned the young distribution clerk, "Stay away from this guy. He's going to snap and kill somebody."

The girl had worked nights for 18 months and had changed to the day shift just the day before the shootings.

She says Sherrill questioned her closely about her new schedule. She quotes him as having asked, "Are you really sure you never come in before 11 a.m.? You won't come in early?"

She notes that she and Sherrill had often worked alone on Sundays and the deranged man had confided in her his problems with his supervisors. Within a week before the shootings, he complained once more, saying, "They'll be sorry. They'll be sorry and everyone's going to know about it. Everybody's gonna know."

What the young woman cannot forget is that the woman who had replaced her on the night shift had succumbed to the fusillade.

"I worry about that," she says. "That's not fair for me to say. But he sure did grill me."

202

Over the weekend of August 23rd and 24th, with Postmaster General Preston R. Tisch having ordered flags atop post offices throughout the nation flown at half mast in honor of the slain workers, burial services are held.

Says the Reverend Finley at the funeral of Patty J. Husband, "We've experienced pain, haven't we? You bet we have. But think of pain being the threshold of peace. It is because of pain that God moves to us and brings us his peace."

At services for Rockne, the Reverend Marvin Leven says, "Everything that has been done in this last week has been unusual and has been cruel, but we know that his soul has been called to God, our Father."

For relatives of Bill Miller, there is some comfort in knowing that he died a hero.

Says one close relative, "Everything I can gather indicates that Billy was trying to take the gun away from him (Sherrill). I know of four people who have told me their lives were saved because he gave his."

While thousands of mourners turn out to pay last respects to the martyred, only 25 are at the gravesite of Patrick Sherrill's parents at Watonga, Oklahoma to watch his cremated ashes interred beside those of his mother and father.

Meanwhile, the city of Edmond summons up its courage to face the immediate future.

The Edmond post office has reopened and stricken employees are back at their appointed duties.

Says former Edmond Postmaster Bill Shockey, "I couldn't be more proud of any group of people I have ever been associated with. They came in here and performed like champions."

The post office lobby is filled with flower arrangements.

Says one resident, "Most people want to do something. That's the one nice thing you can say about this. At least people really care."

JERRY "ANIMAL" MCFADDEN:
"THE 'ANIMAL' IS LOOSE! HE'S A RAPIST! HE HAS A WOMAN HOSTAGE!"

by Bill G. Cox

The scene was like one from a suspense movie. Red-and-blue emergency lights on patrol cars flashed in rotating patterns as powerful searchlights from helicopters above probed the jungle-thick piney woods of East Texas. Spreading through the woods and heavy brush as the dusk gave way to darkness were 800 lawmen involved in one of the biggest manhunts in Texas history.

The object of the desperate search in which the officers feared time was running out was a hulking, bearded and tattooed triple-murder suspect who appropriately called himself "Animal." A few hours earlier on this Wednesday, July 9, 1986, the huge and fierce-looking suspected sex-killer had escaped from the county jail at Gilmer, Texas, abducting a pretty, 24-year-old woman jailer as a hostage.

Members of the huge modern-day posse were well aware that the welfare of the kidnapped woman jailer hung in the balance. They knew the criminal record and the psychotic temperament of the giant escapee: Since 1973, he had gone to prison two different times after conviction in three brutal rapes. Only months after his release on parole in 1985, he had been arrested as the prime suspect in the slayings of three youths—two of them girls who had been sexually assaulted.

One of the officers pressing the massive search was especially filled with gut-fear and dread. He was a Texas Highway Patrol trooper, and the young female jailer now the captive of the convicted rapist and sex murder suspect was the trooper's wife.

The searchers' darting flashlight and spotlight beams lighted up the woods like hundreds of big fireflies. Taking part in the manhunt were Highway Patrol troopers, Texas Rangers, officers from several sheriff's departments, city policemen from nearby towns, FBI agents and other federal officers, and even game wardens. All of the officers knew that every minute counted, that, at the least, the pretty hostage faced a terrifying ordeal and, in all probability, violent death. They could also imagine the wracking emotional agony their lawman colleague was experiencing as they searched for his helpless mate.

The "Animal" was at large with another potential victim and armed with the .38-caliber revolver he had taken from one of the overpowered jailers.

The 6-foot-1-inch-tall, 250-pound jailbreaker with long, bushy hair and beard, his upper body covered with tattoos of women and satanic-looking symbols, indeed had the appearance of a wild man from another age. At gunpoint he had forced the female jailer into her own car to flee from the county jail.

Events leading up to this night of unbelievable tension and fear began quietly enough five weeks earlier when three young people went on a weekend outing at one of the scenic lakes in the lush area located about 100 miles east of Dallas. The East Texas area is hunting and fishing territory, full of pine woods and fish-filled lakes.

The trio left their hometown of Hawkins, a community of 1,000 residents some 20 miles north of Tyler, Texas, to drive around Lake Hawkins, only about five miles out of town. They were Suzanne Denise Harrison, 18, who had been an honor student and cheerleader at Hawkins High School; a friend, Gena Lee Turner, 20; and a male companion, Bryan Boone, 19. They departed in Boone's pickup about 7 p.m. to spend the evening of Sunday, May 4, 1986 at the Lake Hawkins park area, a favorite spot for the town's young people.

Relatives of the youthful trio started worrying when the three had not arrived home by midnight, after saying earlier they planned to eat supper, drive around the lake awhile and wouldn't be home too late. It was about 1:20 a.m. Monday when a relative of one of the youths discovered Boone's pickup parked at the lake.

The searchers found no other trace of the three missing students. They combed the area in the vicinity of the pickup, calling their names without receiving any response. Now thoroughly worried, the relatives placed a call to the Wood County Sheriff's Department at Hawkins.

Deputy Noel Martin responded to the call. Flashing his light inside the blue pickup, he made another discovery that increased the concern for the youths. The deputy's torch spotlighted two purses inside the truck, which were identified as belonging to Suzanne Harrison and Gena Turner. There was a small amount of money in each purse, but the relatives and officers doubted that the young women, had they gone somewhere on their own, would have left their purses behind.

Moreover, the deputies were aware of an earlier reported attempted armed robbery at the lake. It had taken place about the time the three Hawkins youths were supposed to have been driving to the lake. A Tyler couple, badly frightened but unharmed, had notified the sheriff's office that they had been sitting in their car at the lake when they were approached by a large, bushy-haired, bearded man brandishing a handgun and demanding money and drugs.

The man and woman had told the gunman they had neither. He had searched their car and decided they apparently were telling the truth. The young man had tried to appear friendly toward the stickup man, who had said his name was "Animal" and that he was a former member of a motorcycle gang.

The gunman was shirtless and the couple saw that he was covered with ghoulish tattoos of women and peculiar-looking symbols. The badly shaken man later told officers that he even remembered a tattooed slogan on the bearded man's chest that said, "Death Before Dishonor for the Lonesome Loser."

The frightening-looking would-be robber had stayed around a short time, during which he made sexually suggestive remarks regarding the young woman. Reporting the incident to officers later, the Tyler man recalled that the large man had "pulled a gun before I knew it. He looked like he wouldn't think twice about using it."

But, for some reason the armed, lewdly talking man had left without further incident. The couple, still terrified by their experience, considered themselves lucky, as did the officers who investigated.

Now, called to the lake again, the sheriff's officers noted immediately that the abandoned blue pickup in which the missing Hawkins youths had been riding had been located only a half mile from where the earlier attempted robbery of the young couple had taken place.

Driving around the lake shores, the deputies stopped and quizzed all fishermen or campers encountered, seeking information on the Hawkins trio. The officers picked up a report that the three had been seen at the boat launch area and other places around the lake that evening.

As far as could be determined, they had last been seen in their pickup about 9:30 p.m. Sunday. Witnesses remembered having seen the blue pickup with three young persons inside parked next to two other vehicles — one a silver pickup and the other a van or bus.

The officers searched for vehicles matching these descriptions, but found none.

As daylight came to the lake area, more officers were brought in and the search intensified. A private aircraft was used to fly low over the lake area, searching for signs of the missing trio or vehicles that might be parked in remote locations of the dense woods.

Checking in Hawkins, officers learned that the two young women and the young man had eaten at a restaurant in town just after leaving their homes. They apparently had driven to the lake after eating. No one had been seen with the three while they were in Hawkins. If they had been abducted, as it increasingly appeared as the hours passed, it probably had happened at the lake, and the bearded, tattooed man who had tried to rob the young couple from Tyler might easily be involved in the disappearance of the Hawkins trio, officers surmised.

No further trace of the big, shirtless man had been reported in the area, however, after he drove away from the attempted robbery scene in a blue Ford Bronco. A description of the man who called himself "Animal" was broadcast to all law enforcement agencies in nearby counties.

Although sought for the attempted robbery, there was nothing other than conjecture at this point to connect him with the disappearance of the Hawkins students.

The officers were told that the missing trio would not have been away from home for this long voluntarily. All three were known as highly responsible and respected individuals.

One deputy sheriff, who attended the same church as Suzanne Harrison, was acquainted with her two friends as well. "These are nice kids," he said. The principal of the Hawkins High School said the youths had been top students, "the cream of the crop." Their background and the assurance of parents and other relatives that the young people were highly dependable and would have called about any change of plans just added to the growing concern for them.

In a rural community, everyone rallies when news of an emergency spreads. Within the morning, scores of volunteer searchers were assisting lawmen.

It fell upon members of a state cleaning crew to make the discovery that confirmed the worst fears of families and officers. The crew that had gone to Barnwell Mountain recreational park six miles northeast of the little town of Gilmer on State Highway 155 to clean up weekend litter found the semi-nude body of a young woman, who was quickly identified as one of the missing trio—Suzanne Harrison.

The tragic discovery was made shortly after noon on Monday. The girl's body was only a few feet below the paved area at the top of the mountain park. She was nude from the waist down. The cleanup crew called the Upshur County Sheriff's Department in Gilmer. Within a short time, Sheriff Dale Jewkes and several deputies were at the scene. Jewkes also notified Wood County Sheriff Frank White, whose department joined in the ever-widening investigation.

The officers saw that the young woman apparently had been strangled with her own panties. There were numerous bruises on the body, indicating that she had put up a terrific struggle with her assailant. The officers theorized that she had been sexually assaulted.

The officers took photographs of the body and crime scene and searched the area for possible evidence. At a picnic table only a short distance from the body, the investigators found the slain girl's clothing. At another picnic table nearby, foreboding evidence of additional violence was found. Recovered there were shorts and a pair of panties soon identified as those of the other missing young woman, Gena Turner.

Officers had little doubt that Miss Turner had met with foul play, but a search of the area failed to turn up any more evidence related to the missing youths. It was not immediately determined whether Suzanne Harrison had been killed at the spot where the body was found, or elsewhere; the recreational park is about 30 miles from Lake Hawkins, where the trio had last been seen on Sunday night.

After the preliminary investigation was finished at the scene, the body was ordered removed to a forensic laboratory in Dallas for an autopsy.

"This is a brutal murder," Sheriff Jewkes told reporters. "The body has been sent to the forensic lab for an autopsy, but it looks like she was strangled to death. But she put up one hell of a fight. I'm not a forensic expert, but I would say she couldn't have been out there more than 30 hours. I would estimate she was killed between 12 and 36 hours ago. The body wasn't decomposed."

The sheriff said he had ruled out robbery as a motive in the girl's violent death, because of the women's purses left in the pickup. He also said that jewelry on Suzanne Harrison's body obviously had been left by the killer.

As for the fate of the missing young people, Sheriff White of Hawkins said, "It doesn't look good.

Right now, we have just one body, but it looks like we might have three before this thing is over. We don't know yet if she was killed in Upshur County, or killed here and then taken over there."

As the search for Miss Turner and Boone continued Tuesday with no results, officers did get a break in the attempted robbery of the young couple from Tyler. A Wood County deputy saw a blue Ford Bronco and pulled it over to question the driver. At the wheel was a large, bearded man whom officers identified as Jerry McFadden, a 38-year-old parolee. McFadden was taken to the sheriff's office for questioning about the attempted holdup and later identified as the gunman by the two victims. The suspect, however, denied knowing anything about the slaying of Suzanne Harrison or the disappearance of her two friends. Later, investigators said that McFadden's fingerprints did not match any of those found on the abandoned pickup, which didn't necessarily clear him. But at present, there seemed to be no evidence to link the ex-con to the Hawkins youths.

Yet, McFadden was far from being a stranger to the Wood County officers—just the opposite, in fact. Sheriff Wood recalled that he had been downright apprehensive when his office was notified by the state board of pardons and paroles that McFadden was being paroled to his county. That had been only a few months earlier, it seemed.

McFadden's criminal activities had started in Haskell, Texas with a burglary in 1966 and felony destruction of private property in 1968. He received probated sentences for both offenses. But these crimes were insignificant compared to what would

213

follow, officers recalled.

A 24-year-old school teacher at Haskell was raped at knifepoint in her home in January, 1973, and later identified McFadden as her attacker. The rape victim told officers that the hulking assailant had talked his way into her home by saying he had been in an accident close by and needed to call a tow truck. After McFadden was arrested, the officers learned during the course of their investigation that he had another rape charge pending against him in Denton County. The sex attack there had occurred in April, 1972. He had viciously assaulted a young woman at Lake Grapevine.

Eventually, McFadden pleaded guilty to the rape charges in both Haskell and Denton County. He was given 15-year prison terms for each charge, to run concurrently. It wasn't much for two sexual assaults, but as the prosecutor later told lawmen, "I would have gotten him a longer sentence, but the little school-teacher was scared to death. She didn't want to go through a trial." Thus, the rapist was permitted to plead out for the 15-year prison terms.

After serving five years of the sentences, McFadden was paroled in 1978. The ex-con managed to get a job as an oilfield roughneck in the West Texas area. He did his job with no trouble for a while, but on June 22, 1979 he struck again.

He entered an office where an 18-year-old secretary he had met two days earlier worked. After first determining that she was alone, McFadden asked the young woman to accompany him outside to his truck to obtain serial numbers on some equipment. When she went to the truck, the big man pulled a knife and put it to her throat.

He shoved the terrified girl into his truck and began a day-long drive through three counties, during which he stopped and raped the kidnap victim repeatedly, officers learned later. He also forced her to perform oral sex. Finally, in a secluded area along the Brazos River, the oilfield worker forced the girl to stand against a tree. Then he reached around from behind her and choked her into unconsciousness, leaving her for dead. But after McFadden drove away, the victim regained consciousness. A motorist found her running hysterically down the highway near the small town of Lueders. McFadden was arrested later. He was charged with kidnapping and aggravated sexual assault. But once again the ordeal to which he had subjected his victim worked to his advantage when the accused rapist came to trial.

The young woman's hysteria returned. Prosecutors said the young woman "just went to pieces." She couldn't stand the recollections of her day of horror. Her mind "blanked out." Faced with the emotional condition of the victim, the authorities had no choice but to make another plea bargain deal with McFadden. He once again drew only a 15-year prison term.

After serving five years of the sentence, he was released under the state law of mandatory supervision that requires an inmate to be freed after serving one-third of his sentence. He was paroled to Wood County, where he had relatives living.

When Wood County Sheriff White heard of the plans to parole to his jurisdiction a thrice-convicted rapist with a record of such violence, he had a sense

215

of foreboding. He immediately filed a protest with the Texas Board of Pardons and Paroles, telling the parole commissioners that Wood County did not need McFadden's type there and suggesting he be sent to Haskell County where his crimes had originated. But the sheriff's protest was to no avail.

Jerry McFadden was released under the mandatory supervision program — which meant he would have to check in with a parole officer only periodically — on July 17, 1985.

The state parole officer in the county called Sheriff Wood when McFadden arrived and told him apprehensively, "He's here." The parole official, a woman, expressed fear of the parolee, and said she wouldn't go to McFadden's home to check on him without an armed escort.

However, McFadden had not crossed the law's path again until eight months later when he was arrested in the attempted armed robbery of the man and woman at Lake Hawkins. An assistant district attorney in Wood County verbally blasted the mandatory release program under which McFadden had been freed.

"Obviously, you see what the program does," said the prosecutor. "He was sentenced to fifteen years and he served five. It has put a dangerous, violent person back on the street."

And, because of his background of violent sex crimes, McFadden could not be eliminated as a suspect in the strangulation and sex assault of Suzanne Harrison, the investigation officers realized.

The autopsy conducted on the Hawkins teenager revealed she had been raped. She had been struck in

216

the head with an unknown blunt instrument, but death was attributed to strangulation. As officers had surmised, she had been strangled with her own panties. The autopsy also revealed that she had been killed where her body was found.

Meanwhile, investigators were thwarted in their efforts to question McFadden further about the death of Suzanne Harrison and the disappearance of her two friends. The suspect was advised by his attorney not to answer any more questions about the Hawkins youths, Sheriff Jewkes told newsmen.

However, McFadden was charged with two counts of attempted aggravated armed robbery in the episode involving the man and woman at the lake. He was ordered held in lieu of $100,000 bond in the attempted robbery and for violating his parole.

By this time, the search for Gena Turner and Bryan Boone had been intensified. Hundreds of volunteers joined with law enforcement officers, and a special plea for information was issued by relatives of the missing youths.

Rewards totaling $10,000 were offered for information on the murder of Suzanne Harrison and the whereabouts of the other two young people.

Four days of searching the wooded areas in Wood and Upshur Counties failed to locate the missing pair. The search parties concentrated in the areas where the trio last had been seen around Lake Hawkins and where the body of Suzanne Harrison had been found on Barnwell Mountain.

Sheriff Jewkes gloomily told reporters, "Every day that goes by means a less chance of finding the other kids alive. It is my personal opinion that they are somewhere in a five-county area. We keep looking in the obvious places, because that's where we at least know they have been. It is always possible, and I hope it is, that they could still be alive. But so far we haven't turned up much more than we had the first day."

Most of the town of Hawkins and mourners from the surrounding region turned out for the funeral services of Suzanne Harrison. The grief-stricken crowd packed the auditorium of Hawkins High School. Most businesses in town were closed in respect for the slain schoolgirl.

By Saturday, May 10th, more than 500 volunteers and officers launched a massive search for Gena Turner and Bryan Boone. The day dawned gray and rain poured down on the determined search parties. Volunteers were divided into smaller groups and given maps with their search area marked in yellow.

Because it appeared that the youths had been kidnaped, FBI agents also were on the scene, and Texas Rangers had joined the investigation to assist the two sheriff's departments.

The intensive search came to an end at 11:15 a.m. Agent Jim Hayes of the Texas Alcoholic Beverage Commission discovered the two bodies in a ravine alongside Farm Road 1649 about one-and-a-half miles west of Ore City, a small town in Upshur County. The man's body was fully clothed, but the body of the young woman was nude from the waist down. Both appeared to have been shot to death. The officers noted that the two bodies could not have been seen by anyone passing along the road because they were lying about 10 feet down the sloping ravine. The officer who found the slaying victims had been searching on horseback earlier, then got into a pickup truck to go to another area. He had slowed down near the ravine, got out to take a look and made the tragic discovery.

The young man's body was sprawled face up; the girl lay on her side. After photographing the crime scene and searching the site as best they could for possible evidence in the rain that continued to fall, the officers summoned an ambulance to take the two bodies to a Dallas forensic laboratory for autopsies and positive identification. There had been little question anyway about the identities of the pair, but positive identification of the bodies as those of Gena Turner and Bryan Boone came several hours later from the forensic laboratory.

It was believed that Miss Turner also had been sexually assaulted, according to the preliminary autopsy report. Three days after finding of the bodies, Hawkins citizens again attended en masse the funeral rites for Gena Turner in the high school auditorium. Services for Bryan Boone were conducted the next day.

With the community in an uproar over the killings of the three popular young people, officers continued to work around the clock to gather evidence, maintaining a silence about their findings.

But on Thursday, May 22nd, Sheriff Jewkes broke the silence. He announced that Jerry McFadden, the bearded and tattooed suspect charged in the attempted armed robbery at the lake, had been charged with capital murder in the rape and strangulation death of Suzanne Harrison.

He was not charged in the other two killings.

The sheriff told reporters that the decision to charge McFadden in the one slaying came only after "all the evidence began to point in only one direction, over a period of time.

"It was really a process of elimination," the sheriff explained. "We decided only after all the evidence had been compiled, all of it put together. I think we have a good case. If I didn't think that, we never could have filed charges."

The sheriff said he could not give details of the investigation and the evidence at that time.

The hulking suspect was taken before Upshur County Justice of the Peace Robert Crowder and arraigned on the capital murder charge. The justice of the peace denied bond, and McFadden was returned to the Upshur County jail.

Confirming that Boone was shot twice and Miss Turner once, the sheriff said that no gun had been found so far that might have been the weapon in the slayings. Nor had the caliber of the bullets been determined.

On June 9, 1986, a newly empaneled Upshur County grand jury returned a capital murder indictment against McFadden, charging him with the rape and murder of Suzanne Harrison. The indictment alleged that McFadden killed "by strangling and striking the head of the said Suzanne Denise Harrison with a blunt instrument, the type of which was unknown to the grand jury, and the said defendant was then and there in the course of committing and attempting to commit the offense of aggravated sexual assault on Suzanne Denise Harrison."

Capital murder under Texas law is a killing committed during the course of another felony offense, such as rape. It carries a penalty of either life in prison or death by lethal injection upon conviction.

The previous week, McFadden also had been indicted on two counts of aggravated assault and one count each of aggravated robbery and attempted aggravated robbery by a Wood County grand jury in connection with the attempted armed robbery of the couple at Lake Hawkins.

Although McFadden still was not charged in the slayings of Gena Turner and Bryan Boone, Sheriff Jewkes said that he remained a strong suspect in those cases as the investigation continued.

The following day, McFadden was arraigned on the capital murder indictment before State District Judge Virgil Mulnax, who set bond of $500,000 for the burly defendant. Even though bond had been set, McFadden still could not be released, even if he posted bail, because of a pending hearing to revoke his parole. A defendant held for parole revocation proceedings cannot be freed on bail.

An attorney was appointed to represent McFadden, who also was held in lieu of large bonds in the Wood County attempted robbery indictment.

Meanwhile, the fact that McFadden, a three-times convicted rapist, had been paroled under the state law that requires that an inmate be released after serving one third of his sentence, brought a wave of outrage from residents in Hawkins and the rest of the population in the two counties where the latest violent offenses had been committed.

Residents began an organized move to do away

with state laws that permitted a potentially violent convict to be released because of having served one-third of his sentence, plus credit for "good time" served behind the walls.

Hundreds of the handbills seeking information on the killer of Suzanne Harrison and the disappearance of the other two youths had not been distributed at the time the two bodies were found, but were now being handed out.

But with the finding of the latest victims, residents who were growing madder by the minute about a convict with such a proven record of sexual violence having been turned loose to not only rape but to kill this time, had an idea. They would use the undistributed reward posters for petitions to be signed by taxpayers urging a change in the criminal system of Texas, particularly in the parole of violent criminals. The growing momentum in the community to "do something" snowballed into an organized movement to petition the state legislature for changes in the laws.

Residents formed a group called "We, The People," which supported the drive to do something about repeat violent offenders who are freed to once again prey upon society. The newly organized group printed up an additional 5,000 circulars, these bearing the law changes proposed as a result of the tragedies in Upshur County. The proposals listed on the petition included abolishment of the mandatory release program; serving of "real time"—no parole or probation—for those convicted of murder, rape, sexual assault and kidnaping; substantial input by county sheriffs and other officials as to whether criminals should be released to their counties; protection of victims' rights and release of funds to strengthen law enforcement by building more prisons and hiring more personnel.

The handbills bore the heading: "This is a statewide petition to change the criminal system. 'We, The People,' are citizens of Hawkins, Texas, and surrounding areas who have been forced to question the flaws in our Criminal Justice System because of the violent murders of three of our youths. We feel that the following changes need to be made in our laws."

A spokesman for We, The People, said of the reform campaign, "When the Legislature convenes in January, we will be there."

State Senator Ted Lyon, who represents the area, said the Hawkins tragedies might be the catalyst for statewide reform in the system.

"This case has had an effect on me personally," he said. "You've got three outstanding, really top-flight young people who were just senselessly murdered. And if this man was the guilty party, then the crime was committed by a person who should have still been in prison. That's outrageous, and I intend to do something about it."

But if the residents were incensed over the slayings in which Jerry McFadden was suspected, what happened next was tantamount to throwing gasoline on a raging fire.

The events that were to throw a large part of the East Texas into near pandemonium began about 6:30 p.m. on Wednesday, July 9, 1986, on the fifth floor of the county jail in Gilmer.

Three members of the Gilmer County Sheriff's

Department were on duty on this hot but quiet July evening following the holiday hubbub of the July Fourth weekend. They were Jailer Ken Mayfield, 53, a former longtime member of the Dallas Police Department before joining the sheriff's department; Mrs. Rosalie Williams, 24, a combination radio dispatcher and jailer, and Mrs. Stacy Mullinix, 27, also a radio dispatcher and jailer.

Since his arrest in early May as a suspect in the attempted armed robbery at Lake Hawkins, Jerry McFadden had been what sheriff's officers termed a model prisoner in the county jail. Even after his indictment and arraignment on the strangulation-rape murder of Suzanne Harrison, the big tattooed man's demeanor showed no change.

In the routine of the jail procedures, and in compliance with a rule of the Texas Commission on Jail Standards, McFadden and all of the county jail inmates were permitted to use the phone in the jail corridor on occasion. Fairly regularly since his arrest, McFadden called his wife when the day's activity in the jail had quieted down.

When the huge prisoner made a request to use the phone on this Wednesday evening, Jailer Mayfield removed his service revolver from its holster and placed it in a compartment outside the jail area. No officers were ever permitted to carry their weapons inside the jail area. Mayfield then unlocked the door to McFadden's cell and escorted him to the telephone in the corridor, which is within the barred jail area.

The two women dispatcher-jailers were in the jail control room when the triple murder suspect was taken to the phone by Mayfield. Both women are efficient at their jobs. Rosalie Williams, a pretty young woman who had worked for the sheriff's department for over a year, was the wife of Trooper Eddie Williams of the Texas Department of Public Safety. The couple were the parents of a 3-year-old child. They were a happily married pair intent on advancing their own individual law enforcement careers while also keeping up the domestic chores of home life.

Stacy Mullinix, just one month before this fateful evening, had attended the East Texas Police Academy, studying the latest in law enforcement procedures, including hostage situations.

As she would recall later, the shocking action that took place within seconds blotted out all memory of the things she had been taught about what to do in hostage incidents.

She saw McFadden suddenly lift his arm and send some object he had concealed at his side crashing down on Jailer Mayfield's head. She saw the jailer fall to the floor, bleeding profusely from two gaping cuts on his forehead.

The jailer had been knocked unconscious with an L-shaped piece of metal the prisoner somehow had wrested from his cell window frame.

Unfortunately, the door to the jail control room was not locked, and the apparition who called himself "Animal" was inside the control room before the startled women could act.

The big man who had so savagely attacked the jailer with the piece of metal bellowed orders at the women, following one command with another before the first could be carried out.

McFadden grabbed Stacy Mullinix immediately

after flooring the male jailer. The huge prisoner shouted at her to get the handcuffs and put them on Mayfield, then quickly changed his mind and ordered the two women to move Mayfield into a jail cell even if they had to drag him.

At the same time, McFadden was ordering the bleeding jailer to "get up." Somehow, the women helped Mayfield to his feet and half carried him into the detention cell.

Demanding the key to the cell, the murder suspect then had Rosalie Williams lock the wounded jailer and the woman dispatcher-jailer inside.

McFadden grabbed Rosalie Williams by the arm and propelled her to where the prisoners' jail commissary money was kept. He took $162, the amount credited to his name, leaving the rest of the money behind.

Next, still keeping the badly frightened young woman jailer in his grasp, the burly inmate took Mayfield's .38-caliber service revolver from the locker where the jailer had left it before entering the jail. He also found a T-shirt and blue-jean cutoffs belonging to another prisoner and exchanged them for the white jail clothing he was wearing.

Stacy Mullinix watched in numbed shock as McFadden pushed Rosalie toward the jail elevator, which she had a key to operate. Uppermost in Stacy's mind were the brutal crimes for which McFadden had been jailed, the rapes and the three murders in which he was a suspect. She watched helplessly from the locked cell as the escaping prisoner and his hostage disappeared into the elevator. Jailer Mayfield groaned as he began to regain consciousness . . .

McFadden and Rosalie Williams left the elevator on the second floor of the courthouse (which is actually ground level because there is a basement floor below) and exited from the south door of the courthouse. The armed escapee forced the woman jailer into her Datsun 280ZX parked not far from the door. With the bearded inmate driving, the maroon-and-gold automobile sped away—heading west on Highway 154.

Meanwhile, the radio and telephones in the sheriff's office were unmanned. When a Gilmer police officer radioed the sheriff's office and received no response to his repeated efforts to contact the dispatcher, he quickly notified other officers that something must be wrong. The policeman and two sheriff's deputies arrived at the courthouse about the same time and rushed to the fifth floor. About 30 minutes had elapsed since the breakout when the officers freed Jailers Mayfield and Mullinix from the locked juvenile detention cell.

The injured jailer was rushed to the hospital, where he was treated for concussion and the head wounds. Sixty-six stitches were required to close the cuts.

Notified of the escape, Sheriff Jewkes took charge, organizing one of the biggest manhunts in many years in the northeast Texas region. Within the hour, scores of city, county, state and federal officers from 10 surrounding counties were pouring into the area. Radio and TV news broadcasts quickly alerted the public to the escape of the triple-murder suspect described as armed and extremely dangerous and holding a woman jailer as a hostage. Descriptions of the fugitive and the car in which he was riding with Rosalie Williams were relayed by police radio and teletype networks.

Roadblocks were thrown up at intersections of all major highways in the immediate area, each manned by two or three heavily armed officers. Among the searchers in spite of his fear and emotional state was Trooper Williams, praying to himself that the huge and violent rapist-murder suspect could be found before something happened to his pretty young wife. The trooper believed his wife—as a trained law enforcement officer—would keep her wits even as a hostage of the escapee who fondly referred to himself as the "Animal" and who was described as "psychotic." The distraught husband only hoped that time would not run out before his wife could get help and, Lord willing, be rescued unharmed. Yet, as a professional and practical lawman, the trooper knew that the odds were not good that his wife and mother of their small son would escape unharmed, even if she managed somehow to escape with her life.

Colonel James Adams, director of the Texas Department of Public Safety, promised by phone all the state help and equipment needed to locate McFadden and his hostage. Under his command are troopers of the Texas Highway Patrol, a crack force of Texas Rangers and state intelligence agents. Adams assured Sheriff Jewkes that all resources would be placed at his disposal. The DPS director also advised that he was flying to Gilmer to personally direct state forces in the manhunt.

Even before darkness fell, four helicopters were in

228

the skies, flying low over the woodlands with their crews making a binocular scan of the densely wooded region and its scores of backroads. On the ground, officers in patrol cars and on foot began a mile-by-mile shakedown, their car spotlights and their flashlights and the red-and-blue emergency rotation lights flashing through the thick brush and dense cover of trees.

On the chance that the desperate fugitive and his hostage might be afoot after ditching the woman jailer's car, prison bloodhounds were brought in and given the scent from clothing of the pair that was obtained by officers.

The mammoth task force soon had grown to between 700 and 800 officers.

As for Sheriff Jewkes, he spoke of the heavy burden now riding on his shoulders.

"I've never had an officer taken hostage before," he grimly told newsmen gathering at the scene from the newspapers and TV stations in the East Texas area. "You seem to forget how dangerous this job is until something like this happens. Rosalie is a good officer, and we can only hope that we can get her back alive. She is one of the sweetest persons you could ever meet, and she was very good at her job." Some of the reporters noted that the tense lawmen had inadvertently referred to his jailer in the past tense.

Officers who spread over the area also quizzed residents in Gilmer and learned that there had been several sightings of McFadden and his woman hostage as they left the courthouse in the woman's car. Two witnesses had seen the two driving along Highway

154, headed west, almost immediately after the break. Another witness, who had been on foot, reported having seen the fugitive and the female jailer in the Datsun near a Gilmer shopping center, which still indicated that they were driving west out of town, the sheriff noted. If the escapee had continued his flight in that direction, it would take him into neighboring Wood County, where he had been living near Ore City at the time of his arrest.

The search was concentrated in that county in addition to Upshur County, with teams of lawmen driving to the homes of known relatives of McFadden's to see if he might have fled there.

The Gilmer Police Department also received a report on McFadden and Rosalie Williams having been seen at a store on the outskirts of the town. According to the tip, McFadden had bought $10 worth of gas at the store's gas pump.

Sheriff Jewkes warned residents not to try to apprehend McFadden themselves, but to notify officers if he were spotted. Residents also were warned to keep their doors locked and take precautions to protect themselves should the bearded, tattooed murder suspect try to get into their homes.

With the coming of daylight on Thursday, the huge force regrouped to beat the bushes. Colonel Adams arrived on the scene. He and Sheriff Jewkes mapped the day's strategy, studying maps of the area that had been spread on the hood of a patrol car.

In a jungle of trees and brush near the little town of Big Sandy, Rosalie Williams and her barefooted captor left her automobile at 6 a.m. that day. The car had overheated about four miles outside the town of 1,200 people.

As the haggard young woman deputy and her abductor left the car and started pushing through the woods, they heard the sound of helicopters overhead as the day brightened. The fugitive and his hostage ducked under brush in a creekbed at one point, hiding at McFadden's harsh command until the sky searchers moved on. They resumed their plodding through the underbrush, some of which was poison ivy. The humid heat became almost unbearable. Insects singing in the thick woods stopped abruptly as the pair passed by. In the distance could be heard the sounds of the intensifying search. As the big man urged his captive on through the heating day, he seemed strangely docile. He was intent on evading the lawmen, but he did not threaten the young deputy nor try to harm her in any way. Still, the pretty young woman was in fear for her life all of the time. The huge escapee had often and without warning exploded with violence and lust in the past.

They continued to walk through the woods until they reached an empty boxcar on a siding in an isolate area.

Near exhaustion, they climbed into the boxcar. As McFadden shoved the door shut, he told Rosalie, "Do as you're told and you won't get hurt." The big man even seemed to mellow to a point and told her that the reason he had chosen her as his hostage was because she had been kind to the prisoners in the county jail.

The young woman could hear the helicopters overhead throughout the day, the longest in her life. Help was so near, yet so far.

Hunger was one thing, but more nagging was the thirst for water that built as the hours passed. The two were beginning to feel the effect of dehydration. Rosalie wondered how long she could survive, even if the armed man did not harm her. The growing heat and the desire for a drink of water were almost unbearable.

As darkness descended, the fugitive decided to seek water.

Throughout the day, the woman deputy had learned that by talking quietly to the huge escapee, she could keep him calm. The big man droned on, talking about his wife and his children, saying he hated that they had to go through all the turmoil he had caused.

As the man talked, Rosalie thought a lot about her own family, her husband, her little boy, her mother and father. She wondered if she would ever see them again.

She listened to the man talking and prayed to herself. She even prayed for help for Jerry McFadden.

"He's not well. He needs treatment," she prayed silently . . .

In the stifling boxcar where she huddled with her menacing captor, Rosalie Williams was beginning to suffer in the extreme from her lack of water. She was beginning to see things that weren't really there. Her breathing began to increase. It became rapid.

McFadden seemed to be shook up by the physical change in his prisoner.

Moving toward the boxcar door, he told her, "You stay here, and I'll go get us some water."

McFadden slowly slid open the boxcar door and

dropped to the ground. Over his shoulder, he warned Rosalie to keep quiet and not try to leave. She heard him move away into the darkness.

With her heart pounding, the spunky young woman deputy knew that now was her chance to escape, maybe her only opportunity. She had continued to feel that any moment, at any whim, she might die at the hands of the hulking escapee.

Peering cautiously out the door, she saw that McFadden had walked a good distance down the tracks. In her desperation, she decided it was now or never.

McFadden still had the gun with him, and she knew that she had to move quickly and carefully, must keep a "low profile." Then, almost providentially, she saw that McFadden had been set upon by a barking, snarling dog.

The dog was snapping at the man's feet. McFadden was trying to fight off the animal with a stick. Taking advantage of the commotion, the deputy dropped from the boxcar and began crawling away in the tall grass. The dehydrated and weakened woman stayed in the grass, making her way toward a house she saw some distance down the railroad tracks.

Fearing that McFadden might see and overtake her at any minute, the woman deputy ran through the unlocked front door of the house. She was met by a young boy in the living room and told him to take her to his parents. The boy's father, who was asleep in a bedroom, awakened immediately. He recognized the woman from her picture that had appeared in the newspapers and on TV.

The homeowner quickly grabbed his shotgun and assured the frightened, crying woman, "No one is going to hurt you here." He sent one of his teenaged sons to a nearby service station to call the police department in Big Sandy, having discovered that his own phone was dead. The man stood guard with his shotgun while awaiting the arrival of authorities.

Big Sandy Police Chief Richard Lingle was at the house within minutes. He quickly relayed word to the sheriff's department in Gilmer that Rosalie Williams had escaped from the fugitive jailbreaker and appeared to be unharmed other than dehydration and some scratches and cuts suffered from her forced walks with McFadden through the woods.

Lingle also alerted all searching officers that McFadden was in the area.

As officers converged on the Big Sandy location, the kidnap victim's husband, Trooper Eddie Williams, and his partner, Officer Jackie Warren, were preparing to drive to another area to press the search. Warren got out of the patrol car and was walking up to a house to talk to Williams when he turned around to hear something being broadcast on the unit's radio.

"They've found Rosalie, and she's safe!" Warren yelled to his partner.

Williams reacted with unrestrained joy. As he would tell newsmen later, "I just grabbed him." Then the trooper sped to Big Sandy to be reunited with his wife.

After they embraced happily, the trooper drove his wife to a hospital to be treated for her dehydration and near exhaustion. He had been assured by his wife that other than those discomforts, she had been unharmed by the escaped murder suspect during her

28 hours as a captive.

When news of the woman deputy's escape reached residents of Gilmer, they clapped and cheered, those who had congregated in groups.

As the anxiety enveloped the small community of Big Sandy, Sheriff Jewkes moved his command post to a spot near where the big, tattooed murder suspect had last been seen. A witness was located who had seen a man matching McFadden's description running toward a wooded area along the Sabine River.

With dozens of county and state patrol cars scouring the area with spotlights and searchlights, a helicopter took to the air and circled over the terrain where it was thought the escapee might be pinned down. Officers surrounded an area near the railroad yards and the Sabine River just south of town and off Texas Highway 155. The search was slow and dangerous in the darkness, but teams pressed into the woods as other lawmen threw up a perimeter around the area.

Jewkes called for bloodhounds from the Texas prison system.

But the night's search failed to turn up any signs of McFadden, who, according to Rosalie Williams, was suffering from badly cut and swollen feet, since he had fled the jail only in socks. The tattered socks were found in the boxcar where the escapee had hidden with his hostage. The woman deputy told officers that McFadden was having difficulty walking, and officers figured he had taken cover for the night.

By Friday morning, the manhunt for the murder suspect/convicted rapist had hit the national TV news shows. Some broadcasts reported that Big

Sandy had a "circus" atmosphere.

The officers pushed their search with grim reality. Boxcars and even a slow-moving freight that came through the town were searched for the fugitive. During the day, Sheriff Jewkes announced that a house-to-house search in Big Sandy would be made, to make sure the escapee had not taken someone hostage and was holed up in a home.

Meanwhile, Rosalie Williams had been released from the hospital after staying overnight, and rejoiced with her husband and son. Ironically, her escape had come on her husband's 33rd birthday.

By Friday night, the elusive McFadden still was free in spite of the intensive search by the weary officers.

Sheriff Jewkes, who hadn't been to bed since the night before the escape, told newsmen dejectedly that the search was being expanded to a greater area on the possibility that McFadden had slipped through the search perimeter.

"Apparently, he must have gotten a larger jump on us than we thought. We believed he had only 15 to 20 minutes on us before we were able to block all roadways leading from Big Sandy. We didn't figure he had gotten very far, but apparently he did." He said the search sector was being enlarged to cover about 30 square miles.

But, about 10:30 p.m. on Friday, Sergeant Randy Norton of the Collin County Sheriff's Department, and two of his deputies, were driving along a road near the Big Sandy High School. They drove by an abandoned house. Suddenly, one of the deputies exclaimed the thought he had seen someone moving inside. The officers turned off their car lights to approach the house. Quietly trying the doors, they found them locked.

Trying the windows, the officers found a side window that wasn't locked. They raised it quietly, and crawled inside, guns ready. Then they stepped into a room where they confronted a large, bearded man wearing shorts, a shirt and two unmatching shoes.

The man had a gun in his hand, but when he saw the three armed officers he dropped the gun and said, "It's me."

"Who are you?" Norton asked.

"Me, McFadden," came the reply.

Thus ended the three-day manhunt, with no resistance offered by the escapee.

After handcuffing the prisoner, Norton notified Sheriff Jewkes that McFadden was in custody. Two investigators from Upshur County were rushed to the scene to make a positive identification of the man in custody. Then Jerry McFadden was driven back to the Upshur County jail.

News of the arrest had swept through Big Sandy as police scanners throughout the town announced the welcome news. By the time the car bearing McFadden arrived at the courthouse, a crowd of some 200 gathered. The crowd made no attempt to harm the prisoner, who was rushed into the courthouse by a squad of officers.

But the mass of people loudly cheered the arresting officers as they emerged. And, for the first time since the massive manhunt began, Sheriff Jewkes was smiling broadly.

One woman in the crowd said, "Thank God, I can

now sleep at night. I haven't slept good in three days."

The next day, Saturday, a country fair atmosphere prevailed at the courthouse square in Gilmer as hundreds of well-wishers gathered to celebrate the safe return of Rosalie Williams and the capture of McFadden. Yellow ribbons tied around trees and on signs decorated the area. A brass band played. Firetrucks with sirens blowing escorted a red convertible in which the woman deputy, her husband and son were brought to the celebration. Both the deputy and the trooper spoke to the crowd, expressing their gratitude.

Meanwhile, under heavy guard, McFadden remained in the Upshur County jail, facing a battery of new charges including attempted capital murder in the assault on the deputy who was slugged; kidnaping; escape from jail and unauthorized use of a motor vehicle. He also had been charged with federal kidnaping in U.S. District Court.

He subsequently was transferred to the state prison to await trial. Under the laws of the state, he must be presumed innocent of all charges unless and until proven otherwise at his trial. But until then, the man who called himself "Animal" was caged again.

CARLTON GARY
"HUNT FOR THE PHANTOM STRANGLER OF SEVEN!"
by Bob Spurlin

A 16th-century poet once wrote, "Life is a tragedy to those who feel and a comedy to those who think." If you think about the trail of pain, anguish and terror left behind by the Silk Stocking Strangler you will recognize the tragedy immediately; the comedy only comes into play when you consider our great legal system and what it has evolved into.

It was late morning on September 16, 1977, when a relative found the body of Mrs. Ferne Jackson in the bedroom of her 17th Street home in the Wynnton community of Columbus, Georgia. The relative immediately phoned for the police. When Patrolman Al Danns, of the Columbus Police Department, arrived on the scene, he took the normal precautions to seal the home and protect the crime scene. He then radioed for a detective car. Neither Patrolman Danns, nor Detective Steve Wright had any idea that they were the first of more than 2,500 law enforcement officials who would work directly on this case before it was finally solved.

Police noted that the killer had gained access to the old house by forcing open a window in one of the back bedrooms. Mrs. Jackson was found in her bed and had apparently been strangled with one of her own stockings.

Muscogee County coroner Don Kilgore also told police that it appeared the 60-year-old widow had been beaten and raped. Samples of pubic hairs and semen were taken for further analysis and sent to the Georgia State Crime Lab in Atlanta.

Detectives immediately began questioning the neighbors to determine if anyone had seen or heard anything which might give them a clue. This avenue quickly proved fruitless, and another team of sleuths began questioning relatives to determine if anything had been taken from the house which might be traced to the killer. Again there was no luck.

Probers covered all of the bases in their investigation. They checked for all physical evidence and found a single fingerprint on the window sill, but the one print was not enough for a match. They interviewed everyone in the neighborhood on multiple occasions and talked with family members repeatedly, but after a solid week of investigation, the trail was cold.

On the morning of September 24th, the police were once again summoned to the Wynnton community, this time to the home of Jean Diamondstein, on 21st Street, just 12 blocks away from the scene of the first murder. When the police arrived they found that Diamondstein had also been strangled with a stock-

CHARLES WHITMAN

STEVE JUDY

RICHARD SPECK

JUAN GONZALES

JOHN LIST

PATRICK SHERRILL

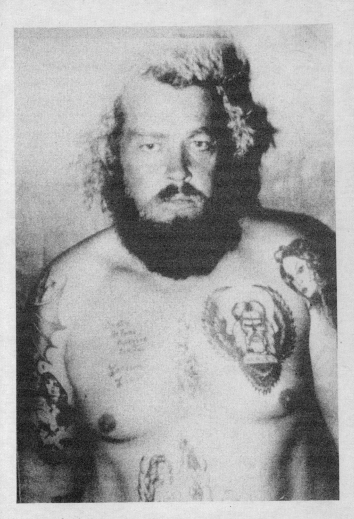

JERRY "ANIMAL" MCFADDEN

JAMES SCHNICK

WILLIAM CRUSE

JAMES HUBERTY

HOWARD UNRUH

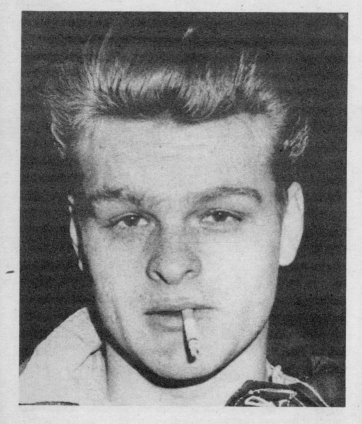

CHARLES STARKWEATHER

ing and had been severely beaten and raped. Again detectives found evidence of forced entry, this time through a side window, but no prints were found at the scene. According to the detectives and coroner Kilgore, there was no doubt that the two murders were related.

Investigation continued, but no solid evidence developed. Detectives couldn't come up with a single lead on who the killer might be. Then on October 1st, police were called to investigate the death of 55-year-old Beatrice Brier. Mrs. Brier did not live in the Wynnton area, and when they began their investigation, the police had no reason to suspect her murder was related to the other killings.

Mrs. Brier was beaten and stabbed, and the method of the killing was quite a bit different from the other two. Working from information gathered from friends of Mrs. Brier, police arrested Jerome Livas on October 2nd. Livas had been dating the victim. After several hours of questioning detectives were satisfied that he was Brier's killer. Meanwhile, community concern was putting a lot of pressure on local government officials to make some headway on the stocking stranglings.

On October 3rd, Mayor Jack Mickle appeared on a local television talk show and, when questioned about the Wynnton stranglings, told the commentator that there was a suspect in the case. Within hours, the news services in town had learned that Livas was that suspect.

The community breathed a little easier during the next ten days because no new killings had occurred, and then on October 4th, Public Safety Director

Gordon Darrow made an announcement that Jerome Livas had told them details about the Wynnton murders that only the killer could have known. Even though no charges were formally filed against Livas in the other murders, the city wanted to believe the terror was over. But their hope was short-lived.

On October 21st, a relative found the beaten and raped body of 89-year-old Florence Schieble in her duplex on Dimon Street in Wynnton. The modus operandi was a duplicate of the first two murders, and police were again unable to come up with any hard evidence to lead them to a suspect.

Shortly after the announcement of Ms. Schieble's death, a rumor began to circulate that Jerome Livas was still a suspect and that Schieble's murder could have been a copy-cat killing. Police did, however, report that there were some differences in this case from the other.

More probing by reporters, however, made it clear that there were enough similarities — the beating, rape, and even the type of knot used in the stocking — to convince almost everyone that the strangler was not Jerome Livas, who was still sitting in the Columbus Jail.

The community was almost in a state of panic now, and a reward of $15,000 was established for information about the killings.

The Wynnton community is made up of mostly older homes, and many of its residents are either elderly or widows living alone. The community began beefing up its security.

One woman, Mrs. Martha Thurmond, retired schoolteacher, had a new deadbolt lock installed on her door, and began locking herself in every night at sundown.

The problem Mrs. Thurmond didn't anticipate was that the lock had been installed backwards. She was found murdered in her Marion Street home on October 25th, just four days after the Schieble murder. The method and crime scene were almost identical to the other three stranglings.

The first break in the case for police came four days after Thurmond's death. Detective Steve Wright talked with a neighbor who told him that she had seen a young man near the Thurmond home several times in the last few weeks. The woman was able to describe the man to a police artist, and a composite drawing was made. Police hoped this drawing would lead to a speedy conclusion of the case.

They were wrong, however.

The composite was released to the public on November 1st, and police received several calls. At least 700 persons were interviewed, but no solid evidence or suspects were uncovered.

In the meantime, Jerome Livas was still a suspect in the first two stranglings because of his apparent admission of inside facts about the case. On November 7th, *The Columbus Ledger-Enquirer* ran a story that shocked the community and verified the gruesome truth that the strangler was still on the loose.

In a jailhouse interview, Jerome Livas supposedly admitted to the stranglings. However, he also admitted to the assassinations of Presidents John F. Kennedy and William McKinley.

When this news was released to the community, a new wave of terror engulfed the city. Locksmiths and security companies began receiving ten times as many calls as normal, and sales of security systems and locks soared. One locksmith who had served the city for over 26 years told the press, "Never has business been so good for such a bad reason." He said that he was getting locks from an eight-state area and still had a tremendous backlog of orders. He was interviewed on a national television news show about the demand problems and, that evening, he received calls from as far away as New York and California, offering to ship him locks for the emergency. Many locksmiths who were on the verge of shutting down were kept in business because of the Silk Stocking Strangler.

Many elderly women in the area also had security alarms installed and panic buttons placed beside their beds. Some of the alarms would ring directly to the police stations while others were connected to an alarm at a neighbor's house. The residents banded together and were instructed by police to look out for any suspicious persons in the area and were told how to establish protection cells — small groups to look out for each other.

Police worked doggedly on the case but still had no new information. Finally, when it was clear that conventional investigative techniques were not bringing results, city officials asked the Georgia Bureau of Investigation (GBI) for assistance. The GBI agent assigned to the case was Dave Bascomb.

On December 22, 1977, Columbus Mayor Jack Mickle announced at a news conference that a special "Strangler Task Force" was being organized. He told reporters that it was necessary to form a special unit made up of local and state officials who could operate independently of the regular department in order to disseminate the vast amounts of information and to coordinate the hundreds of investigative activities related to the case.

Police also placed special patrols in the Wynnton area during the evening hours, and there were at least three extra cars assigned to the beat since the third murder had occurred.

Despite these precautions, however, the Silk-Stocking Strangler struck again. On the morning of December 28th, police found the body of 74-year-old Kathleen Woodruff in her Buena Vista Road home. There was no doubt that it was the Silk Stocking Strangler.

The next day, Mayor Mickle announced that Detective Ronnie Jones would head up the task force to nail the strangler. Jones announced the establishment of a special strangler hotline where citizens could call and give information without revealing their names. The task force would also tell citizens how to protect themselves from attacks.

The 36-member task force began an investigation that rivaled anything in the history of the South. Drawing from law enforcement agencies around the country, police tried to find a similar method of operations. Inquiries were sent out to every police force in the country. Locally, more than 5,000 interviews were conducted and filed away. The regular task force members were aided by state and federal officials every step of the way. But even with this massive effort, no significant clues were uncovered.

Police asked psychiatrists to come up with a profile of the killer, hoping that it might narrow down the search. The psychiatric profile stated that the killer was probably a male between the ages of 15 and 25. The fact that he had spent what appeared to be an inordinate amount of time disassembling the door of Florence Schieble's house indicated the killer might have a youthful determination. In addition, the killer was probably right-handed, based on the evidence of wounds on the left sides of the victims' faces. Also, since the car of Kathleen Woodruff had been stolen, it was evident that the killer was able to drive one and possibly had a record of car theft.

Based on other physical evidence at the scene, and the earlier witness's description, the profile stated that the killer was at least five-feet, ten-inches tall. Psychiatrists felt that the killer was probably quiet and even withdrawn, a person who rarely displayed anger, particularly with girls, and was probably a loner.

The fact that all the attacks had been committed on elderly women led experts to believe the killer might have been raised by his grandmother or perhaps an elderly aunt or other elderly relatives. It was almost certain that the killer lived alone and had not discussed the killings with anyone. This was based on the fact that the reward fund had now grown to over $100,000, yet no one came forward to give information and claim the reward.

In all likelihood, anyone who knew the killer would probably not believe him to be capable of such violent acts. "It is quite possible," stated one psychologist, "that the killer has lived or worked in the Wynnton neighborhood. He could have been a delivery boy or a transient yard worker." It was also apparent that the killer was very intelligent, for after the fourth murder, police found traces of peppercorns and coffee along the killer's escape route, probably being used to cover his scent.

The coroner's reports added quite a bit of information to the profile. The killer was reported to have a blood type common to 20 percent of the population, and both his hair and spermatazoa were normal. It was estimated that he wore a size ten shoe, based on partial impressions found at two of the murder scenes.

Meanwhile, on January 4th, a burglary was reported in the Wynnton area. No one had been home at the time of the break-in. The victims told police that several items had been taken, one of which was a handgun. They gave police the serial number, and the detectives entered it into the NCIC computer. Many of the sleuths working the strangler case felt that this burglary was his work because of the similarities in entry. Based on this, a copy of the case file went into the strangler records.

The first 40 days of the new year brought no more violence, and city residents almost started to relax. Then, on February 12th, an elderly widow was attacked in Wynnton. The woman apparently awoke as the attacker entered her bedroom. She was able to fight him off by striking him with a bookend. She was also able to reach her recently installed panic button which sounded an alarm in a neighbor's house. The neighbor called the police, and the first squad car arrived at the Carter Avenue house within two minutes, but even that excellent response time wasn't fast enough. More than 30 officers were on the scene within minutes, searching the entire Wynnton neighborhood for the assailant but without results.

After several hours of searching with blood-hounds, the police admitted that the strangler had gotten away.

"We were so damn close!" commented one officer. "We were here within minutes and he still got away. Whoever he is, he must be extremely familiar with this neighborhood."

During the canvass, other detectives were concentrating on interviewing the woman, the first known intended victim to survive the strangler's attack. The woman told police that the attacker had been wearing a mask and that the room was dark. She was unable to give any description of the man.

Because of the attacker's swift "vanishing act," Det. Jones, the task force leader, stated that the assailant may have been inside the house when the police arrived and had probably stayed hidden until the searchers fanned out away from the house. This became an even greater possibility when, the next morning, relatives discovered the body of Mildred Borom, 78, in her home on Forrest Avenue, just 200 yards from the surviving victim's home. There was no doubt that the strangler had left one residence and had immediately broken into the Borom home.

Up to this point, police had kept their profile and knowledge of the killer out of the press. Rumor had it that the police were looking for a young white male, who had grown up in the Wynnton area and who had recently been released from a mental institution. Other reports hinted that police knew who the killer was but were trying to cover up the man's identity because he was related to a prominent local family. All the rumors were squashed and the city became a racial time bomb, when, on February 15th, coroner Don Kilgore told the press that the pubic hairs found at the scene of the Borom murder were definitely "negroid."

The head of the local chapter of the NAACP immediately responded by condemning the announcement. He said that blacks were being placed in a bad position because racial prejudice, which he said was already high in the Columbus area, would be worsened by the announcement that a black man was terrorizing old white women in the community.

Police officials explained that it was now necessary to release as much information as possible to the public, because the normal routes of investigation were failing. The officials emphasized that there was absolutely nothing racial about the case. They were looking for a killer, not a black or white killer. The fact that the physical evidence pointed that way would increase their efforts in the black community, but they said they would conduct all investigations according to the law, and innocent people, whether black or white, were urged to cooperate with authorities.

This answer did nothing to dissuade local black leaders from constantly complaining about the release of information. For almost 30 days, the papers were filled with each side taking verbal swings at the other.

The community had, in fact, been putting a lot of

pressure on local police officials and on the mayor's office. Public opinion polls indicated that most of the community believed the killer would have to walk into police headquarters and surrender for the police to catch him. Dissent came not only from the general public but from highly placed local government officials as well.

On February 24th, local Superior Court Judge John Land, in an interview with the *Washington Post,* stated that he had lost all confidence in the local authorities' ability to solve the case. He said, ". . . The only way they'll catch him is if he runs a traffic light."

On March 31st, the police and the *Columbus Ledger* received a letter from a man claiming to be the chairman of a terrorist group called, "The Forces of Evil."

The letter warned that if the city didn't solve the murders of the elderly white women, black women would soon start dying. The author of the letter also demanded a $10,000 ransom.

Police naturally ignored the ransom demand, but three days later, a young black prostitute was found dead just across the city limits of Columbus on Fort Benning, Georgia. Many people believed that the strangler was responsible for this murder and that he was simply trying to throw police off track by switching his method of operation.

Detectives, however, had a different opinion and, just five days after the murder, Specialist Fourth Class William Henry Hance, a soldier at Fort Benning's 197th Infantry Brigade, was arrested for the murder. Police released a statement that Hance was apparently not only the chairman of the so-called "Forces of Evil," but was, in fact, its only member.

Sleuths focused on Hance's whereabouts during the stranglings. After several interviews with the soldier and hundreds of other people, the police released a statement saying that Hance was definitely not the Silk Stocking Strangler.

Meanwhile, patrols in Wynnton were still very active even though it had been two months since the strangler's last strike.

Detective Steve Tims explained, "We had the area covered like a blanket. We were positive that nobody could get in who didn't live there without being stopped and questioned."

The beefed-up security, though, was once again ineffective against the wily strangler. The killer went totally against his original pattern when, on April 20, 1978, the body of Janet Cofer, a 61-year-old schoolteacher, was discovered in her Steam Mill Road home. The neighborhood in which Cofer lived was about five miles east of Wynnton. It was the first time the strangler had left the Wynnton area, and many questioned whether or not it was the same killer.

But sleuths didn't take long to confirm that the strangler had struck again. Based on the physical evidence at the scene and the M.O., which showed that the window of Mrs. Cofer's home had been forced in almost exactly the same manner as the other strangling victims, detectives knew the strangler was responsible. Also, the beating and rape fit the pattern of the strangler.

The city, which had already been concerned about

a small community being terrorized, was now in turmoil. Nobody in the city was safe now. The strangler could strike anywhere, any time, and the police couldn't seem to stop him. The citizens demanded a change.

On July 27th, acting on information from several sources, police circulated to the press a sketch of the man they believed to be the strangler. The composite was based on descriptions from people in Wynnton who had seen a suspicious man in the area on various occasions. The drawing was also based on a description given by a woman who had been attacked and beaten about two weeks before the first strangling. The drawing was all the police had to go on.

At this point, over $1,000,000 worth of manpower and equipment had been expended on the case. Over the next year, police continued their dogged pursuit of what seemed to be a ghost killer. More than 5,000 people were interviewed in the city and hundreds more from out of town. Anyone who resembled the strangler's profile was questioned. The result was still zero.

A year after the last murder, Police Chief Curtis McClung told reporters that the stranglings ". . . have been the biggest disappointment in my career." McClung added that the police were not giving up and that the case would remain a number one priority.

Indeed, Columbus law enforcement officials pursued the case with everything they had. Friends, relatives, and acquaintances of the victims were requestioned, and the files of sex criminals were scrutinized in hopes of making a connection.

During this time, the city of Atlanta, just 100 miles north of Columbus, was being terrorized by the Atlanta child murders. In March, 1982, when Wayne Williams was arrested as a suspect in that case, Columbus police traveled to Atlanta to interview him, because many of the officers involved felt that he might fit the profile of the strangler.

After two interviews, this, too, proved to be a dead end. Wayne Williams was definitely not connected to the Columbus murders.

Meanwhile, the original suspect in the case, Jerome Livas, was now serving a life sentence after being convicted of Beatrice Brier's murder. And Specialist Fourth Class William Henry Hance was tried and convicted for the murder of the young black prostitute and sentenced to die in Georgia's electric chair.

A new mayor, Harry Jackson, and a new police chief, Jim Weatherington, seemed to have little impact on breaking the Silk Stocking Strangler case. Detectives were still dedicating time and effort, but the results were all negative.

Another new mayor, William H. "Bill" Feighner, took office in January, 1983. Feighner vowed that the case would remain a top priority of the Columbus Police Department and ordered Chief Weatherington to assign as many probers as necessary to try to break the case.

Police reopened all of the files and reinterviewed hundreds of witnesses. They reprinted and recirculated the composite of the suspect, and republicized the reward being offered. The results, however, did not change. The investigation was stone-walled until

January, 1984.

Columbus police were notified that a man in Kalamazoo, Michigan, had filed for a gun permit. The serial number of the gun matched that of the gun taken during the Wynnton burglary in January, 1978. Since the description of the man seen near the home resembled the description of the strangler, police contacted the Michigan man.

The man told police that he had bought the gun from a friend in Kalamazoo, and he gave the police his friend's name and phone number. Detective Mike Sellers called this man and asked him where he had gotten the gun. The man told Sellers that he had bought the gun from a man in Phoenix City, Alabama, located just across the Chattahoochee River from Columbus. He gave Sellers the man's name and told him the area where the man lived.

Police searched through the Phoenix City phone books and found the man's address. Working with Phoenix City authorities, detectives went to see the man. He first told police that he could not remember having a gun. When they assured him that their informant had not been mistaken in his identification, the man admitted to having sold the gun to him. When asked where he had gotten the gun, the man said he could not remember.

"I felt like he knew where he had gotten the gun," said Detective Sellers after the case was over. "I told him that we had traced the gun all the way to Michigan and through two other people to get to him and that I couldn't believe that he didn't know where he had gotten the gun. I told him that he had very probably been talking to the Silk Stocking Strangler when he bought the gun."

At this point, the man commented, "He's just a petty thief. I don't think he would do that."

When Detective Sellers asked him who was just a petty thief, the man realized that he had to cooperate. He told them that he had gotten the gun from a relative of his named Carlton Gary.

Sleuths tried to ascertain Gary's whereabouts from the man but were told that he wasn't sure where Gary was. He said he thought he might have been in jail, ". . . somewhere up in the Carolinas."

Meanwhile, back at police headquarters, detectives ran Carlton Gary's name through the NCIC computer. The report came back that there was a warrant out on Gary for his escape from a jail in Gaffney, South Carolina. Upon making contact with South Carolina authorities, police learned that Gary had been convicted of three counts of armed robbery in different South Carolina cities, and that he had escaped about two months before.

The next step for probers was to find out as much as possible about Gary. Working from his police records in South Carolina, police began questioning many of Gary's relatives and friends.

The more investigators learned about Carlton Gary the better he looked as a suspect in the Columbus stranglings. Gary had been born and reared in Columbus, Georgia. According to various sources, Gary had a lot of problems as a child. His family had been poor and he had reportedly been a discipline problem in his later years of high school, transferring several times.

One of Gary's teachers told police, "Carlton was a

very smart, but very troubled, young man. He wanted too much too fast, and he was willing to take any shortcuts he could to get it."

The teacher added that Gary had been a very popular student with his peers, and all the teachers tried to help him reach his potential.

Scrutiny of Gary's criminal record revealed a life of crime. The first incident was a charge of breaking and entering an automobile in October, 1967, when Gary was only 17 years old. From that point on, his criminal record escalated. Gary was charged with two more counts of breaking and entering in December of the same year, in Gainesville, Florida. Just four months later, he was charged with arson of a building in Gainesville.

From this point, Gary moved north, but his life of crime followed him, and in November, 1969, he was charged with assaulting a police officer in Bridgeport, Connecticut.

Many police officers believe that crime is a disease with an escalating pattern, and this certainly seemed to be the case with Carlton Gary, because in July of 1970, he was charged with an armed robbery in Albany, New York. A woman had been killed in this robbery, but through plea-bargaining, Gary received a reduced charge and was sentenced to 10 years in prison.

After five years, he was released on parole into the custody of the Syracuse, New York, Parole Division. Less than four months later, Gary was charged with a third-degree escape, resisting arrest and a violation of parole. Gary went back to jail, but only for nine months.

After being out again on parole for less than 60 days, Gary was charged with assault, and a bench warrant was issued for his arrest. Before he could be arrested again it was January, 1977, and, when he was arrested, new charges of possession of stolen property, perjury, resisting arrest, and assault were added to the list.

In August, 1977, while waiting trial in the Onondaga County Correctional Institute in Janesville, New York, Carlton Gary escaped and returned south to his old home of Columbus, Georgia.

As investigators pored over Carlton Gary's life of crime, they became more convinced than ever that he could have been involved in the stranglings. A nationwide manhunt was launched for Gary in connection with the murders.

From April, 1978, through February, 1979, Gary traveled back and forth between Columbus and Greenville, South Carolina, and was responsible for a string of restaurant robberies in both those cities. Finally, in February, 1979, he was arrested for a restaurant holdup in Gaffney, S.C. and was sentenced to 21 years in prison.

Strangely enough, Columbus robbery detectives had traveled to South Carolina to interview Gary in March of 1979, and Gary had confessed to four robberies in Columbus. But at that time no connection had been made between Gary and the stranglings.

In July, 1979, Gary was returned to New York where he pleaded guilty to escape charges and was returned to South Carolina to continue to serve out his sentence for armed robbery.

He remained in prison for almost five years until

March of 1984, at which time, based on his good behavior record, he was made a trusty. Fourteen days after the appointment, Gary promptly walked away from the Goodman Correctional Institute in Columbia, South Carolina.

Police learned a lot more about Carlton Gary during their search for him. They found out that he seemed to have an unlimited supply of girlfriends, many of whom were suspected of being drug carriers for him. Gary was a hero to many of the people in his circle. "Style," said one of his acquaintances. "He always went in style and dressed in style."

Apparently, he even dressed in style when he pulled his robberies. He was always reported as being fashionably dressed, but his fashion ensemble included a .45. He reportedly posed as a traveling road musician and paid cash for an enormous wardrobe at one of the classiest stores in Columbus.

Police also learned that many of Gary's girlfriends would rent cars for him and act as his messengers. Gary reportedly made regular trips between Columbus and Albany, Georgia, as well as to Gainesville, Florida.

On April 3, 1984, Phoenix City, Alabama, authorities were investigating an armed robbery at a local restaurant. Acting on a tip, the officers included a picture of Carlton Gary in the batch they showed to the restaurant workers. Gary was identified as the holdup man.

For the next several days, the police departments of both cities, which are separated only by the Chattachoochee River, conducted massive independent searches for Gary. Finally, there was communication between the departments, and the Phoenix City police were told that Gary could indeed be the Silk Stocking Strangler.

A coordinated effort to locate Gary continued, but he evaded all authorities. It was not that he was in hiding. He was just on the move constantly. It was reported that he had asked an old girlfriend to go to a concert with him in Columbus. The girl apparently told Gary that she didn't have a dress to wear, and Gary told her, "If you'll come with me to Florida, we'll get you a dress."

In questioning the suspect's family and friends, police kept a list of Gary's regular haunting grounds and made regular routine checks of these places. They followed his seemingly endless list of girlfriends and talked with every snitch they could find.

Police would later learn that twice while checking known nightspots Gary frequented, they had actually had him in custody, but had failed to follow up because Gary was using the name Michael Anthony David, and they failed to make the connection that he was really Carlton Gary. On the second occasion, he was arrested and booked on a disorderly conduct charge, and was released from jail after paying a $500 bond.

A Phoenix City woman later told police that Gary and a woman had knocked on her door the morning after his arrest and told her that Mike (Gary) had just gotten out of jail. He said that a couple of teenage girls had been in his car smoking pot and that he had distracted the police so they wouldn't get caught.

"During the month of April he was like a shadow,"

259

said one frustrated Columbus officer. "He was here, and everywhere, and every time we got close, he was nowhere to be found."

On another occasion, police learned that Gary had been staying in a Phoenix City motel. They quickly coordinated with the Phoenix City authorities and burst into the room. There was no Carlton Gary, just a half-pound of cocaine and nearly $1,500 in cash.

Police also learned, although again too late, that Gary showed up at a relative's house whom he hadn't seen since he was a boy. He asked the relative if he would rent a car for him, explaining that he wanted to take his girlfriend to Florida, but the car rental agency rejected him because he didn't have a permanent address.

"He looked all clean-shaven and neat, and he had the money for the car, so I helped him," the relative would later tell police.

Columbus sleuths conducted routine checks of Gary's girlfriends and found a Lincoln parked at one of their houses. The car had been backed in so as to hide the license plate, and the probers were suspicious.

After verifying that the car was a rental and convincing a judge of the connection between the girl and Gary, a phone tap was authorized. Police monitored the tap for three days before they finally hit paydirt. Gary called the woman and sounded frantic. He told her that he was in a motel in Albany, Georgia and that he needed her to bring him a stash of drugs he had left behind. He then gave her his address and room number.

Columbus police were now almost obsessed with

capturing Carlton Gary. They remembered how close they had been to him before at the Phoenix City motel and at the nightclub. Many of the officers wanted Captain C. T. Kirkland to authorize them to go to Albany to make the arrest. After some discussion, Kirkland and Police Chief Weatherington decided to let the Albany police handle the arrest.

The Albany police force responded to the challenge. They had been briefed by Columbus police that Gary often traveled with accomplices and that he would rent several rooms in a motel, sometimes not staying in any of them. When the Albany police SWAT team arrived at the Holiday Inn at approximately 4:30 on the afternoon of May 3rd, they finally found Carlton Gary.

He had rented three rooms and then had gone back to the desk to rent a fourth. Gary was relaxing across the bed in the room waiting for the Phoenix City woman to deliver his cocaine. There was a woman in the room with him. When she left to get some ice, police officers took her into custody.

Once they determined that Gary was in the room alone, four SWAT team members burst in. Police carried rifles and handguns, and all were cocked. They were naturally nervous about the arrest since Gary had a record of assault and armed robbery. Even outnumbered four to one, Gary lunged for a .38-caliber pistol on the bedside table. One of the police officers pounced on him before he could reach it.

After an intensive 50-day, three-state manhunt, the prime suspect in the Silk Stocking Strangler case was finally in custody.

It was almost 10:00 p.m. when Gary was escorted into the Columbus Police Department. A reporter who was on the scene that night recalled that Gary came in like a rock star walking with a rhythmic gait and mumbling constantly to himself. Gary only stopped mumbling once, and that was to flirt briefly with a female reporter.

Although the press knew Gary was a chief suspect in the case, the authorities had not as yet released any real evidence connecting him with the stranglings except for the fact that the gun had been traced back to him.

Police Chief Weatherington and District Attorney Bill Smith said no comments would be made about the evidence against Gary until the trial.

With that short statement, Gary was taken in for questioning and reporters gained no further information until the next morning, when D. A. Smith took his evidence to a grand jury, behind closed doors, and emerged only three hours later, telling the press that he felt sure Gary would be indicted for murder, rape, and burglary in the cases of Florence Schieble, Martha Thurmond, and Kathleen Woodruff. He again refused to give any specifics of the case against Gary.

Two weeks later, Carlton Gary was arraigned in Superior Court before Judge Rufe McCombs. At that time she appointed Columbus attorneys Gary Parker and Bruce Harvey as the defense team. Gary entered pleas of not guilty to all charges, and Judge McCombs ordered him held without bond until trial. A preliminary trial was scheduled for July.

The team of attorneys immediately filed various

motions requesting that Gary be released on bail. The petitions complained that Gary was being held in solitary confinement and was not being allowed any exercise or outside time at all.

Muscogee County Sheriff Gene Hodge told the court that, with Gary's record of escapes in the past, he was hesitant to let him outside. Hodge also explained that there had been several threats to kill Gary before he could be taken to trial and, therefore, it was for Gary's own safety that the solitary confinement had been imposed.

The defense attorneys argued that Gary was becoming depressed and was, therefore, unable to contribute to his own defense, thus making it impossible for him to receive a fair trial.

For six months, Gary's attorneys asked for, and were granted, continuances, telling Judge McCombs that this was a very complex case and that they needed the extra time to examine all the evidence Prosecutor Bill Smith was planning to present. When they finally showed up for trial, attorney Parker told the court that he would have to be removed from the case because he was unable to devote the necessary time to ensure a fair trial for his client.

In the meantime, Atlanta attorney August "Bud" Seimon, a well-known death penalty opponent, had approached Gary. Gary asked Judge McCombs if she would allow Parker to back out of the case. and let Seimon take his place. McCombs reluctantly agreed, and the case was postponed again.

During all these preliminary court strategies, Gary, although in prison, had not remained docile. On one occasion he had attempted suicide, and on another, he had removed the leg of his bunk in an attempt to dig the mortar out of the concrete blocks in his cell wall. Hodge assured the public that Gary hadn't even come close to escaping, and that he had been moved and placed under more stringent observation to prevent any future attempts.

After more than two weeks of bickering with defense attorneys, Judge Followill announced that the jury selection process would take place in Spalding County, Georgia, about 100 miles north of Columbus. Immediately, Gary's attorneys began objecting, arguing that the percentage of blacks in Spalding County was not high enough and that Gary would not receive a fair trial. But Followill stood firm on the decision and, during the last week in July, 1986, the court reconvened in Griffin, Georgia.

As soon as Followill opened the court proceedings, Gary's attorneys filed a motion requesting a hearing to determine whether or not Followill should be allowed to hear the case. The attorneys stated in their motion that Followill's rulings in the preliminary hearings had been prejudicial, and his refusal to grant funds for Gary's defense should disqualify him.

Followill agreed to the hearing and, within three days, it was held. The court determined that Followill could indeed hear the case because there were no grounds for removing him. The opinion further stated that Followill acted properly in all matters of the case

The process of selecting a jury took more than two weeks. Most of the prospective jurors had never heard of Carlton Gary and, therefore, had not been influenced by the press. Since District Attorney Bill Smith was seeking the death penalty, each prospective juror was asked if they could vote for the death penalty should the evidence in the case warrant it.

Gary's attorneys filed another motion, arguing that the prosecution was excluding those jurors because of their anti-death-penalty beliefs, and were, therefore, discriminating against them.

Followill ruled against the defense on this point. He told the defense that discrimination only existed when a person was singled out because of a trait or belief that was beyond their control. Since each potential juror had the option to be for or against the death penalty, no discrimination was involved.

With a jury finally seated and four alternates chosen, the trial began during the second week of August. It began, however, without the jury present. The first order of business was a hearing to determine whether or not District Attorney Bill Smith would be allowed to present evidence which was not directly related to the three killings Carlton Gary was charged with.

Smith told the court that he wanted to link Gary to several other crimes, including the other stranglings and the robberies. He also planned to introduce evidence that Gary may have been involved in the death of an Albany, New York, woman who was killed by someone using an M.O. similar to the strangler's.

Reports had been circulating that Smith would call as many as 125 witnesses in the case and that it could last as long as three months. When Followill ruled that Smith could proceed with his evidence, everyone braced themselves for a long-drawn-out courtroom battle.

Smith began his case with a bang and never let up. He produced two fingerprints and a palmprint that definitively placed Carlton Gary at the scene of three murders. He presented an eyewitness who said Carlton Gary had been the man she had seen in the Wynnton neighborhood shortly before the body of Florence Schieble had been found. Smith also presented testimony from Albany, New York, detectives who stated that they had thought Gary was the perpetrator in a similar killing there in 1977.

The only inconclusive evidence against Gary were the pubic hair samples taken from the crime scenes. Lab technicians told the court that the samples of Gary's hair were not an exact match.

Besides the fingerprints, the most damaging evidence against Gary came from the testimony of Columbus police. Several officers testified that, on the night of Gary's transfer to Columbus, he had taken detectives to Wynnton and had pointed out all six of the houses where the killings had taken place. Police were careful to point out that Gary never admitted to the killings, that he only would point to one of the houses and say something like, "That's where he did one."

Gary had told police that the killer was actually a man named Tom Perkins. Gary, however, didn't deny being at the scene of the slayings.

District Attorney Smith refuted this testimony by producing New York detectives who told the court that Gary had also tried to implicate Perkins in a killing in New York several years before. Perkins had

266

been tried and acquitted of the murder.

Perkins also testified that he had not been involved in the killings and was able to verify his whereabouts at the time several of the stranglings occurred.

Just 13 days after beginning his prosecution, D.A. Smith rested. This move surprised everyone, including the defense attorneys.

Defense Attorney Seimon called only relatives and friends of Gary to vouch for his character. He portrayed Gary as a thief and a petty drug dealer and argued that the killings didn't match Gary's long criminal behavior pattern. After just three days of this defense, Seimon rested.

During his closing arguments, Smith told the jury that Carlton Gary was a hardened sociopath and a remorseless killer. He recapped the physical evidence and Gary's inside knowledge of where the crimes had occurred and then he told the jury, "If there ever was a crime that the death penalty was specifically written for, this is it."

The jury must have agreed with Smith because it took them less than 45 minutes to return a guilty verdict.

On the morning of August 27th, the jury heard arguments in the sentencing phase of the case. When both sides were through, the jury took less than three hours to return with a recommendation of the death penalty on all three counts.

Followill followed the jury's recommendation and imposed the death penalty. He also sentenced Gary to a life sentence in each of the rape convictions and 20 years on each count of burglary. Followill imposed the sentences to run concurrently.

It took eight years, three suspects, and the questioning of more than 18,000 people, but the Columbus police, through dogged persistence, finally cleared what has been the most terrifying and bizarre case in its history.

JAMES SCHNICK
"WEIRD TWIST IN THE MARSHFIELD MASSACRE!"

by Barry Benedict

To the local officials, the farm crisis experts and a good many farmers, the killing frenzy that took place outside Marshfield, Missouri, on September 25, 1987, made a tragic sense.

The suspect was a 14-year-old Marshfield Junior High student named Kirk Buckner who, seemingly pushed to the breaking point by searing poverty and relentless workload, apparently loaded his gun and killed as many people as he could before he, too, was gunned down.

Residents felt sadness for the boy as well as his victims. "Kirk was a fine young man," said a farmer over a coffee at a Marshfield coffee shop the day after the killings. "We can't condone what he did, but we can understand it. These are tough times and that could have been any one of us pulling the trigger."

But the killings didn't make sense to students at

Marshfield Junior High. "Kirk just couldn't have done it," said a classmate, who knew the boy about as well as anyone. "He didn't have a mean bone in his body."

No one seemed to be listening to just a bunch of kids—except for police. Initially, they went along with the theory that Kirk had just snapped. But when the evidence didn't add up they started agreeing with what the kids had said all along—that Kirk just couldn't have done it.

At 6:45 in the morning of September 25, 1987, the Webster County Sheriff's Office received a call for help from a man who said he and his wife had been shot.

Deputies raced to a farmhouse near Elkland and about 10 miles east of Marshfield. Pulling into the gravel driveway, they saw a man curled up in the doorway, holding his side. He was moaning in pain and his fingers were pressed against his bloodstained shirt.

As a medic attended the moaning man, deputies ran into the house. They found a teenage boy in front of the bedroom door, a pistol clutched in his right hand. He had been stabbed and shot and lay dead in a huge blood pool.

In the master bedroom, they found a woman sprawled across the bed. She was dressed in a white nightie that was stained with blood.

In another bedroom, they found two kids. They were dressed in nightclothes and were huddled together terrified, but otherwise unhurt.

The deputies returned to the front porch where the medic worked on the wounded man.

"What happened here?" asked one deputy.

"The boy just went crazy," the wounded man said. "He shot me, he shot my wife. He would have killed us all if I hadn't killed him first."

The wounded man was James Schnick, 36. He said he had been the one who made the call for help. The woman in the master bedroom was his wife, Julie, 30, and the boy lying dead in the hallway was his nephew, Kirk Buckner, 14.

"The boy just went crazy," the shocked farmer said. "He started spraying bullets everywhere. Damn, I am lucky to be alive."

Schnick was bandaged and loaded into the back of a waiting ambulance. A deputy accompanied him on the short trip to the hospital to take down any statements Schnick cared to make.

Investigators under Sheriff Eugene Fraker arrived at the farmhouse. After locating a relative to take care of the children, the sheriff dispatched an investigator to the Buckner home to notify the family that Kirk had been shot to death.

Several minutes later, the excited deputy reported back that there had been a shooting at the Buckner place—"I count three dead children."

Investigators raced to that farm, seven miles from the Schnick place. Inside the farmhouse, they found 2-year-old Michael Buckner lying in his playpen, and his brothers Dennis, 8, and Timothy, 7, in an adjoining bed. All had been shot to death.

The sight of the murdered children sent a chill up the investigators' spines. "Where are the parents?" asked a deputy.

The shocking answer came after deputies searched

the barn directly behind the front house. In one of the stalls that housed the milking cows, they discovered the body of 36-year-old Jeanette Buckner. She lay face-down in the straw, shot in the back of the head. Near her was an overturned pail. She was apparently getting ready to milk the cows when a bullet dispatched her to an early grave.

Deputies frantically searched for 36-year-old Steve Buckner. He was not in the barn or anywhere on the property. Investigators hoped that the man had gone to town and escaped the slaughter.

Then a deputy reported that he had found the body of a man lying off a road near the local cemetery a half mile from the Buckner farmhouse. Steve Buckner, dressed in bib overalls and work shoes, lay face-down in the earth. Like the others, he had been shot to death.

Sheriff Fraker set up a command post at the Buckner home and ordered every available detective to assist in the investigation. He also made a request to the Missouri Highway Patrol office in Marshfield to send lab technicians to the Buckner and Schnick farms.

Reporters and photographers swarmed over the rural farmhouses. They were joined by farmers and townfolk who knew the Schnicks and the Buckners and could not believe what had happened.

The murder of seven persons—including the wholesale slaughter of a family of five—was overwhelming, even for the case-hardened deputies.

"They were slaughtered like cattle," one deputy told a reporter. "Them little kids look like they were shot while they slept."

272

Autopsies on the seven victims were conducted that evening. The preliminary results showed that Jeannette Buckner and her sons—Dennis, Timothy and Michael—had been shot once each in the head, while Julie Schnick and her brother, Steve Buckner, had been shot twice in the head.

Kirk Buckner had been shot twice and stabbed four times with a steak knife found protruding from his chest.

Ballistics confirmed that the seven victims had been shot with the revolver found clutched in Kirk's right hand.

Investigators reasoned that Kirk shot his parents and three brothers, then hauled his father's body to the graveyard before driving to his uncle's home and murdering his aunt.

Late that evening, detectives received word from the hospital that James Schnick felt better and wanted to make a statement.

Sheriff Fraker found him propped up in bed, a thick bandage around his middle, but otherwise okay.

"I still can't believe it," the 36-year-old farmer said. "Kirk was like my own flesh and blood. Why did he want to kill me or my family?"

Schnick said he rose early that morning as he always did and staggered from his home in the darkness to repair a broken stretch of fence.

When he returned to the house for breakfast his brother-in-law's pickup was in the driveway. Suddenly, he saw muzzle blasts come from the house. "I ran into the house and saw Kirk," Schnick said. "He looked kinda' crazy and wild and I asked him what happened and he pulled out this gun and pointed it at me."

Schnick said he grabbed a steak knife from the table and lunged at the boy as he fired. The slugs ripped into his gut, but he managed to wrestle the boy to the ground.

The struggle continued into the hallway, where Schnick said he overpowered the boy and killed him with the knife.

He said he ran into this bedroom and saw his wife lying on the bed with blood on her nightie. He checked the kids before stumbling to the telephone.

"You have any idea why he did it?" the sheriff asked.

"I can't think of none," Schnick said. "We have been close for years. Kirk was just the nicest kid you can imagine. We would have him over here anytime."

"How did he get along at home?"

"As far as I know, okay," Schnick replied. "Life might have been kinda' tough on him. My brother was having hard times — but we all were. I don't have to tell you these are tough times for the little farmer."

Even in good years, farmers in Webster County had it tough. And these weren't good years. Investigators learned that Steve and Jeannette Buckner were two years behind on payments to the FHA and Federal Land Bank and were in hock up to their necks.

Their house was run down, the farm machinery was old and always breaking down, and there was no money to fix anything, even if they had the time, which they didn't.

"I'd see Jeannette and Steve ten times a day and they were always working," a neighbor told investigators. "They never complained, not even the kids, but I think it had to get to them after a while."

As the oldest, Kirk spent every spare minute working. He rose two hours before school to milk the cow then did a full day's work after school.

On weekends, he worked on the farm or hit up neighbors for part-time jobs. "The boy did the work of ten men," one neighbor remarked. "I would hire him to slop the pigs and feed the cows and he would finish what I gave him and ask for more."

Kevin worked as hard at school as he did on the farm. While he was no "brain," he did his homework every night and eked out a "B" average.

But exhaustion was starting to show. Instructors said that Kevin showed up at school with big bags under his eyes and sometimes fell asleep during class.

"I guess he was just worn to a nub," said one instructor.

Funeral services were held on September 28th at the First Baptist Church in Elkland. Mourners jammed the modest church and filed past the caskets that held Julie Schnick and the six members of the Buckner family.

Jim Schnick was brought to the funeral by his wife's parents. He wore a white shirt and dark jacket and hobbled on crutches. He was visibly moved by the emotional eulogy and, toward the end of the service, appeared to slump.

Afterward, he stood by the door and thanked mourners as they filed out the door.

Several hours later, Sheriff Fraker contacted the Missouri Highway Patrol office in Springfield and talked to his hunting buddy, Sergeant Tom Martin.

"Tom, I need your help," the sheriff said. The MHP is the largest law enforcement agency in Webster County and lends out investigators and lab technicians when requested.

"Sure thing," the sergeant said. "We've been following that mass murder case like everyone else. I guess the kid just snapped."

"Maybe," the sheriff said. "But we got a lot of things here that don't add up."

"How is that?" Martin asked.

Fraker said that initially he was ready to accept the story that Schnick had murdered his nephew after Kevin had turned a gun on him. He was also ready to believe that Kevin had wiped out his family before driving to the Schnick farm. It was a wild, crazy story, but it did make sense. A few years earlier, a deranged man had walked into a McDonald's in San Diego, California, and wiped out 25 women and children before he was finally cut down. If that could happen then it was logical that a kid stretched to the breaking point could turn on his own family.

"I bought it for a while," the sheriff said. "And it still might be true. Except a lot of things just don't add up."

The sheriff explained that he first suspected something wasn't right when the search of the two farmhouses did not turn up a single cartridge casing.

"There were eighteen shots fired in the rampage," the sheriff said. "If Kirk had gone crazy, why did he have the presence of mind to pick up the casings? And what did he do with them?"

There was also the question of body weight. Fraker said his investigators had discovered blood in the

276

back of the Buckner pickup, indicating that it had been used to haul Jim Buckner's body to the graveyard.

"But how did Kirk get his dad's body in and out of the truck?" the sheriff asked. "Kirk didn't weigh more that 130 pounds, while his dad weighed almost twice that. There was no way he could have moved him."

Another clue that cast a shadow of doubt on Schnick's story surfaced after a deputy returned from conducting interviews at Marshfield Junior High School.

The deputy told the sheriff that none of the students who knew Kevin believed he could have committed the murder.

While questioning a teacher, the deputy happened to glance at some of Kirk's recent schoolwork and noticed how the handwriting slanted to the left.

The deputy told the sheriff that he showed the schoolwork to the teacher, who told him that Kirk wrote that way because he was left-handed.

"If Kevin was left-handed,' the sheriff asked Martin, "what was he doing clutching the murder weapon in his right hand?"

Martin agreed. The gun should have been in Kevin's left hand.

"What kind of guy is your suspect?" he asked.

"That's the strange part," Fraker replied. "Everybody we've talked to likes him."

James Schnick was from near Billings, Missouri, which was southwest of Springfield in Christian County. He'd moved to Elkland eight years earlier, where he married Julie Buckner and raised his two children.

He tended a small herd of 30 dairy cows on his 95-acre farm and also worked part-time at a feed company.

Quiet and easygoing, Schnick had few outside interests. Unlike his neighbors, he didn't like to hunt or fish and showed little interest in firearms.

"Jimmy kept guns in the house like we all do," one farmer told investigators. "But he never used them, not even at target practice. They just didn't hold his interest."

Most of Schnick's energies, investigators learned, were directed toward work. He labored sunup to sundown, rarely with a break, and worked on weekends.

About his only outside interest was the Elkland Volunteer Fire Department. Schnick attended the meetings on the first Monday of every month and was on call if needed.

Firefighters said Schnick loved hanging around the fire station and had applied for a full-time position with the Springfield Fire Department. He passed the physical and written requirements and was expected to be hired within the month.

Not exactly the portrait of a mass murderer, Sergeant Martin agreed. But why was he lying?

The detective reached that conclusion after more inconsistencies in his story emerged.

Paramedics said Schnick held his sides and screamed in agony on the way to the hospital. Yet a doctor who examined him said the wounds were superficial and barely cut the skin.

When asked if the wounds could have been self-inflicted the doctor nodded. "It is possible," he admitted.

Schnick also told detectives that during the struggle in the house he stabbed Kirk with a steak knife, then shot him by turning Kirk's hand that held the gun around so the barrel pointed at his nephew's chest.

But, according to the coroner's preliminary report, the angle of the bullet wound through the boy's heart wasn't consistent with the struggle Jim had described.

Perhaps the most damning evidence came after investigators discovered that Schnick was the beneficiary of a $100,000 life insurance policy on his wife. Schnick had also co-signed a bank note that in the event of Steve Buckner's death, would have given him debt-free title to his brother-in-law's farm. Moreover, Schnick was a possible beneficiary of his father-in-law's large holdings and a 24-acre farm which had been willed to the Buckner children and grandchildren.

"By killing those people, he eliminated seven heirs," Sheriff Fraker cursed between tight lips.

"I can't believe someone would be that cold-blooded, but I guess it is possible," Sergeant Martin agreed.

Schnick also had someone to spend it on. Police discovered that the hardworking farmer had a mistress whom he had been seeing for the past two years.

They learned that the mistress had learned Schnick was married and had threatened to go to his wife. The ultimatum was given shortly before the murders.

"Money and sex," Sergeant Mason said. "Two

powerful motives."

On October 5th, police contacted Schnick and asked him if he was up to coming to the station and answering a few more questions. Schnick said that was okay with him and hobbled into the station.

The 36-year-old farmer told investigators the same story he had a week earlier. Sergeant Martin watched him closely; he didn't believe a word of it.

Martin then asked Schnick if he was willing to take a lie-detector test. He said it would involve sitting in a chair and having electrodes attached to his nipples and other parts of his body. The test would take about an hour.

"Why do you need that?" Schnick asked.

"Because I think you are lying and this machine will tell us if you are or are not," the sergeant snapped.

"I didn't hurt anyone," Schnick shot back. "That boy was trying to kill me."

"Then you won't mind taking the lie box," the sergeant said.

"No," the farmer said. "Let's do it."

Schnick rose from his seat then appeared to slump. He grabbed his side and sat back in the chair. He remained silent for several moments before saying, "I guess you would find out sooner or later."

Schnick was advised of his constitutional rights. He was asked if he wanted a cigarette or something to eat before he made his statement.

Schnick shook his head. "No, I'm fine just as I am."

The worst mass murder in Missouri history began when Schnick went to Buckner's home on September

25th to help him with some chores. He said he arrived early as always, then waited for his brother-in-law to meet him outside before he shot him in the back of the head. He then shot Jeannette and turned the gun on Kirk and the other kids.

Schnick said he dumped Buckner's body in the graveyard, then drove seven miles to his house and shot his wife while she slept. He dragged Kirk's body into the house and shot himself superficially before calling for help.

"Once I started I couldn't stop," Schnick told detectives.

"Why did you do it in the first place?" Sergeant Martin asked. He already knew about the money, but the answer surprised him.

Schnick said that Jim Buckner had raped his wife Julie when they were children. He said the incest had scarred Julie and was a reason for the deterioration of his marriage over the past two years.

Schnick said he had confronted his brother-in-law about the alleged rape. That had resulted in a series of arguments.

Schnick said he did not expect trouble when he went to Buckner's house the morning of the murders. However, he had another shouting match with his brother-in-law which led to the shooting.

Schnick was arraigned on seven counts of murder on October 6th. Wearing bib overalls and a white tee-shirt, he told the judge he understood the charges against him and that he believed he had the money to hire an attorney. Judge Max Knust then ordered him to appear in court and to be held without bond in the county jail in Marshfield.

County Prosecutor Donald Cheever said it was likely that his office would seek the death penalty. "If there were ever a death penalty case, this one is it," he remarked.

Schnick went on trial in April, 1988 in Webster County Circuit Court before Judge John Parrish, with Donald Cheever as prosecutor. Schnick had been charged with seven murder counts but would stand trial only for the murders of his wife and nephews Kirk and Michael. The other counts were severed in case Schnick was found not guilty and it was necessary to try him again.

Eighty spectators and two dozen reporters packed the small courtroom to hear testimony and see in person "Missouri's Worst Mass Murderer."

Schnick was not much to look at. Bushy-haired and overweight, he was dressed in a jacket and slacks and slumped next to his attorney for much of the proceedings.

Prosecutor Cheever told the eight-woman, four-man jury that the defendant had carefully plotted the seven murders, then attempted to blame his nephew Kirk in order to collect on the insurance policy and to inherit property.

He said that Schnick had been cheating on his wife for two years and that Jeannette Schnick had learned about the mistress just before the killings.

Cheever speculated that Schnick had killed his wife because she threatened to divorce him because of the affair.

Jurors watched the lengthy video-taped confession Schnick had given in the police station. On tape, the defendant wiped sweat form his forehead, fidgeted with his fingers and occasionally broke into tears as he described in grisly detail how he'd committed the murders.

The jury then listened to Schnick's attorney, who asked them to forget what they had heard and seen on the tape and not to make any conclusions until they had heard all the witnesses.

He said that his client did not know what he was doing when he made the video-taped confession, and that he had been coached by police into making the statement.

Thirteen witnesses took the stand to testify that Schnick was a hardworking, much-liked person in the community who always went out of his way to help others.

A teenager also testified that he had been a friend of Kirk Buckner's and had gone hunting and fishing with him many times. On these occasions, the witness said, Kirk used his right hand as often as his left when he shot and fished. The testimony was apparently to cast doubt on the theory that Schnick had planted the gun on the body to make it look as if Kirk were the killer.

The defense also put on the stand two friends of the defendant's who testified that they had helped Schnick put his financial affairs in order after his wife's death and suggested he apply for the $50,000 benefit from the life insurance policy on Julie Schnick's life.

Courtroom observers later said that they thought the purpose of the testimony was to cast doubt that Schnick committed the murders for the money.

The jurors were not swayed. They found Schnick

guilty of three counts of first-degree murder on April 14th after just one hour and 45 minutes of deliberations.

"It was overwhelming," a juror said later.

The same jury was then asked to determine in the penalty phase of the trial if Schnick should be sentenced to death or to prison the rest of his natural life.

A psychologist testified for the defense that Schnick's violent behavior on the morning of September 25th had been completely contrary to a life of compassion and caring for others. He said it was likely that the defendant had simply "exploded" because he had difficulty expressing anger and sought acceptance through hard work.

"Most people have outlets for anger, fear and hurt," the psychologist said. "His outlet was to work harder. He had nowhere to go if you pushed him into a corner or up against a wall."

Friends testified that Schnick was a hardworking, loving father, while members of the Elkland Volunteer Fire Department said that "he was one of the best."

One man who had known him for 30 years said, "Jim never lost his temper and was the type of guy who would stop a truck from moving across a field so he could remove nests of baby rabbits rather than run over them."

Prosecutor Cheever reminded jurors that there was ample evidence to vote for the death sentence. "Think about Julie Schnick and the two children," he told jurors. "The defendant showed them no mercy."

He then described 2-year-old Michael lying dead in the crib. "It's difficult to imagine anything more defenseless and helpless than a two-year-old asleep in his bed."

The jurors returned to chambers on April 16th. This time they spent two hours and 30 minutes before returning to the packed courtroom.

"Have you reached a verdict?" the judge asked.

"We have," the jury forewoman said.

A slip of paper was passed to the judge, who quickly read it and passed it to the court clerk.

"We, the jury, find that James E. Schnick should die in the gas chamber," the clerk read aloud.

James Schnick wept as the jury sealed his fate. Bailiffs removed him from the courtroom.

Schnick became the 57th person on Death Row at the Missouri State Penitentiary. It is unlikely that his sentence will be carried out in the near future. His case is on appeal to the state supreme court and it could be years before a ruling is made.

Missouri is also slow to act on capital cases. No one has been executed in Missouri since 1965.

Schnick is currently on Death Row waiting the outcome of his appeal.

WILLIAM CRUSE
"THE MAN WITH A RAGE TO KILL!"
by Don Unatin

"I heard the shots across the street. About twenty rounds. Just bam, bam, bam. We opened the door and looked out. The look on his face was just like suicide."

Palm Bay is a typical Florida community. It features the strong ties of middle-class family life and well-kept lawns. Kids enjoy a type of freedom which blossoms among caring adults.

Located just 30 miles south of the Kennedy Space Center at Cape Canaveral, Palm Bay has known the triumph and tragedy of historic events there. But Palm Bay itself has had little or no reason to make its own headlines.

For the most part, life is even and placid in Palm Bay. What bustle there is occurs along Babcock Street, which cuts a path between the Sabal Palm and Palm Bay Shopping Centers. It is to Babcock Street's parking lots that young families and older retirees come in search of the clothing and household goods values offered by the 30 or so stores of the twin shopping centers.

There is a sense of well-being and camaraderie among the merchants and consumers who make Babcock Street the focal point of retail activity.

The general feeling is that nothing really bad could ever happen in these civilized surroundings. After all, this is a mushrooming high-tech community where salaries are good, education is highly regarded and being civilized is a way of life.

Take any sampling of four shoppers who happened to be in the parking lots or shopping centers along Babcock Street at 6:30 p.m. on a lovely April evening and they would be likely to resemble these four in age, customs and social outlook:

Ruth Green, a 67-year-old divorcee, who on Thursday evening, April 23, 1987, is about to enter the Winn Dixie supermarket to buy lettuce for her pet hamster. Mrs. Green is a devout Baptist who has shown an increasing consciousness of her own mortality. Just moments ago, she has confided to a woman friend her most intimate thoughts on dying. "It'd be so beautiful to be with Jesus," she has commented.

Lester Wilson, a 51-year-old quality-control inspector, who is walking out of the Publix Supermarket, his arms laden with two shopping bags. The Syracuse, New York native, who moved to Florida 20 years ago, is on a routine shopping expedition for his family.

Nobi Abdul Alhanell, 25, and Emad Al Juwakuly, 19. The Kuwaiti natives are students at Brevard

Community College and Florida Institute of Technology, respectively. Their studies are being subsidized by the government of Kuwait. Usually, they do their weekly shopping at a supermarket in Melbourne, Florida. For some reason, they have decided on coming to Palm Bay this afternoon.

None of the four have any knowledge of an incident that has just taken place about a half mile away. Nor do any of the others who are going about their appointed tasks at this very moment.

Nobody is aware that two youngsters scant minutes before have run across a neighbor's lawn. They know nothing of the rage that has been triggered in a rumpled, gaunt-faced, wild-eyed 60-year-old man's mind by the sight of the two teenagers on his property. They can't imagine that anybody could have been so provoked by such an incident to begin firing a high-powered .223-caliber rifle at the inadvertent trespassers.

As yet, nobody has become suspicious of the white Toyota now sliding into the Palm Bay mall parking lot, or its driver. Not until the first shots smash the early evening calm do they realize something unbelievably horrible is erupting all around them.

As pandemonium suddenly erupts, Ruth Green, Lester Watson, Nobi Abdul Alhanell and Mohammed Al-Juwakuly fall to the ground, their lives snuffed out by the fusillade of rifle fire.

Now the driver of the Toyota eases his vehicle across the four lanes of Babcock Street. His objective apparently is the Winn-Dixie Supermarket, where about 100 people are either working or shopping.

It is approximately 6:35 p.m. The man with the rifle is firing at random. There is panic everywhere. It will be days before all the gory details of what is happening in these minutes will be sorted out. They will come from the shocked and hushed accounts of those fortunate enough to have survived the onslaught.

They will tell of the terror as the Toyota circled, stalking victims. They will recall the bullets skipping across the facades of storefronts and splintering as shoppers dove for cover and doors were slammed and locked.

One young woman who works for a card shop will say, "This guy was shooting at anything in sight. He didn't care. He was amazing. He was just shooting at anything.

"I saw a little boy, maybe seven or eight, get shot. And a man in the car who had just been shopping. The gunman shot him down."

A supermarket employee will recall an elderly couple who were gunned down as they left the store. "He (the sniper) shot both of them. They were lying on the ground and he just kept shooting them."

A stockboy who works for the same supermarket will remember running out of the store when he thought the crazed gunman had left.

"I looked down and saw all these bodies on the ground. Then I saw the gunman. He was about five-feet-eight with gray hair, about 50 years old and wearing a tan jacket. He just kept looking around, like he was looking for someone.

"Then the lady pulled up in a car. He turned and

289

saw her and he shot her. I knew that she was dead."

A retail jeweler will say, "I heard the shots across the street. About twenty rounds — just bam, bam, bam. We opened the door and looked out."

He will tell of seeing a man with reddish-gray hair stepping out of a white compact car about 20 feet from the jeweler in the parking lot. He will describe the man's clothing as being a light T-shirt and vest. He will note that the man was carrying a rifle. But most of all, it will be the look on the assailant's face which will conjure up the true feelings of dread. "The look on his face was like suicide," he'll comment.

Another jewelry-store employee will tell of having been at a pay station adjacent to the Winn-Dixie Supermarket. The retailer was calling his wife when the gunman opened fire on the supermarket. Then, as the jeweler stared in disbelief, the rifleman turned toward him.

The retail jeweler will say, "I just hit the door and hit the floor."

A third jewelry-store employee will tell listeners, "I felt one bullet go right through the top of my hair."

The three jewelry-store men will reveal how they made good their own escape from the line of fire.

"We were running with our backs turned," one will say. "I opened the back door and I said, 'Get out of here! This guy's shooting people!' I saw people running and I saw a guy drop. He (the assailant) shot him in the back."

"We ran across the street, ducking and hiding behind cars."

As the first bursts of rifle fire are to be replaced by

the ominous tension of a hostage standoff, the three jewelers huddle with 25 others who have been lucky enough to make their way to safety in a shopping-center drugstore.

One of the jewelers will best express the mood of all those who have taken refuge there by saying, "I'm not going anywhere until they shoot that guy."

There will be a quaver of shock remaining in the voice of the owner of a coin-operated laundromat as he describes a portion of the firefight. Not only has the man witnessed the assailant firing from the hip at any moving target—he will tell of just how two young Palm Bay police officers have been murdered in cold blood.

His attention attracted by the first bursts of gun-shots, the laundromat owner is outside his own establishment when it happens.

He'll give this graphic description:

"The first police car pulled up about forty feet away. I looked to my left. There was this man with reddish-gray hair aiming his rifle at the cop behind the wheel before the car stopped. He was just standing there calmly squeezing off shots into the windshield. The cop never had a chance. He just slumped over at the wheel."

As the first officer, Gerald Johnson, a 28-year-old cop with one year on the Palm Bay police force, lies dying in the front seat of his car, a second police cruiser drives into the parking lot. This vehicle's driven by Palm Bay Officer Ron Grogan. The 27-year-old man had only been hired by the department a scant seven months prior to the shopping-center massacre.

291

Grogan brings his police car to a screeching stop directly behind Johnson's squad car. This places Grogan squarely into the sights of the deranged killer's .223-caliber rifle.

The laundromat owner will give the position of the rifleman as being some 30 feet from Grogan. The assailant, he will say, was partially screened from Grogan's view by the overhang of the Winn-Dixie Supermarket. The rifleman squeezed off at least two shots. Grogan was dead before he could get out of his own car.

There is some conjecture as to whether Grogan actually died instantly. Some will say the intrepid officer did manage to get six shots of his own off and had at first merely been hit in the leg by his adversary's bullet. But when Grogan crawled behind his patrolcar to reload, the witnesses will report, the killer-on-a-spree stepped around the car and shot him in the head.

Now two fine young men who chose careers as keepers of the peace and protectors of the community of Palm Bay have been added to the list of those who are to be mourned. In all, there are now six to be counted dead.

The Palm Bay Police Department and the community at large will not soon forget the valiant way in which the two cops met their doom.

Nor will they forget what Johnson and Grogan stood for.

Each man had been embarking on a splendid career of public service.

Johnson had served in the United States Army. He had joined the Palm Bay force eleven and a half months before his death. Married for two and a half years, he and his wife had not as yet had any children.

Grogan, who at one time had been a corrections officer, had received his Palm Bay badge in October, 1986. He was a newlywed, having gotten married a scant two months before the shopping-center tragedy.

Not satisfied with the havoc he has wreaked thus far, the gunman now seeks out new targets for his rage.

Firing his weapons as he moves into the Winn-Dixie Store, he drives scores of panic-stricken potential victims before him.

One young woman, who brought her infant son to the shopping center on the fateful evening, will later be interviewed at her hospital bedside. She will say, "It was like we was ducks at the fair, or something, male or female or children." The woman, who has been wounded in the abdomen, is listed in satisfactory condition. Her baby has been grazed by the gunfire, according to police. However, he has not been seriously injured.

Terrified shoppers and employees sprint from the back of the supermarket. The man with the rifle follows in hot pursuit. Some of the throng are picked off as they clamber across a wide ditch and flee into the back yards of homes. In the general hubbub can be heard the urgent screams of those seeking help.

And help is on the way. It comes in the persons of 200 police officers who flood into Palm Bay from nearby communities. (The deaths of Grogan and Johnson have cut the Palm Bay police force in half.

Of the four officers who comprised the community's constabulary, only two now remain alive.)

The lawmen now taking up positions around the stricken shopping center are backed by United States Air Force canine units. Overhead, police and military choppers crisscross the sky as crews seek to determine the current position of the crazed sniper.

The man with the reddish-gray hair, the camouflage pants, vest and white T-shirt has now carried his arsenal of weapons and ammo back into the supermarket.

Aware of his presence, some Winn-Dixie employees seek whatever cover is available to them within the store. Three lock themselves inside a cold-storage room. They will remain there for hours, benumbed by the intense cold and the fear which grips them. Eight terror-filled hours will pass before they will be able to leave their improvised barricade.

A young woman store clerk manages to hide in a bathroom. She crouches in terror as she hears a man's footsteps approaching. She sees the bathroom door handle begin to move. The door opens. She is confronted by the gunman.

Later, she will say, "I was preparing myself for a bullet." However, she will remember the assailant as being almost gentle with her, despite the fact that he kept a revolver pressed against her head.

She will tell of the note of apology in the sniper's voice as she quotes him as having said, "I'm sorry to have to do this to you," but informed her that he needed a hostage.

The store clerk, along with two others, will be forced to fill the hostage role throughout a good portion of the night.

The crisis has turned into a stalemate. Police snipers take up strategic positions but cannot use their weapons because of the peril to those inside the supermarket. SWAT teams, their rifles equipped with telescopic sights, their supply of tear-gas shells and stun grenades ready for instant use, can do nothing but stand and wait.

For the paramedics, the frustration of the ensuing hours is mind-boggling. They can see the dead and wounded sprawled in the parking lots. But because of the sporadic fire of the rifleman they are pinned down.

Peter Wahl, director of community services for Brevard County, is at the scene. He reports that ambulances have been unable to reach the victims because the vehicles have "drawn fire" each time they approach the bodies.

There is much confusion. First reports have eight dead. Later, it is said 12 have died. (Final count will be revised downward to six.) The number of wounded is thought to be 12. (It turns out to be 14.)

The prime concern is to prevent any further loss of life. This will be the responsibility of highly skilled members of a police negotiating team. To do their job, they must gather as much information as they can as quickly as possible about the rifleman. If they can keep him talking, there's the hope he will listen to reason and cool it.

The negotiators are informed that the man in question is 60-year-old William B. Cruse, an unemployed loner. Cruse has a history of erratic and antisocial behavior. There have been complaints from

Cruse's neighbors in the past of his aggressive and hostile forays against children and young people. He is said to have been a resident of Palm Bay for two years. It is thought he might have migrated from Kentucky because his Toyota carries license plates issued by the Blue Grass State. Cruse is said to be caring for his wife, who is reported to be suffering from either Parkinson's or Alzheimer's disease.

Armed with this information, a police officer uses a bullhorn to talk to Cruse, trying to calm him down. An 18-year-old high-school student takes notes which will document the delicate give-and-take between the lawman and the suspected killer.

According to the notes, which will be released later, the officer tells Cruse, "Bill, we called your wife—she is real disturbed. We are not going to hurt you."

The officer suggests that Cruse use the woman hostage to communicate his thoughts to the police.

Later, the woman hostage will report that the gunman had begun talking about committing suicide. She will say, "I told him to go somewhere else to do it."

She would also relate how, in the middle of his rampage, Cruse had allegedly asked for a tally of the number of people he had killed. The woman will say he forced her to ask the police over the phone for the figures.

She will comment, "He said he was sorry he had to do this to me. Then he had me go ask the police officers (by phone) how many people were killed. That's what he wanted to know. He really does regret what he did."

As the touch-and-go negotiations between the police and Cruse continue, five buses are able to roll out of the shopping center. They're crowded with people who had been trapped by the lethal gunfire. Waving and cheering from the bus windows, the evacuees are taken to a nearby parking lot for debriefing interviews with police. Then they are conducted to Palm Bay's city hall for family reunions. An armored personnel carrier is also used in the rescue operation.

There is a new thrill of terror in the area as a report circulates that a second armed man has been picked up in the vicinity. Rumors circulate that the alleged sniper may have a confederate. Everyone breathes easier when it is learned that the second man is a law-abiding citizen who has taken up a rifle as protection from the rampaging killer.

The strain continues to grow as midnight passes and there still is no break in the situation.

Then, at approximately 1:00 a.m., it comes.

Cruse, who has been demanding a car and an airplane for safe conduct out of Palm Bay and has been incoherent at times, finally relents. He agrees to give up his hostages.

Police spokesperson Louise Brown will quote him as saying he "didn't want to hurt any more women."

It is shortly before 2:00 a.m. that the woman hostage is released. She runs frantically through the police lines to safety.

Still the standoff has not been resolved. Cruse shows no sign that he is about to surrender. Instead, he remains holed up in his improvised barricade.

There is a hasty conference among those in charge

of the police action.

It is decided that the time has come to send in SWAT teams to flush the suspect out.

The tactical officers move with overwhelming speed. There is the sound of exploding shells. Dense clouds of tear gas fill the supermarket. A stun grenade is hurled.

Cruse bolts. He tries to escape through a rear supermarket exit. The police are waiting. There is a fierce struggle as the distraught man tries to wrestle his way free.

The word goes out. It is given by Police Lieutenant Candice Leek. The officer says, "They chased him down and caught him. He is being brought to the station right now."

Cruse is handcuffed and, despite his struggles, taken in for questioning. An eyewitness will report, "The cops started to cuff Cruse when they grabbed him and he fought them all the way to the car, knocking one of those guys down."

Those who had locked themselves in the supermarket refrigerator room and others who had remained pinned down in the store throughout the night are led to freedom and treated for exposure.

Intensive interrogation of the suspect reveals a lack of remorse on his part.

Palm Bay Police Chief Chuck Simmons will comment, "It does not appear he is concerned one way or another with what he has done."

As Friday wears on, details of Cruse's history begin to surface. Some who have had dealings with him refer to the killer as a "walking time bomb." He is described by many as "both a tormentor and a tor-

298

mented man."

Although neighbors are well acquainted with his temper outbursts and his solitary ways, they report they don't know a great deal more about him. Nobody can say for sure whether Cruse is unemployed or retired.

Cruse's contact with other residents seems to have been limited to his skirmishes with children who tried to use his lawn as a shortcut. One neighbor, who had recently issued a police complaint against Cruse, alleges that the elderly man was always the first to utter the insult. Says the neighbor, "It was always him saying something and them responding."

It is said that in the fall of 1986 some neighbors signed a petition that charged Cruse was dangerous, and asked authorities to help him. Others report they had called police when Cruse allegedly drove after their children in his car.

More recently, the neighbors report, Cruse was sighted at least twice with a rifle in his possession. Each time he appeared at his door toting the weapon, he is alleged to have shouted, "Get off my land!"

For their part, police cannot say when Cruse obtained the .223 rifle which uses the same ammunition as the Army's M-26.

It is said that Cruse's rages were not directed toward youngsters alone. One 39-year-old man recalls an occasion when a co-worker dropped him off at his home across the street from the one occupied by Cruse. The neighbor relates that Cruse aimed his rifle in the man's direction.

Says the construction worker, "He pointed it right

at us." He quotes Cruse as shouting, "You made me lose my job. I'll get you for this!" The man did not report the incident to the police.

Experts study the reports coming out of Palm Bay to gain new insights into the rash or random massacres which have afflicted the nation in recent years. They cite similarities in the shopping center rampage and these bloodbaths:

The July 18, 1984, massacre of 21 people at a McDonald's Restaurant in San Ysidro, California. The killer, James Huberty, was himself shot dead by the police.

The August 1, 1966 rampage on the Austin Campus of the University of Texas in which 14 people were shot to death by Charles J. Whitman. (Whitman had killed his wife and mother on the night before the University of Texas mass slayings. He in turn was shot to death by police.)

The Edmond, Oklahoma slaying of 14 postal workers by Patrick Sherrill on August 20, 1986. Sherrill, who had been threatened with being fired, shot himself to death after slaying the others.

The experts hold that while mass killings are not unique to the United States, the loss of life in such incidents here is much heavier because of the ability of pathological killers to easily obtain guns.

Says Jack Levin, a sociologist, "Other societies may have lots of frustrations, people who lose their jobs, but they don't have the guns around and you don't hear about people being massacred. You can't take six people out with a knife."

Comments Dr. Park Elliot Dietz, professor of law and psychiatry at the University of Virginia, "In order to be a successful mass murderer in America, one must have the hardware."

Levin and James A. Fox, a criminologist, have recently collaborated on a book on mass murder. They hold that several trends in American culture, including divorce and rootlessness, contribute to the loosening of social controls that might otherwise restrain a violence-prone society.

The two Northeastern University professors, in their book, *Mass Murder; America's Growing Menace,* list four tendencies which they say are common to mass murderers. They say the killer is usually the product of a life of frustration. (His rampage is often triggered by a single incident, however. Loss of a job or a divorce are cited as examples.)

Usually the killer is familiar with guns. He is likely to be a veteran of the armed forces, a hunter or a target-shooting enthusiast.

In most cases, the killers did not have other people around them to stop them and get them through bad times. This was because they either lived alone or they had recently pulled up roots.

On this point, Levin says, "They've left their friends, relatives and families."

Over the weekend following the shopping-center carnage, flags fly at half-staff over Palm Bay in memory of the dead.

Funerals are held for Lester Waster Watson and Ruth Green. The bodies of Nobil Al-Hameli and Emad Al-Tawakuly are flown back to Kuwait for burial. Preparations go forward for hero funerals for Officers Gerald Johnson and Ronald Grogan which are scheduled for St. Joseph's Catholic Church.

For his part, Cruse insists that he has no memory of the lethal events of the bloody evening.

However, the young and plucky store clerk who spent six and a half hours as his hostage is strong in her belief that the accused man knew exactly what he was doing at every point throughout the tragedy.

She says, "I know he remembers. He told me he knew he was going to be dead because he had killed and paralyzed people.

"He knew he fired those shots. He asked me to find out how many people he had killed. He opened up to me. He said I was his friend. He told me he wanted to get revenge on everybody who bothered him."

It is expected that the young woman will be the state's star witness in court proceedings pending against Cruse.

As Florida State Attorney Norm Wolfinger indicates that prosecution strategy is likely to call for seeking the death penalty against Cruse, Brevard County Public Defender James Russo meets with the accused killer.

Following the session, Russo comments, "We are looking at all possible defenses and certainly we are looking at a psychiatric defense."

Meanwhile, Palm Bay tries to cope with the tragedy which has left its indelible mark on the community.

It won't be easy.

Says one 17-year-old resident, "A nice neighborhood like this . . . Nothing ever goes wrong in a place like this."

The words echo those of the widow of martyred

302

Officer Ronald Grogan. She comments, "I always thought, 'This is Palm Bay—that kind of thing just doesn't happen here.'"

The grieving young woman noted her own reservations about her hero husband's having become a police officer. She comments, "To some extent, I didn't want him to be a cop, but I thought he should do what he wanted to do.

"It was very important to him.

"He could have died doing anything that day if it was his time."

As this is being written, William Cruse is awaiting trial on the six counts of first-degree murder and 10 counts of attempted murder with which he has been charged.

It is his constitutional right to be considered innocent unless and until proved otherwise under due process of law.

JAMES HUBERTY
"I'M GOING HUNTING HUMANS!"
by Tom Basinski

For Albert Leos, July 18, 1984, was just another beautiful summer Wednesday. The 17-year-old boy lived a busy life. He would soon start his senior year at Chula Vista High School.

Albert was spending the summer working as a fry cook at McDonald's in San Ysidro, a small community in the city of San Diego on the Mexican international border at Tijuana.

Leos also worked out daily, getting in shape for the football season only four weeks away. Albert had lettered as a junior defensive back and was courting thoughts and hopes of a college scholarship if he turned in a solid performance this year.

Albert was 5 feet 9 inches tall and weighed 155 pounds. But he was very fast and tackled with teeth-rattling impact. He knew that he was too small to play for any of southern California's "football factories," but he hoped that some smaller school would trade him an education for four years of solid football.

During this summer, Albert worked 30 hours a week at the famous fast-food restaurant. However, Albert was no workaholic, in spite of his goals and his resolve to realize those goals. Albert had many friends and he loved to go to the beach, attend parties and enjoy life.

On July 18th, Albert was scheduled to begin cooking burgers and fries at 2:00 p.m. This particular shift virtually ruined a day at the beach. Had he started at four, or ended at noon, he could have salvaged some fun out of the day. But the two o'clock starting time ended any thoughts of the beach.

For this reason, Albert Leos considered not going to work. But Albert's training at home and on the football field dictated that he must go to work. He knew that nothing tangible was ever realized by a day at the beach. When it came time to go to work, Albert did.

At the time Albert was punching the time clock, a man who lived in an apartment two blocks away from McDonald's was walking with his family inside San Diego's famous zoo. Earlier in the day, the man had pleaded guilty to a traffic ticket in municipal court and had eaten lunch with his family at another McDonald's.

The man was an unemployed security guard who had the usual fascination with camouflage clothing, literature about mercenaries and high-powered firearms. There was a small arsenal of weapons in his car trunk. The man was 42-year-old James Oliver Huberty.

Albert Leos had worked at McDonald's for about six weeks and knew the ropes very well. There was always the big rush of customers at noon and at five o'clock. Things were so busy at these times that all the workers moved as fast as he or she could.

Albert kept a full grill of hamburgers going, constantly turning the patties and adding new ones as orders came over the speaker.

This particular McDonald's was the busiest in San Diego. The familiar golden arches were one of the first landmarks that weary travelers saw after driving through United States Customs.

Many McDonald's customers had waited in overheated cars in long lines for more than an hour in order to be questioned by federal law enforcement officers about their citizenship and what they were bringing into the United States.

Some travelers had been reluctant to eat in Mexico. Others were just thirsty. McDonald's welcomed them all.

By four o'clock, James Huberty drove home from the zoo, stayed a while and then left. His last words to his wife were: "I'm going hunting humans!"

By four o'clock, Albert Leos was fully in the swing of things. He had forgotten about the beach and was "in rhythm," moving the beef patties on the grill. He made sure there was a good supply of beef ready to be cooked as the five o'clock rush was approaching and that all were there and ready. Cartons of buns and cases of tomatoes and lettuce were stacked off to the side.

Albert was standing at his station with three of his co-workers, also high school students. All four of the youths had mastered their duties. They could work with rapid efficiency while carrying on a conversation.

Since they were in the back of the building, Albert and the three other teenagers did not even notice when James Huberty walked in the front door carrying a 12-gauge shotgun and a 9 mm semiautomatic Uzi submachine gun. He had a 9 mm semiautomatic pistol in his belt.

Albert heard some commotion in the front of the restaurant. The store manager, 22-year-old Neva Caine, was doing paperwork in one of the booths near the counter. She often did this so she could monitor the level of service while keeping up with her managerial duties.

Suddenly, James Huberty yelled out, "Everybody get down on the floor or I'll kill somebody!"

Neva Caine bounded from her seat at the booth, next week's work schedule fluttering to the floor in the wake of her movement. Neva had dealt with troublemakers before. However, none had ever entered carrying weapons. Somehow, this entire thing did not seem as though it was really happening.

Some of the customers hit the floor. Some headed for the door, and still others, anesthetized by television gunplay, turned back to examining the overhead menus as if nothing had happened.

Neva Caine said to the man, "All right, you can't come in here and act like this." Those were to be her last words. The strange intruder leveled the shotgun at her head and pulled the trigger.

When Caine went down, Huberty definitely had everyone's attention. He fired a few more shots into the ceiling and then started spraying with the Uzi.

More than 50 people were inside the restaurant at the time. The bullets flew indiscriminately, flying into people, the walls, and breaking the heavy, tinted window glass.

Some people were killed in their booths. One family had just sat down with their tray of food. Their drinks were untouched and the hamburgers were still tightly wrapped in waxed paper. Their bodies slumped forward, riddled with bullets. The gunman yelled, "Shut up, all of you."

Some people hit the floor and remained motionless. The man pointed at those on the floor and pulled the triggers. Some were hit. Some played dead and others really were dead.

Huberty shot and walked about the restaurant. He did not run and he was not frantic. He shot outside through the windows. He walked behind the food counter and fired at the overhead menu and then once into the milkshake machine. The bullets ricocheted and rattled in the steel and cement building.

The gunman walked to the grill in back. There, huddled on the floor, were Albert Leos and three coworkers. Huberty held the 12-gauge shotgun under one arm and the Uzi under the other.

Albert Leos looked up at the gunman. Huberty smiled and said, "Thought you could hide from me, eh?" Leos only gave him a solid stare. The people on the floor were sobbing quietly.

Huberty's grin suddenly dropped from his face, replaced by a stone-like expression. Using both hands, he fired his weapons at the four people on the floor. Shotgun pellets and 9 mm bullets ripped into the

308

people. Huberty continued to fire.

Two of the girls were hit with shotgun blasts and died immediately. Albert Leos crawled away after being hit and tried to take cover under a small metal table. The fourth employee had been shot with the Uzi. She tried to crawl away as she screamed and cried, "Don't kill me! Don't kill me!"

He shot her two more times. Then the firing stopped and the triggers clicked on empty chambers. Wordlessly, Huberty walked back to the front of the store and began reloading.

Albert Leos had been hit four times, once in the left arm and once in the right arm. He was also hit in the upper right leg and once in the right side of the stomach. He was not aware of his stomach wound, however.

While Huberty was reloading up front, three 11-year-old boys came up the driveway, pushing their 20-inch bicycles. Each had a dollar and they were going to get a milkshake and play on the playground equipment.

The boys put their bicycles down and started waking toward the door. Someone yelled something at them from across the parking lot. One of the boys turned to see who it was.

Bullets flew into them from inside the restaurant. Two of the boys were killed immediately and the third lay on the cement, wounded but still alive. He played dead and waited. He hoped his two friends were playing too.

The official police reports indicated the first call for service was received at 4:03 p.m., on the 911 emergency lines. The first police car arrived at Mc-

Donald's at 4:07 p.m. As the responding officer got out of his patrol car, his windshield shattered and his overhead emergency light bar disintegrated in a barrage of gunfire.

Coincidentally, the responding officer was on the SWAT team and was also a member of the Primary Response Team that performed hostage rescues and assaults on buildings containing suspects. This officer requested a full contingent of SWAT and alerted radio dispatch that a full-scale siege was under way.

The officer could see the three boys, but could not get to them. For two of the boys it did not matter.

The restaurant is a healthy stone's throw from Interstate 5, a heavily traveled eight-lane freeway. One vehicle was hit by James Huberty's gunfire and as a result, the freeway was subsequently closed down.

Meanwhile, officers continued to arrive at the scene and Huberty from inside greeted them with a hail of bullets. Two officers returned fire, but missed. The officers were reluctant to fire wildly because of the likelihood that hostages might be hit. Also, no information had been received on how many suspects there were or why this was happening. Was it a Middle Eastern political move by a terrorist group? Or was it a crazed gunman?

The diversion created by new targets wearing police uniforms allowed Albert Leos to crawl to the rear of the restaurant and down a few steps to the storage basement. He had tried to walk but the 9 mm bullet in his leg had penetrated the muscle, rendering it useless.

Albert knew that the gunman would come back and finish him off when he reloaded. Albert's goal at

310

this time was to get into the storage room in the basement. He pulled and crawled his way along the floor and down the steps. Blood was flowing freely from all four wounds.

Because of his intense desire to save himself, Albert was not conscious of pain at that moment, only of a hot metal inside his skin in the area of his wounds.

When Albert arrived at the storage room, he reached up to open the door. It was locked. He knew there were people inside because they were down there when the shooting started. The room was also an unofficial employee lounge where the workers took breaks.

Albert banged on the door, but not too loudly. He hoped the gunman had forgotten about him. Yet he feared that the gunman was now slowly stalking him with a fresh supply of bullets.

Albert called, again not too loudly, that it was Albert and to let him in. The door opened up and those inside rapidly pulled him in. They closed and locked the door. Albert looked around the room and saw five familiar faces. The girls were crying and the boys had a look of glassy-eyed, bland-faced, terror.

Albert was bleeding profusely. His co-workers removed his shoelaces and made them into tourniquets for his arms.

Once Albert was in the comparative safety of the storage room, he started to realize how much pain he was in. A few moments earlier when he had been eight feet away from Huberty, looking into his eyes while bullets were ripping into his body, he had not been aware of pain, only of his need for survival.

Now it was time to feel the hurt.

The burning sensation of before now gave way to feelings of flesh on fire inside his body. The heat did not diminish, but rather seemed to get even hotter.

Albert was bleeding at an alarming rate, in spite of the shoelaces around his arms. The pain was so great that Albert thought he would break some of his teeth from clenching his jaw.

Someone placed a small hand towel in Albert's mouth. Albert held it there so his screams would be muffled and his teeth protected.

What would happen next? Would the gunman kick his way through the door and ring up six new victims? Albert thought that the police must know by now that something was going on. Would they come through the door and rescue everyone? Or, would Albert lie on the floor, surrounded by his co-workers, and bleed to death?

Upstairs things were happening fast. The 500 block of San Ysidro Boulevard is the main drag of the little community of San Ysidro. The street has only two lanes and it is always filled with cars. Late afternoons are worse. The street often looks like a parking lot.

The police had blocked off San Ysidro Boulevard for three blocks on either side of McDonald's. The Highway Patrol had closed down Interstate 5. To the south of McDonald's was a United States Post Office annex. To the north was a donut shop. Officers began scrambling to contain the area so that no suspects could escape.

No one outside knew how many suspects there were. One report had described one gunman as wearing camouflage pants, dark T-shirt, and dark glasses. Were there more?

McDonald's had tinted windows so the police could not see inside. Some of the bullets had caused a "spiderweb" effect on the glass, making visibility even worse. Every few minutes some shots came from inside the restaurant, slamming into something inside.

At 4:46 p.m., two people inside McDonald's were able to run out the back door while Huberty was in front reloading. The people had been there when the incident started. They survived by getting down on the floor when the first shots rang out.

They curled up as small as they could and huddled under a table. It was just not their day to die.

SWAT officers debriefed the couple. The two escapees told them the attack was the work of only one man with a lot of guns and a lot of ammunition. He had a transistor on which he was listening to commercial stations from time-to-time.

The couple told of the carnage inside. They could not even estimate the number of dead. They said they knew others were alive, however. One of the escapees, a man, had watched and had eye contact with at least two people who shared his fate, hiding on the floor.

This last fact caused the SWAT commander to decide against an assault on the restaurant. According to the two escapees, the gunman was no longer shooting occupants of the restaurant. He was trying to get police officers on the outside.

This was good. If he was aiming outside, he would be coming closer to a window or a door and a police officer on the perimeter could do his job.

From a tactical point of view, McDonald's occupied what is called "high ground." The building was elevated about three feet when it was built. A brick retaining wall went around the front and two sides. This height gave the gunman an advantage, albeit a slight one.

A SWAT sharpshooter, Agent Chuck Foster, and a SWAT spotter, Officer Barry Bennett, had scrambled to the roof of the post office.

The roof had a gentle slope and had an 18-inch raised ridge around the perimeter. Foster and Bennett belly-crawled to the edge. Periodically, Bennett used a hand-held mirror to peer over the top to monitor what was going on inside. Because of the tinted glass, the trained spotter was unable to make out what was happening. The sounds of sporadic gunfire let Bennett know that there was activity, however.

At one point, Bennett became impatient with the restricted visibility of the mirror. He put his cap on backward like a baseball catcher and peeked carefully over the top.

One shot rang out, slamming into the brick wall below him. Bennett ducked immediately, but not before he was able to see the tinted glass crumble to the floor. Bennett said, "All right, mister, now we can do it."

Up until this particular time, the SWAT team was operating under a "red light" condition. This term meant there was to be no firing unless the gunman tried to make an escape.

No one would have shot anyway since there was no visibility inside. However, with the intelligence information offered by the two late escapees, and the fact that one large window was now shot out, the condition was changed to "green light" at 5:05 p.m.

The "green light" meant that if anyone had a clear shot he could take it. Before the "green light" was given, a detailed clothing and physical description was put out over the air.

History has shown that hostage takers will change clothes with a hostage and then parade the hostage in front of a window. History has also recorded tragic results.

The officers were aware that, if they shot someone, they had to be correct. News media from all over the world had assembled outside the restaurant in the hour that the siege had been under way.

The Democratic National Convention was in session in Los Angeles and political reporters from everywhere were told to go to San Ysidro and do a "hard news" story. If a police officer made a mistake now, the entire country would be put on trial in the same manner that all of Dallas had been tarnished by President Kennedy's death.

Barry Bennett's partner, Chuck Foster, had checked his weapon, a .308-caliber sniper-rifle, once again. At 5:17 p.m., Bennett told Foster, "There he is, right in the window. It's him." It was the same person Bennett had seen firing from inside.

Foster rose up, found the man in his sights, took a deep breath, held it and squeezed the trigger. The single shot traveled at a slight downward angle for 112 feet. The bullet hit James Oliver Huberty in the chest, ripping open his aorta and knocking him back.

The bullet exited the body. Huberty was dead on impact. Bennett said over the radio, "This is Sniper Two. Suspect has been hit. He's on the floor by the cash register. Does not appear to be moving."

The incident, however, was far from over. The Primary Response Team made entry and began summoning paramedics and other rescue personnel.

Meanwhile, the six people huddled together in the storage room downstairs were only aware of sporadic gunfire. The basement survivors heard a commotion outside. The doorknob turned a little but stopped because the door was locked. A boot crashed through the wooden, hollow-core door near the handle.

Albert Leos looked up from his agony and saw a camouflage pant leg. That sensation was chilling. Then Leos saw the entire person was clothed in camouflage and had on a camouflage helmet. Leos sighed in relief.

Leos looked up at the police officer and asked, "What took you so long?" The burly officer did not speak immediately. Then he replied, "We got the son of a bitch."

Albert Leos had lost a great deal of blood. The police knew Albert was in the room by following his bloody trail. Albert was put on an ambulance and rushed to Bay General Hospital in nearby Chula Vista. He finally lost consciousness in the ambulance.

Albert began receiving intravenous fluid immediately. A team of doctors, on alert since the incident began, examined him on arrival. Emergency steps were taken to stop the bleeding. Antibiotics were given to counteract infection from the bullet. The location of the bullets was monitored by X-ray to determine what should be done with them.

Albert Leos drifted in and out of consciousness, his periods of waking filled with the white-hot burning pain. Leos had not even known he was shot in the stomach. His arms hurt so badly and his leg muscle was ripped open and useless. It was only when the paramedics lifted his shirt at the time of rescue that he saw the hole in his stomach.

During one of his waking moments, he heard one of the masked emergency room doctors order whole blood. Leos woke up and said, "Get it from my family. No blood from strangers." Albert had read about AIDS and was fearful even in his semi-conscious state.

The young man had been following the progress of the killer disease in its early stages of public knowledge. He wanted no part of blood from the general population. In spite of the pandemonium of the moment, the hospital acceded to Albert's wishes.

What irony that situation offered! To survive the bullets of a madman, only to be done in by a blood transfusion. Albert lapsed back into unconsciousness. A relative was located and a direct transfusion was made.

The doctors determined there was no internal bleeding. The bullet that entered his stomach had lodged near his spine. The bullet was in no danger of touching anything vital.

A decision was made to monitor Albert's vital signs and perform surgery to remove the bullets at a later date. The unfortunate sidelight was that no painkillers would be administered. In order to accurately assess and treat his injuries, it was necessary to have the patient free of any medication. So whole blood, glucose, and antibiotics were all that came through the tube into Albert Leos's arm.

Meanwhile, homicide teams from the San Diego Police Department swung into action. No prosecution would result from this case, but the whole world wanted to know how and why this happened. Every detail of the incident would be questioned and examined.

Lieutenant Paul Ybarrondo made the assignments and the gruesome work began. When the investigative work was completed, the details of the atrocity were numbing, absolutely shocking.

More than 50 people had been inside when the ordeal began. Twenty-one were killed. Fifteen people were shot, but survived. The victims ranged in age from 18 months to 74 years.

James Huberty had fired 251 9 mm rounds from his Uzi and the handgun. He had fired 12 shotgun rounds. The police department had shot five rounds at Huberty.

More information was sought on "hero" Agent Chuck Foster, 28, who had ended the harrowing ordeal for everyone. Foster had been on the police department for five years and been a SWAT member for just over two years. Foster said, "I don't feel like a hero. I did my job, what I'm supposed to be ready to do. The situation called for it."

Foster did not want to go on any further or make any more statements to the press. Foster's own comments to the contrary, that is the way real heroes talk and act.

Two days later, Albert Leos was put in an ambulance and transferred to another hospital 20 miles away. Preparations were made to remove the bullets. The projectiles in his left arm and right leg were removed during one surgical session. The following day the bullet next to his spine was removed.

Albert Leos stayed in the hospital for a total of three weeks until the fear of infection and internal bleeding was over. The tedious process of rehabilitation was begun. This process was two-fold. The arm muscles were so damaged that Albert could not move his wrist. His leg muscle had been destroyed and needed to be built up again.

The mind of Albert Leos was also examined. He had stood five feet from a man who had looked him in the eye and said, "So you thought you could hide from me, eh?"

Why did this have to happen to the people in McDonald's? Another question Albert asked was, "Why was I spared?" He had been standing shoulder-to-shoulder with three others and they were all dead. This was pretty heavy baggage for a young fellow to carry who was starting his senior year of high school.

Gruelling three-hour physical therapy sessions were held in the mornings. Albert had suffered during past football seasons. Two-a-day practices were tough and Albert had learned his limits of pain and endurance under the scorching late summer sun.

Those drills were a stroll in the meadow compared to his rehabilitation sessions. He was not learning how to take down a fleet-footed, hard-hitting halfback. He was trying to move his wrist, raise his arm and walk.

In the afternoons Albert went to another kind of therapy: the kind that helped him deal emotionally with all that had happened. The routine was the same. Tell the doctor how he felt about everything. No aspect of the nightmare was overlooked. Even though Albert showed no sign of being bothered by what had happened, doctors and health care officials wanted to avoid the "post-traumatic stress syndrome" that affected so many Vietnam veterans.

The doctors wanted to avoid problems for Albert Leos in the future. The best method was to get all of the pent-up feelings that simmered within him out on the table now. They wanted Albert to look at those feelings. Examine them. Question them. Were the feelings normal? Were the feelings rational?

How about guilt? Could Albert have done anything to change the outcome? Albert was young and unarmed. Huberty was in there for an hour and 17 minutes. Was saving himself Albert's only option? Could the police have come sooner? Could they have shot sooner? And on it went.

One day about a year later, Albert told his therapist he was tired of talking about it. There was nothing more to say. The doctor knew that when a patient said that, it was time to stop.

During that time of rehabilitation, Albert started his senior year of high school. He even rejoined the football team near the end of the season. Colleges can juggle five years of eligibility, allow players to "red shirt" and sit out a year if they want to or need to. There was no such benefit for Albert Leos.

320

His senior year came but once, and he had to make the most of it, as much as he was able. He practiced. He dressed for the playoff games. For now, Albert had lost his speed. What good is a defensive halfback without speed?

For a young player, this was a bitter pill to swallow. Albert loved football and this was his last chance. Yet the disappointment of not being a real contributor to the football team was tempered by the fact that he *was* out there on those autumn Friday nights, wearing the uniform and hearing the band play the national anthem.

After all, Albert had looked down Huberty's gun barrel and was still alive.

During Albert's senior year, he continued with another extra-curricular activity that he had been involved in for more than a year: that of police explorer scout for the National City Police Department.

The explorers do a type of voluntary work for the police. They have uniforms that are similar, but different, from the officers. They receive training in criminal law and evidence. They perform some functions, such as crowd control at parades. They go on outings with the advisor, who is a sworn police officer. Like all scouting activity, being an explorer is work and it is fun.

While Albert was doing all of the things he had to do during his senior year, he was thinking that he wanted to become a police officer. Albert knew there would be roadblocks in his path. He was no stranger to adversity. When Albert was 12, he and his family lived in Los Angeles. Albert, his sister, and another friend were outside playing. A huge Great Dane dog attacked the trio. Albert, in a heroic act, threw his sister and the friend over a fence, allowing them to escape.

While this was going on, the dog was savagely ripping away at Albert. Often dog bites are not stitched up for fear of infection. These tears were such that Albert had to be sewn. His wounds required more than 100 stitches.

Two years after that incident, Albert took up motocross motorcycle racing. He was with his family in Mexico on a three-wheel motorcycle jumping hills and sand dunes.

Another motorcyclist going the opposite direction from Albert attempted to occupy the same space as Albert. There was a head-on crash. Albert was wearing the usual safety equipment. His helmet cracked and he suffered a broken collarbone.

He had headaches for some time after. But Albert Leos was tough. Just as in the dog-bite incident, he fought back and became well. Albert had fought back from everything and had prospered. He turned one adversity after another into a type of victory.

After graduation from high school Albert enrolled in Southwestern Community College, a two-year school in Chula Vista. After graduating, Albert signed up for the San Diego Sheriff Academy as an "open enrollee."

This method of preparation for a law enforcement career is growing in popularity. In former times, a person would be hired by a police department. The agency would send the recruit to a police academy, paying both the cost of the academy, plus a salary.

The trend in California now is for a prospective peace officer to go through an academy at his or her own expense. When the recruit graduates, he or she can walk into whatever agency is desired and fill out an application.

The fact that the recruit is almost "street ready" increases the marketability of the recruit. All the hiring agency has to do is teach the recruit the particulars demanded by that agency.

So Albert Leos entered the Sheriff's Academy and began to progress. He handled the physical training thanks to his mental and physical toughness. He handled the gunfire on the range with no problem.

As graduation time came nearer, the sheriff's department actively recruited Albert to join their ranks. The sheriff's recruiters knew of Albert's past experiences. They had watched Albert closely during the 16-week academy session and they were ready to take him on board.

But Albert had strong emotional ties to the National City Police Department. The chief at the time was Terry Hart, a man revered by street cops from all over the area. Albert wanted to join the National City Police Department because he had been an explorer there and because he thought so highly of Terry Hart.

Albert went through the usual battery of tests administered to a police recruit. There is a four-hour multiple-choice psychological test followed by an extensive interview with a psychologist. These tests are designed to identify those people who have overly aggressive personalities and other defects which would make them unsuitable for law enforcement.

Albert waltzed through the tests and interviews with no problem. He was also given a rigorous physical exam and battery of fitness drills, which he passed easily. He was hired and began working in National City, a somewhat wild, rollicking town stuck in the midst of laid-back southern California.

There is a high concentration of Hispanic, black, Samoan, and Filipino communities in National City. The police department has a greater than average number of officer-involved shootings and assaults on officers per capita. This phenomenon is hard to explain, not that it has not been examined by sociologists, attorneys and members of the liberal press.

The National City Police Department has been investigated by the district attorney, the attorney general, and the U.S. Department of Justice. So far, all of the findings have cleared National City police officers of misconduct. The simple fact is that it is a tough town.

Albert Leos did not mind all of this. He could take care of himself out there. However, as a probationary officer he saw some things that frightened him.

Second, there were a lot of rumblings and rumors from City Hall about police layoffs due to budgetary constraints. Albert knew he would be among the first to go since he was newly hired.

Two miles down the road stood Chula Vista. The department was twice as large as National City. Police Chief Bill Winters had been in his position for more than 24 years, something unheard of in the ranks of San Diego County.

Within the County, the chief with the closest tenure had about five years of service. The City Council of Chula Vista got along well with the police and the citizens generally supported the Chula Vista cops.

Albert Leos reasoned he should leave National City for the relative stability of Chula Vista. He applied there in August 1988. He was qualified by the same pre-employment tests and was hired. Leos is currently assigned to the night shift patrol.

Police officers everywhere have that uncertain feeling about facing a gunman. They wonder what it is like. How will they react? Will they panic?

Albert Leos knows. Albert proved that to survive you must never give up, never stop trying, never give in. To do so is to invite defeat and in some instances that is the same as death.

Albert Leos never talks about the incident at McDonald's, but will answer questions if asked. He has put that day out of his mind. He stays in contact with some of the McDonald's employees who survived. They stay in contact not because they survived, but because they are friends. These friends never talk about that day.

Albert did not sue anyone. He is still awaiting a Workmen's Compensation judgment and will abide by that decision. In the meantime, he is busy trying to be the best police officer he can be. He has taken that terror-filled 77 minutes and turned it into a positive force in his life.

Albert said, "If you give up, you're going to lose. Even if you're on the floor and a gun is pointed at your head, don't give up or you're going to lose."

In spite of being shot four times at point-blank range, witnessing the deaths of friends and co-workers, and lying in a pool of his own blood for more than an hour, Albert Leos did not lose. He never gave up. And he never will.

WILLIAM RYAN
"HORROR OF THE HUNGERFORD MASSACRE!"
by Brian Marriner

To US British, the idea of a gunman on a murder spree is something typically American, and we've prided ourselves on the fact that it couldn't happen here. We had watched the movie *Rambo* with enjoyment and cynicism. We had read about Charles Whitman, who in August 1966 climbed the university tower in Austin, Texas, and killed 16 people by rifle fire and wounded another 31, having already shot dead his wife and mother (he was eventually killed by a police marksman).

We knew that in 1982, in WilkesBarre, Pennsylvania, prison guard George Banks shot dead 13 people; that in April 1984, 2 women and 8 children went shot dead at their Brooklyn, New York home by Christopher Thomas. Even more horrifying, in July of that same year, mad gunman James Huberty walked into a McDonald's in San Diego and blazed away for 83 minutes, shooting dead 20 people and wounding 17, before being shot by police.

From Australia, in early August 1987, came news about a 19-year-old gunman, Julian Knight, a former officer-cadet, who went berserk in Melbourne's suburbs and killed 6 people and wounded another 18 before surrendering quietly to police.

We've had some history of gun deaths in Britain, of course, but nothing on that scale. In 1980, bachelor Barry Williams were berserk in the Midlands and shot dead five people. In July 1982, two policemen were among the three victims of fugitive gunman Barry Prudom, before he was shot dead by police after an 18-day manhunt. Jeremy Bamber, a cool and callous killer, shot dead five members of his family in 1984 so that he could inherit a fortune. And in April 1986, former Cornish police detective Colin Gill shot dead his four sons and his wife, after he discovered she was having an affair. Then he turned the gun on himself.

For the main, these crimes were "domestic" — sad and sordid crimes of passion with the victims either known to or related to the killer. We remained smug, convinced that "it couldn't happen here." But it did, and as a nation we have lost our innocence.

This is a record of the bloodiest day in the history of British crime . . .

Wednesday, August 19, 1987, began quietly enough in the small market town of Hungerford — population 4,000 — in the county of Berkshire. Hungerford lies between Marlborough and Newbury, and is a town of ancient tradition. John of Gaunt gave the town its lands, and the local school is named John O'Gaunt Comprehensive School. A few miles away is Greenham Common, site of a U.S. Air Force Base, armed with cruise missiles. Women from all over Britain have made a permanent "peace camp" outside the base, protesting against the missiles and demonstrating for peace by lighting candles at night in vigil, and placing flowers and dolls on the barbed-wire of the perimeter fence.

That Wednesday, August 19, 1987, was a market day. The early morning began with housewives seeing their husbands off to work, and newsboys delivering the daily papers. The weather was fine, a warm summer's day, and children, on the long holiday from school, played in gardens. Later on, the streets of the town became packed with people shopping. The market stalls displayed fresh fruit and vegetables, fish and eggs, and gaily-colored clothing. And the clock had begun ticking away the last minutes of peace in the town.

Police Constable Roger Brereton, 41, a traffic cop with 14 years service, was cruising around in his patrolcar. Mrs. Susan Godfrey, 32, had set out from her home in nearby Reading to picnic with her children in Savernake Forest, a few miles from Hungerford. With her in her car were her two children, Hannah, 4 years old, and James, 2. They reached the forest at about 10 a.m. and soon found a suitable picnic site.

In his home at No. 4 South View, Hungerford, 27-year-old Michael Ryan was getting ready to go out. He was dressed in U.S. military fatigues, along with a Rambo-style headband. He carefully slipped ammunition clips into the pockets of his camouflage flak-jacket, and lovingly fondled his Chinese-made

329

copy of the Kalashnikov AK47 assault rifle, a weapon highly regarded by the IRA in Ireland, who call it the "widow-maker." This semi-automatic rifle had cost Ryan #295 by mail-order. In the trunk of his car was a survival kit consisting of a Swiss Army knife, waterproof matches, a flask of brandy, wound dressings, thermal underwear and a gas-mask. He also had an arsenal of weapons in the trunk, including an M-I Carbine, and three handguns. One of these, a 9 mm Beretta, was attached by a lanyard to his wrist.

He was ready and feeling high. A member of two gun clubs, he had practiced the previous day with the Kalashnikov, and was pleased with the results. He lived with his mother, Dorothy, 61, a waitress at a local hotel. His father had died of cancer two years earlier. His mother was good to him, bought him presents and gave him generous pocket money, even though he did hit her from time to time.

Sure, he knew some people regarded him as a wimp, a mama's boy. But with the AK47 in his hands, he was more than a match for anybody. He had done badly at school. His work record — drifting from job to job — suggested that he was a failure. But he would show them. Smiling slightly, the blond, bearded man got into his car and drove away.

At some time between 11:00 and 11:45 a.m., he was in Savernake Forest, confronting Mrs. Godfrey. He spoke with her, gesturing with his rifle, then marched her 100 yards into the forest, out of sight of the children. Then came the sound of gunfire. When the children investigated, they found their mother lying still, covered with blood. She had been shot 15 times in the chest.

At 12:40 p.m. the children were found wandering along the main road between Bristol and London, near the forest. They went up to their grandmother, clutching each other's hands. They told her, "We have been looking for you. The man in black has shot our mummy, and he has taken the car keys and James and me can't drive the car so we are going home."

It was perhaps merciful that the children were too young to appreciate the full extent of their personal tragedy. The grandmother was to stay with the "babes in the wood" until they could be collected by their distraught father. Police called to the scene started a search of the large forest. It took them one hour and 20 minutes to locate the body.

Even before they found the slain mother, however, events had overtaken them. Reports were coming in over their personal radios about a mad gunman on the loose in the area.

At 12:38, Ryan drove in to the Golden Arrow Garage at Froxfield, six miles from the forest, and filled his car with gas from the self-service pump. Then he walked up to the girl cashier, sitting behind an armoured glass window, and demanded money. The girl ducked as Ryan raised a handgun and fired. The bullet shattered the glass partition, showering her with glass fragments, but leaving her uninjured. Then the gun jammed, and Ryan fled to his car and drove off rapidly.

The cashier dialed the police emergency number with trembling fingers. She told them about the robbery attempt and informed them that the gunman, "dressed like Rambo," was headed east towards Hungerford, some three miles away. The description of the man and the license number of his vehicle went out to all mobile units.

At 12:46 p.m., Newbury Police sent two patrolcars separately to Hungerford. One was driven by Constable Roger Brereton, the other by Constable James Wood. Their orders were to find the gunman's car. At 12:47, a call was logged from South View, the road in which Ryan lived. A gunman was shooting people! After that, emergency calls flooded in.

Michael Ryan had driven to his home at No. 4 South View, where he replenished his stock of ammunition from a shed in the garden, slinging a bandolier across his shoulders. At this point, as he was about to get into his car again, Constable Brereton arrived on the scene. He spotted the wanted vehicle and realized that the quarry was about to drive off. He rammed the vehicle with his patrolcar.

Ryan jumped out of his vehicle, brandishing his weapons. Constable Brereton had just enough time to radio in urgently—"Ten-nine, ten-nine," the code for urgent assistance required by an officer—and his next words were—"I've been shot." Then came silence. Ryan had slipped around the back of the patrolcar and emptied a full clip from the Kalashnikov into its rear window. P.C. Brereton died under the hail of bullets. The carnage was under way.

Ryan's mother ran out into the street, begging him to stop firing. Ryan casually shot her dead. She fell in the gutter between two parked vehicles. Then Ryan went back into the house, shot the family's pet dog and set the house on fire.

When he came back outside, Ryan noticed some neighbors peering anxiously from their windows. He sprayed the house next door with bullets, shattering windows. Then he walked slowly along South View, shooting at every house. There were 16 houses in South View. At No. 1 the family was away on holiday in France. At No. 3, Ryan wounded Alan Lepetit. At No. 6, he shot dead two elderly pensioners—Roland and Sheila Mason. No. 7 was empty—the family was on holiday. At unlucky No. 13, home of the Mildenhall family, daughters Lisa, 14, and Marie, 12, were playing in the garden. Marie fled at the sight of the gunman, but Lisa was seriously wounded in the thigh. Marie was later to say, "I saw him shoot Lisa. He just poked the gun at her. I was so scared." The children ran in to mother Jennifer, 36, and Lisa asked: "Have I been shot, mummy?" There was a large hole in her thigh.

At No. 4 South View, Ivor and Julie Jackson had both been wounded by the gunfire, Mr. Jackson badly. Mrs. Jackson crawled to the phone and called a family friend, George White, 51. A self-employed surveyor, the man, when he learned that his friends were injured, jumped into his blue Toyota car and drove immediately to South View. But he never had a chance to get out of the car—Ryan shot him dead as he sat behind the wheel.

Ken Clements, 52, was out on the common walking his dog when he came face to face with Ryan. He attempted to pacify him, but Ryan shot him dead.

The situation was confused, with eyewitness accounts conflicting, as happens in any sudden tragedy. But at 12:53, the Fire Brigade answered an emergency call to go to a house on fire at No. 4 South View. They had been advised by police to "proceed with caution," as a gunman was believed to be in the area. The firefighters came under attack immediately and were unable to get close to the house. As a result, three houses were totally destroyed by the fast-moving flames.

Mrs. Lepetit arrived home from shopping to find her house ablaze and her husband wounded in the arm by a bullet. "I couldn't believe it," she said. "It was like something on television, not something which happens in Hungerford." The house was not insured, and the Lepetit family were left homeless and penniless, with only the clothes on their backs.

Ryan now made his way along Fairview Road. At the home of Abdhu Khan, a retired shopkeeper, he blasted the locks off the front door, went into the house, and riddled Mr. Khan with a hail of bullets. In Priory Avenue, leading to the High Street, Ryan saw a car coming towards him. The occupants were Douglas and Kathleen Wainwright, who had traveled from their home in Kent to spend a holiday with their policeman son, Trevor. Ryan opened fire with the Kalashnikov, blasting Douglas, 67, dead. Kathleen escaped with chest wounds and the fingertips of her hand blown away. The car began to burn. Ironically, P.C. Trevor Wainwright was in another part of the town, trying to divert traffic from the danger zone. He was not to know of his father's death for some time.

Incredibly, two plucky old ladies confronted the swaggering Ryan as he stalked the streets of Hungerford, shooting at anything which moved. A grandmother, 68-year-old Mrs. Betty Tollady of Clarke's Gardens, was cooking sausages in her kitchen when she heard the commotion outside. She marched down her garden to the sidewalk, walked up to Ryan, and said, "Stop that racket!" As she reported later, "He turned 'round and shot me in the groin. The bullet went right through my body and out the other side. It left two huge holes. I crawled back to my house to get to the telephone and phoned for an ambulance. I was bleeding all over the place, but I had to wait for four hours, until five-thirty, before an ambulance could get to me."

A local pensioner in her 80s, affectionately nicknamed "Smythie," was more fortunate. She approached Ryan and asked him bluntly, "What the hell are you doing to these people, you silly bugger?" Ryan ignored her and the old lady lived to tell the tale. It was the luck of the draw. Ryan walked on down the road.

High Street, Hungerford, became Ryan's personal killing-ground as he stalked along, shooting at random. The street echoed to the sounds of gunfire and screams as people fled the scene or were hit and fell groaning. The dead and injured lay where they fell; unarmed police officers were unable to recover the bodies under fire.

Ryan took delight in firing at moving vehicles. Witness Audrey Vaquez watched from her window as the camouflaged figure took aim at cars. She said, "He just stood there grinning, his gun pointed at the road as he waited. He took one step into the road as a car came round the corner, lifted the gun, and fired it into the driver's window. I heard the sound of smashing glass, and then heard the car crash."

Satisfied that the driver was dead, Ryan strolled casually away to find more human targets. Audrey said, "He appeared so calm, and walked on as if nothing had happened. He treated it like a fairground game. There was no emotion whatsoever."

Next, Ryan shot dead minibus driver Eric Vardy, 51, father of two. Engineer Kevin Lance was luckier. He was blasted by Ryan as he drove through Hungerford. It was his 20th birthday. He said, "I saw this man with a gun raise it to his shoulder and take aim. The next thing I knew there was a hole in the windscreen and he had shot me in the right arm. I managed to keep control of the vehicle and drove back to my plant. Some workmates and I locked ourselves in a shed, and I had to wait four hours for an ambulance to get through to me."

But those ambulances *were* trying. On that day of carnage, with ordinary people caught up in a maniac's mad rampage, there were acts of individual heroism. Two ambulance women, Hazel Haslitt and her partner, Linda Bright, came under fire as they attempted to tend to victims. The ambulance was hit by bullets, shattering the windscreen, and the women had to reverse the vehicle out of the area and leave the dead and injured where they lay. Hazel Haslitt had been injured by the gunfire and had to be treated at the hospital.

A young soldier on furlough, 21-year-old Carl Harries, was in Hungerford that day visiting his parents. He became personally involved in the catastrophe, and saw more action that day than he would probably get in a lifetime in the armed forces. He had served in the Falklands War, but in 15 minutes he was to witness more death.

He came face to face with Ryan, but escaped by diving over a hedge. He had recognized in an instant the distinctive banana-shaped magazine of the Kalashnikov, and knew that no British serviceman would ever carry such a weapon—not even on a military exercise. He said, "I saw a man standing about thirty yards away with a headband around his head, wearing camouflage—just like Rambo. He was holding a pistol in his hand and had a Kalashnikov over his shoulder. He raised the gun and I jumped over the hedge.

"I heard a couple of shots whistle over my head. Later, when I came out from hiding, I saw a woman in her twenties slumped over the wheel of a Renault car. She had been shot in the chest, and she was making gurgling noises, trying to talk. She said: 'I'm dying, aren't I?'

"That was the sick thing about it—she knew she was going. I managed to get her out of the car and laid her on the ground, but she was dead by then. I covered her with a blanket. Then I went across to another car where a couple had been injured. The woman was screaming hysterically, and the man had been shot in the neck. I realized he was dying, but gave him mouth-to-mouth until an ambulance came.

"Then an off-duty ambulanceman who had been shot in the leg hobbled over to me. He said he was worried about his next-door neighbor, and he asked me to take a look. I went over to the house. The crazy man had shot the lock clean off the front door.

"I went into the house and into the kitchen. It

looked as if it had been painted with blood. There was this man on the floor. He'd obviously had it — he'd been shot to pieces — and his wife was leaning over him screaming. She had been shot two or three times, as well." The victims were Victor Gibbs, 66, who had died trying to protect his invalid wife, who was helpless in her wheelchair. Carl Harries did his best to patch the woman up.

As he laid the man out, covering him with a blanket, another man came in yelling, "He's shot my girlfriend!" Harries ran across the road to another house. A girl lay shot through the legs. The soldier was near breaking-point as he started to give her first-aid. "I had never seen anything like this," he was to recall. "Nothing, even in my job, had prepared me for it. It was horror — just horror."

Witnesses in Hungerford High Street that day were later to talk about their experiences. Mrs. Barbara Morley said, "I just couldn't believe it. He was shooting at anything that moved." Mrs. Jennifer Hibbard of Fairview Road, who knew Ryan by sight, came face to face with him. "He was firing his rifle from side to side, and re-loading from a bag of cartridges on the chest of his flak-jacket. He was just strolling around very casually, and shooting."

Christopher Bowsher, 29, said he saw the man holding a Kalashnikov and a pistol. Amanda Grace, 14, who was babysitting at the house next to her own, heard shots ring out. She said, "I looked out of the window and he was right there in front of me. He was wearing a uniform and carrying a gun in front of him which he kept firing all over the place. He had some sort of headband around his head. I couldn't understand at first what was happening.

"Then I realized what he was doing. He was crazy. I dived down on the floor and just lay there, waiting for him to go away. I was so frightened. I finally managed to get out by the back door."

By 1:30 p.m., armed officers had been sent to the scene and were trying to find out exactly where the gunman was. He had abandoned his M-1 Carbine near the town's war memorial, and when police recovered the weapon and had its serial number checked by the police computer, they knew for the first time who they were hunting. Michael Ryan, holder of Firearms Certificate No. 6197.

So far, 12 people lay dead, 11 of them Hungerford itself, but Ryan was not finished. He had more victims to rack up. The shooting of Marcus Barnard, 33, involved a particularly cruel twist of fate. He was a local taxi driver, known to everybody in Hungerford as "Barney the Cabbie." He had been married for 18 months, and his wife Jenny had given birth to their first child, a son, Tom, just four weeks earlier. The baby was five weeks premature. Bernie was in his taxi, on his way to visit his wife and child, when Ryan shot him dead. Had the baby not been premature, Barney would have died without ever seeing him.

Francis Butler, an accounts assistant in his mid-20s, had taken the day off work to be with his wife and two small children. He was walking the dog when he came face to face with Ryan in Coldharbour Road. Ryan instantly shot him dead. The dog remained whimpering by the body of his master. He was another of the victims of Ryan, chosen at random. He happened to be in the wrong place at the wrong time.

The Main Street of Hungerford was littered with brass cartridge shells; the air was heavy with the smell of cordite. Michael Ryan blasted his way along the street, calmly strolling, his face impassive. He paused now and again to re-load his weapons. He shot at a 15-year-old girl in his path and missed. In Fairview Road, he came across 22-year-old Sandra Hill and shot her. She was rushed to a nearby doctor's surgery, but died soon afterwards. She was to be Ryan's last victim.

Back in the town, began the grim task of picking up the wounded and ded which Ryan had left littered behind him in his trail of terror. Fleets of ambulances moved in, and the town was sealed off to the outside world.

At 1:50 p.m., Ryan was spotted by Constable Wood heading in the direction of John O'Gaunt School. At 2:52, the school caretaker phoned police to say that Ryan was approaching the school building. The police advised the caretaker to lock himself and his children in his quarters.

By 4:15, police had thrown a cordon of armed officers around the school, and local residents had been evacuated from their homes. They were taken to the Community Center to be given hot drinks. The police had had to wait for their weapons—these had been under lock and key 40 miles away. No English police officer carries a weapon in public on normal duties. There were rumors that a five-man squad of SAS troops had been dropped by helicopter to aid local police, but this was never confirmed. The

340

SAS—responsible for storming the Iranian Embassy in London—shun publicity and never acknowledge any action. A police helicopter hovered over the school, in case Ryan made a break for it.

By now the Hungerford massacre had made national news. Television programs on all channels were interrupted to bring news flashes.

At 5:00 p.m., police flashed a message to their headquarters: "School secured." Carrying automatic rifles and wearing flak-jackets, they cautiously searched the school building. At 6:20 they reported, "Suspect confined to top floor of building." Some witnesses had reported that Ryan was carrying grenades. As it was, with the weaponry he carried he was fearsome enough. It was understandable that police had to be cautious and patient.

By now the press had assembled in force. Preliminary reports had put the death toll at 9 persons, with 14 injured. Chief Constable Colin Smith of the Thames Valley police said that his men were negotiating with Ryan. He declared, "I hope to end this incident peacefully," adding bleakly, "Enough blood has been shed already."

Trained police officers, experienced in siege tactics, were trying to "talk out" the desperate gunman. They found him to be surprisingly calm and rational, although he did not explain what had triggered off his murderous spree. He expressed regret about killing his mother. At 7:00 p.m. a single shot was heard. Police waited for some time before entering the classroom where Ryan was holed up.

At 8:45 p.m., Mr. Colin Smith held a final press conference. He told reporters that Ryan had committed suicide. Ryan had a "lucid and reasonable" conversation with police before he shot himself. "He expressed the view that he found it strange that he could shoot other people, but found it difficult to shoot himself," Mr. Smith said. "As he had said during these discussions that he had a firearm and a grenade, and we had no reason to know whether he was alive or whether he had a hostage, we still had a situation that was dangerous. Therefore, it required a professional taking of the building." Police occupied the classroom on the top floor of the school at 8:10 p.m. and found Ryan dead.

Mr. Smith named Ryan's 13 victims in Hungerford — Mr. Abdhu Khan, 84; Mr. Roland Mason, 70, and his wife Sheila, who lived next door to Ryan; Mr. George White, found shot dead in a car; P.C. Roger Brereton, found dead in his patrol car; Mrs. Dorothy Ryan, the gunman's mother, found dead in the street outside her home; Mr. Kenneth Clements; Mr. Douglas Wainwright; Mr. Marcus Barnard, found dead in his taxi; Mr. Francis Butler; Sandra Hill; Mr. Victor Gibbs, 66; Mr. Eric Vardy, found dead in a car.

The chief constable praised the people of Hungerford for "their tremendous fortitude during this ordeal." He also praised the dedication of the dead officer and his colleague, P.C. Wood, and the various emergency services. He revealed that Ryan had been granted a gun license for a shotgun in 1978, and this had been varied to a firearms certificate in 1986 when he proved he was a member of a registered gun club. All his weapons had been legally in his possession.

Assistant Chief Constable Charles Pollard said that Ryan had legally possessed three handguns and two rifles. Asked if this included the Kalashnikov, he replied, "The law allows this man to possess such a weapon, and I am here to enforce the law." When it was pointed out that the Kalashnikov was the favorite weapon of terrorists, Mr. Pollard said drily, "I would think there is no type of weapon produced in the world that has not been used by terrorists." He admitted, "It does seem incredible that a man is allowed to keep ammunition at his home," but refused to be drawn on the gun-law question.

In order to be granted a firearms certificate, Ryan had to establish that he had no criminal record, was of good character and had a legitimate reason for wanting a weapon, such as being a member of a gun club. He had satisfied these criteria—police had made stringent checks on his background before granting the license.

As the day-long operation wound down, people began to think of the 15 wounded victims lying in hospitals in neighboring counties. Even after his own death, Ryan was to claim two more victims. Mrs. Myrtle Gibbs, 63, died on Thursday night, August 20th in Swindon Hospital, and Ian Playle, 34, died at an Oxford hospital on Friday, August 21st. Mrs. Gibbs had been unconscious ever since being admitted to hospital with severe abdominal gunshot wounds and had never come out of her coma. The list of wounded also included two ambulance officers.

The task of restoring Hungerford from a battlefield to its usual state of tidiness and calm, was begun by the Mayor of Hungerford, who announced that a fund would be set up to help the victims of the disaster. Local millionaire Peter de Savoury, close friend of Princess Michael, who had once employed Michael Ryan as casual help, immediately donated #10,000. The money was needed to help those families left without a bread-winner, and those whose homes had been destroyed. The fund stands at half a million pounds, many donations coming from the U.S.A.

Social Services moved trained therapeutic workers into Hungerford, stressing that Michael Ryan's victims might need at least a year's counseling to get over their grief and feelings of helplessness. The social workers ran sessions to teach people how to cope with all their confused feelings.

On Friday, August 21, 1987, Prime Minister Margaret Thatcher visited the town to express her sorrow and sense of shock. Accompanied by her husband, Dennis, she was shown the burned-out houses. At Hungerford Vicarage she met 15 relatives of the dead. She emerged ashen-faced and said, "I had to come. It was so unbelievable, and the only thing I could do was to come and be with the people who had suffered." She promised an urgent review of Britain's gun laws. In retrospect it seems that Ryan's actions that day were one long extended suicide. Did something happen that morning or on the previous day to spark-off his death-stalk?

With his death, police began a probe into Ryan's background. He appeared to be an oddball loner with an obsession for guns. His father, Alfred, who had been old enough to be his grandfather, had died

344

of cancer two years earlier at age 80. His death may have affected the son. His mother, Dorothy, doted on him. She bought him expensive presents and gave him generous pocket-money. He always had a new car, and could afford expensive guns, in spite of being unemployed. He had once had a gun-dealer's shop, but the business had failed. He had been an academic failure at John O'Groat School, and, since leaving school, he had drifted from job to job, always of a menial kind.

He had never shown interest in girlfriends, reserving his enthusiasm for guns. Since early childhood he had collected weapons. He had once shot an air-rifle at passersby when only a child. His mother worked hard as a waitress, but Ryan treated her badly.

He hero-worshipped the "Rambo" cult-figure, and his love of guns may well have been a substitute for a deep sense of inadequacy.

Ryan's former boss said, "Ryan was terribly over-mothered. He said he dreaded going home to her." A family friend said, "He was a spoilt little brat. He used to get everything he wanted from his mother, but he made her life hell. He beat her up."

Other people who knew Ryan described him as a "wimp" — "more like Bambi than Rambo," as one person put it. But everyone agreed that he was quiet. One neighbor noted, "He collected all sorts of guns ever since becoming a teenager. His mother doted on him and was always buying him things. He was self-conscious about going bald, and always wore sunglasses in all weathers."

His 60-year-old mother regarded Michael as a

model son. She once told friends, "I don't know what I'd do if Michael went."

An obvious explanation for his terrible actions on that day in Hungerford is that he was insane, despite his cool behavior. One psychiatrist said that Ryan lived in a secret fantasy world until his tortured mind finally exploded with a blinding rage that made him kill. Dr. Stephen Shaw, a psychiatrist who helped police in the Yorkshire Ripper hunt, said he would not be surprised to learn that Ryan had been addicted to "video nasties." According to him, "There is a small band of sick people who get hooked on these films."

Dr. David Nais, a senior lecturer in psychopathology, said, "I believe he was already suffering from a personality disorder when he was hit by a sudden and dramatic psychiatric breakdown. It sent him completely and utterly insane. He probably intended to kill himself—and others had to die because he saw them as enemies."

Dr. John Hamilton, medical director of Broadmoor, said: "Obviously we are dealing with someone who is mentally disturbed. Either mildly psychotic or completely off his rocker. Psychotics are people who have lost touch with reality and live in a world of their own. If it is true that Ryan had this 'Rambo' image of himself, then a psychopathic disorder is a possibility. One does find these kinds of individuals who are 'loners' and have a very self-centered approach to life."

Despite all the psychiatric palaver, the fact that Britain has never before experienced such a shooting tragedy is due solely to our tough gun laws. The Firearms Act of 1920 has been amended many times since, and is very strict. Men who have served a prison sentence of three years or more are banned for life from ever possessing a firearm, and all prisoners are banned for 10 years after release from prison.

During 67 years of strict gun control, we have had no incident comparable to Hungerford. During the last 10 years in England and Wales, the number of homicides involving the use of firearms averaged 44 per year, and the majority of these were incidents involving members of the same family. In 1985, there were only five homicides involving the use of a firearm in the course of an act of theft or robbery, and usually the weapon had been illegally obtained. Legislation has proved effective in containing the incidence of death arising from the personal possession of licensed firearms.

What we cannot legislate for is the insane. There are one million gun licenses held in Britain, with very little trouble. Following Hungerford, there have been calls for the banning of all weapons. This is unnecessary. We do not have too many Michael Ryans, fortunately.

Ryan lived in a fantasy world. He boasted of having been a paratrooper, which was a lie. And, mad as he was, he prepared carefully for his day of slaughter. It is known from the records that he practiced with the Kalashnikov on the day prior to the killings at the Devises Tunnel Rifle and Pistol Gun Club. He was also a member of Swindon Gun Club. He bought the Kalashnikov on July 15th—35 days before the slaughter. He practiced with it on July 23rd, July 26th, August 2nd, August 10th, August 12th and on the Tuesday prior to Wednesday's massacre.

Michael Ryan was cremated on September 3rd, his relatives promising that his ashes would be scattered without any stone or marker. The Vicar of Hungerford gave the service, describing Ryan as, "a poor lost soul who caused the deaths of so many loved ones."

Film director Michael Winner, famous for a string of tough thriller movies, is also chairman of the Police Memorial Trust, which is dedicated to placing plaques at the spots where police officers are killed on duty. Mr. Winner has announced that a memorial will be erected in Hungerford. "P.C. Brereton is someone we would wish to honor," he declared.

Hungerford was a small unknown town, a place few had heard about. Now it has a place in England's consciousness—the scene of the nation's biggest mass-murder. It has left a stain which will take a long time to fade.

The cruel irony is that the names of the victims will fade and be forgotten, while Michael Ryan has assured himself a dubious place in history.

BRANDON THOLMER
"RAMPAGING SEX STARVED STRANGLER!"
by Turk Ryder

In mid-August, after the most recent Hollywood murder, the detectives gathered on the third floor of Parker Center. They were from the Los Angeles Police Major Crime Detail. On this sweltering afternoon they sifted through a batch of crime reports kicked out by the department's computer.

Their attention was directed at a string of murders dating back to 1981. There had been no pattern at first, nothing to connect them, and the murders remained hidden by the 800 or so homicides committed annually in Los Angeles.

But now at the tail end of summer, as kids exchanged surfboards for schoolbooks, and parents prepared for the Labor Day binge, police were hot on the trail of another serial killer.

The first in the string was Rose Lederman. A spritely 80-year-old, she lived in a spacious triplex in Silverlake. The retired antiques dealer had lived there as long as anyone could remember. Even Rose, whose mind was as sharp as a tack, had a hard time pinpointing the date.

Silverlake is a turn-of-the-century neighborhood, honeycombed with canyons and hills on the northern edge of downtown. Rose could remember when, as a young girl, milk came in glass bottles and was delivered by horse-drawn wagon. And when men took the Hoover Street trolley into town.

It was a glimmering jewel of a neighborhood then. Frank Lloyd Wright had designed some of the homes up by the Silver Lake Reservoir. And others, perched on canyons and along the southern border, were no less impressive.

Over the years, Silverlake experienced revivals, the most recent in the late 1970s when yippies discovered the grand old homes.

It was too little and too late to bring the old gal back to her glory years. Graffiti scarred the old buildings, and stores fought a losing battle to stay in business.

Rose's son had moved out of the neighborhood, and he wanted his mother to follow. The neighborhood was no longer a jewel, Frank Lloyd Wright homes or not, he insisted. And besides, it is just too dangerous. Rose shrugged. She was 80 years old and set in her ways. She knew Silverlake like the back of her hand. Her history was there. So was her life. She might be 80, but she still did her own shopping and still travelled by bus. And she wasn't about to change her ways this late in the game.

Rose's triplex was on Plata Street at the intersection of Hoover Boulevard. On August 13, 1981, she failed to keep a dinner date. Her son called to find out why. When no one answered the phone, he jumped in his car and raced across town. Traffic was light and the old buildings of Silverlake stood out like beacons of a forgotten age as he pulled up in front of the Plata Street triplex.

He ran up the stairs. The front door was unlocked. He pushed it open and went inside. The lights were on in the living room and kitchen. That was odd, he thought, because Rose never left lights on when she went to bed.

Then he walked into Rose's bedroom. She was lying face up on the bed, but she definitely wasn't sleeping. Her face was battered and there was blood on the pillow. Bruises lined her slender throat.

The son telephoned the police from the phone in the living room then went outside to wait. It didn't take long. Patrol officers arrived in front of the house and went inside. Ramparts Division detectives soon followed. They took their photos and measurements, and searched the house inside and out.

By late sunrise, they had put a few pieces of the puzzle together. According to the medical examiner, Rose had been dead 24 to 36 hours before her son called. Because she had worn a nightgown and was lying on her bed, detectives figured she had been asleep when the assault began.

The killer had likely entered through an unlocked window or door since sometimes Rose forgot to use the locks and the home showed no signs of forced entry.

Rose had been raped, then strangled. Sometimes it was the other way around, but not in this case. The

351

killer then left, leaving no clues as to his identity, and very little evidence for detectives to follow.

The slaying received scant attention in the morning papers. Three inches of news space in the *Herald-Examiner*, even less in *The Times*. Most residents learned of the slaying on the 10 o'clock news, or by following the sirens and flashing lights of police cruisers to the scene.

No matter how they received the information, it came as a shock. Silverlake was plagued by burglars and drug addicts, but murder was different.

Detectives took down two dozen reports during the neighborhood canvass but nothing, at first, seemed to have any connection to the murder.

Rose's next-door neighbor was a nurse who worked at a community hospital. She had been working the graveyard shift and had not returned home until that morning. She worked a lot and knew the elderly woman next door only slightly.

Rose's other neighbor was a small community theater which ironically presented the play "Little Murders" the night Rose was murdered. Employees were questioned but they had seen nothing suspicious the night of the murder, they told police.

The best clue was found in the apartment. Rose kept little money or valuable jewelry in her tidy triplex. One heirloom she treasured was a lacquered Chinese box in which she kept her jewelry. The distinctive box was gone from the bedroom bureau when detectives searched the room. Relatives drew a picture of the box and said they would be able to identify it if they saw it again.

Less than a mile from the Silverlake neighborhood

where Rose Lederman spent her last day, lived Wolloomooloo Woodcock, a 69-year-old retired teaching aid with the Los Angeles City School District. Her small home was located on Beverly Boulevard in East Hollywood.

When the native-born Australian with the alliterative first name moved into the cozy single-story home, Hollywood was a fabled address. Fifty years later, the neighborhood had lost its luster, but Wolloomooloo wasn't about to leave the place because it wasn't trendy.

Her friends wished she weren't so stubborn. East Hollywood was bad news, not the kind of place you wanted your friends to live out their golden years. Most felt it wasn't even safe to drive through, much less live in. They wanted her to find a place in the Valley where life-styles were tempered by middle-class ethics.

Wolloomooloo wanted none of it. East Hollywood wasn't so bad, she insisted.

In mid-August 1982, a year after police opened the file on Rose Lederman, Wolloomooloo was invited to have dinner with a friend who had recently retired from the city school district. Wolloomooloo didn't show. Her friend was worried. She didn't want to drive to Beverly Boulevard alone so she called her boyfriend.

"I'll be right over," he said.

They arrived at Wolloomooloo's home shortly before midnight. The friend had a key to the apartment but the door was secured by a safety chain from the inside.

The boyfriend put his shoulder to the door and

the chain snapped open. They found Wolloomooloo on the couch in front of the TV.

The medical examiner who was called to the home estimated she had been dead for 48 hours. Cause of death was strangulation. She had also been bludgeoned and raped.

Ramparts Division detectives determined the killer entered the cozy home through a rear bathroom window that had been left open because of the heat. No one heard him go into the house or saw him leave but that wasn't unusual. Beverly Boulevard is bumper-to-bumper traffic and he would have had to make a hell of a racket to be heard over the din.

Lab technicians fared little better. The only fingerprints they found in the house either belonged to the victim or friends later cleared of involvement in the slaying. This wasn't surprising; the fingerprint tech found wipe marks on doorjambs and tabletops—evidence that police were dealing with a pro.

A wad of paper apparently used in the wipe-down was found on the floor. It, too, had nothing on it that could be traced to the killer.

It was a perfect crime except for a single shoeprint found outside the bathroom window. It came from a 9-½-C-size foot wearing a jogging-soled shoe.

Seventy-year-old Dorothy Fain lived alone in a bachelor cottage. The home bordered an alley and was behind a main house on one of Hollywood's busiest residential streets.

The landlord lived in the main house. He liked renting to older people. They took care of the place and were always appreciative. Besides, he liked giving them a break. Getting on in years himself, he knew one day he might be needing a few breaks himself.

August 21, 1983, was a scorcher. Too hot to sleep, the landlord went to the front porch to catch one of the infrequent cool breezes that wash across the L.A. basin.

There was no breeze—just heat. And light. He turned toward the light and saw it came from the cottage behind the house.

The roof was on fire.

"My God, there is a woman inside!" screamed a neighbor when the fire department arrived. Firemen, in black slickers and plexi-glass fitted helmets, pumped enough water on the blaze to refill Mono Lake. But it came too late to save Dorothy Fain.

Her body was on the bed in the combination living room/bedroom, and she had been charred beyond recognition. Firemen discovered the corpse after raising the roof which had collapsed during the blaze.

The fire that took the elderly woman's life and turned her home into a charcoal briquette had been ignited inside, firefighters determined.

Accidental self-immolation due to faulty wall heaters or stoves are common in a neighborhood where most of the homes are wood inside and out and well over 50 years old.

But few people use heaters or fires indoors on hot August evenings. Also, the elderly woman's body was found completely nude on the bed, with her nightgown lying beside it.

The blaze might have been an accident, but investigators were called to the scene anyway. A relative provided a clue when she said Dorothy wore two gemstone rings on her finger. The rings were not on her fingers when the body was discovered. A relative said she could not have removed them herself since they were too small to get over the knuckle.

Dorothy had not died in an accidental fire. She had been robbed, detectives believed, then the fire set to cover the crime.

Sodomy was added to the crimes of robbery and murder after a medical examiner, surgically probing the body orifices, produced a sperm fragment in the victim's anus.

Detectives canvassed the neighborhood for witnesses who might have seen the killer enter or leave the victim's home. They got a few leads that went nowhere, and checked out a dozen or so suspects who turned out to be clean.

The case was still under investigation when firemen were called to a bungalow-style home on Monroe Street less than a mile away from the torched home of Dorothy Fain.

It belonged to Mary Pauquette, a 72-year-old retired social service supervisor. Her small, one-story stucco home was on the 100 block of Monroe near the intersection of Vermont Avenue.

At 5 o'clock on the morning of September 12th, smoke was seen pluming from beneath the eaves of Mary's house by a neighbor walking his dog. He rushed inside his home and called the fire department.

Flashing sirens and piercing sirens soon awoke most of Monroe Street. Residents dashed outside to see firemen dousing the blaze.

The firefighters were in time to save part of the

structure but not Mary Pauquette, who was discovered lying on her bed. The bedding was charred and the rug scorched. It didn't take an arson expert to realize the fire had started there.

It also didn't take a genius to realize the fire was set to hide the fact that Mary had been murdered. She had also been raped.

The ghastly sight of their neighbor zipped into a body bag and carried by gurney to the medical examiner's van struck fear into the hearts of Monroe Street residents. Normally a quiet street in an unquiet neighborhood, Monroe had witnessed the same procession of vehicles and detectives five months earlier.

Lucille Pyle had lived in a small, white stucco home one block down Monroe from Mary Pauquette. On May 10th, a neighbor across the street saw a black and white police cruiser pull up in front of the 82-year-old widow's home. The neighbor walked across the street and asked one of the blue-shirted officers what was wrong. The officer said he couldn't tell him, but it didn't take long for the bad news to circulate.

Earlier, a friend had stopped by to pay Lucille a social call. Lucille didn't answer the door and the friend, sensing something was wrong, tried the door. It was open. She went inside and saw her friend lying naked in the bedroom, beaten and strangled.

Residents learned of the murder after detectives went door to door asking if they had seen any strangers near the Pyle home. After that, they locked their doors and watched the neighborhood through slits in the front curtains. Strangers who once went unnoticed were now reported to the police right away.

Ann Burnett managed a small apartment building a block east of Lucille Pyle's home. She was a tough cookie who faced down trespassers with an icy stare and chased them off her property. The woman she looked after marvelled at Ann's courage.

"Nothing scared her," the woman reported proudly.

Then the 68-year-old apartment manager woke up at 2 a.m. August 29th and saw a man at the front window. A high-pitched scream chased him away. And just in time too. Pry marks on the window found by police showed he was within seconds of getting in.

Reports of the two murders and the attempted break-in were kicked downtown to Major Crimes Detail. Obviously there was a connection: the victims were elderly single women, who lived in detached homes on the same block. In each instance, the intruder chose a rear or side window as the point of entry. In the two murders, the victims were sexually assaulted before they were strangled, and the apartments were robbed of jewelry and other small items that could be worn or easily concealed.

Sexual assault of senior citizens is just another wrinkle in the Los Angeles crime picture. Murder isn't that uncommon either. As any cop who has worked the mean streets knows, the elderly are singled out because they are vulnerable.

The Hollywood division had hundreds of sexual assaults of senior citizens on the books. The statistics were a sad commentary on a society that seemed to treat its older citizens as throwaways.

But why had the two seniors on Monroe Street been singled out? Police went to the computers for other assaults and murders that shared points of similarity with the Monroe Street crimes. The computers came up with 32 unsolved murder cases.

They were spread over a two-year period and covered the neighborhoods of Hollywood, Silverlake and Westlake. The task force, spearheaded by Sergeant John St. John and Detective Kirk Mellecker, pored through the stack of reports, follow-up reports and crime scene investigations, looking for threads that formed the fabric connecting the victims to their killer or killers.

Did the seniors go to the same market? Take the same buses? Know the same people? Go to the same doctors? The same dentists? Visit the same drug stores?

Police knew there were as many kinds of rapists as there were victims. Some were opportunity rapists. Others tracked their victims for weeks before striking.

The one prowling the neighborhoods ringing the downtown area appeared to fit the latter category. Most victims lived within a two-mile radius of each other in single attached homes that bordered alleys or side streets. And all lived alone. The pattern suggested the rapist had followed his victims to their homes. After learning they lived alone, police figured, he struck.

The search continued through October. Detectives Paul Vonlutzow and Sergio Robleto had been assigned to the sex offenders list. It meant going through records of hundreds of convicted sex offenders living or working in the neighborhoods where the murders took place, or who matched the psychological profile of the rapist/murderer. Offenders who were back in jail or who were not in the area when the murders occurred were weeded out. The rest required further work. Sometimes a simple phone call did it. Other times, the detectives had to track the offender through the city, chewing up lots of phone calls and shoe leather.

There was nothing glamorous about sitting at a desk in a room full of smoke trying to locate the scum of the city. Vonlutzow and Robleto wore guns on their belts and carried badges in their jackets but they felt like glorified clerks as they went through the stack of crime reports. Then in November, they came across the file of Brandon Tholmer. The name meant little to the detectives. Just one of hundreds they had checked out since the task force was formed.

Tholmer, 27, had pleaded guilty to rape in 1976 and spent three years in Patton State Hospital as a mentally disordered sex offender. Since his parole in 1979, he had been an outpatient at Gateway Vocational Rehabilitation.

The detectives had heard of the agency. It provided rehabilitation and counselling for the city's mentally ill and was considered a pretty good agency providing a much-needed service. About one third of the patients were sex offenders.

Detectives noted the agency was located in Silverlake, within walking distance of three elderly victims murdered since 1981.

Things got better when detectives pulled Tholmer's

arrest file. In the mid-1970s, West Los Angeles was under siege by another murderer/rapist. Dubbed the Westside Rapist because he struck the Wilshire/Fairfax district, he was linked to two dozen rapes and five murders of elderly single women.

In 1975, police arrested Brandon Tholmer for the unrelated charge of battery against a police officer. The charge was bumped to rape when his fingerprints matched those of a man who broke into a home in Los Feliz on October 22nd and raped the occupant, a 79-year-old widow. Tholmer confessed to the assault, saying he was high on LSD at the time.

He was sentenced to 42 months at Patton State Hospital as a mentally disordered sex offender. Released 37 months later, he was accepted at Gateway Rehab as an outpatient.

A Department of Motor Vehicles teletype showed Tholmer lived on North Normandie Drive in Hollywood. That put the convicted sex offender close to two more victims.

The detectives brought Tholmer's name to the attention of task force leader John St. John. A fabled investigator with over 40 years as a detective, St. John felt a surge of adrenaline.

Brandon Tholmer fit the rapist/murder's profile. And his home and the outpatient clinic he attended put him in the neighborhood of several victims. St. John ordered a surveillance team to follow Tholmer while they dug for more evidence.

For the next five days, surveillance officers tracked the convicted sex offender along the boulevards and side streets of Hollywood. It was no easy task as

Tholmer only travelled at night or early morning and used city buses.

The surveillance team lost him several times over the next five days, causing panic and requiring surveillance officers to "box" the block until they picked him up again.

On Monday evening, November 6th, Tholmer left the Hollywood shoe store where he worked as a clerk and took a bus to his North Normandie apartment. He left the apartment an hour later wearing jeans, a dark knit shirt and a dark windbreaker.

The surveillance team followed him to the apartment of a girl he was dating, then to a coffee shop and up to Hollywood Boulevard where he stopped at a hot dog stand. They watched him hop a bus and head south on Vine Street. Exiting on Santa Monica Boulevard, he took a side street, promptly losing the surveillance team.

They picked him up half a block later and followed him until 1:30 Tuesday morning when he ducked down an alley. A plainclothes officer followed. Standing in the shadows, he watched Tholmer climb a fence into a backyard.

"Freeze, Brandon," the officer ordered.

Tholmer turned from the window he was about to enter and saw half a dozen officers pointing guns at him. No fool, he froze.

Tholmer was brought to Parker Center and grilled about the Hollywood/Silverlake murders. Later he was booked into the county jail charged with five counts of murder.

At a press conference the next morning, Police Chief Darryl Gates praised task force investigators for breaking the case. They were also given a hand of thanks by a relative of Mary Pauquette's who said, "I am very pleased with the LAPD. They solved the case and didn't have many clues to work with."

Meanwhile, therapists at Gateway Rehab were baffled by the arrest. They saw Tholmer as making excellent progress and deemed him an excellent candidate to be returned to the streets cured.

Some wondered if police had the right man. Some of the most seasoned therapists took it in stride. "We aren't mind readers," one admitted. "We do the best we can."

Tholmer was behind bars, but the investigation was far from over. Detectives worked the case into 1984, searching for evidence linking the sex offender to the string of murders.

Jewelry played an important role. Detectives traced a ring stolen from the finger of Dorothy Fain to one of Tholmer's girlfriends. The girlfriend told police he had given it to her as a present which "symbolized their love for each other."

The Chinese-style jewelry box taken from Rose Lederman was later traced to a man who said Tholmer sold it to him in late 1981 when the two were roommates. A 35mm camera was later traced to an elderly woman whose duplex was burglarized while she was gone.

Tholmer was also linked to the murder of Wolloomooloo Woodcock by the shoeprint found outside her bathroom window. The print matched a sneaker found in the suspect's closet.

The lab also matched a palmprint found in Mary Pauquette's apartment to Tholmer's.

The investigators figured Tholmer spotted his victims at supermarkets, on bus lines and on the streets. The house Tholmer was breaking into when arrested belonged to an 85-year-old paraplegic. She later picked him out in a lineup as a man she saw hanging out at the market where she shopped.

Supermarket employees said Tholmer was often at the market talking with his girlfriend who worked there as a bag girl. Mary Pauquette and Dorothy Fain also shopped at the store.

Tholmer denied everything. He hadn't hurt anyone, he claimed. The cops had it all wrong. After a lengthy preliminary hearing in 1984, he was sent back to Patton for psychiatric evaluation to determine if he was mentally competent to stand trial. Defense motions and a crowded court calendar pushed the trial date into mid-1986.

Brandon Tholmer had been a suspect in 34 unsolved murders of elderly women between 1981 and 1984. Though evidence linked him to 12 of the murders, Tholmer was charged with only four.

"We filed only on those where there was the most evidence," explained Prosecutor Lance Ito.

Using charts and diagrams, Ito presented more than 100 witnesses and 100 exhibits to link Tholmer to the killings. On Friday, July 25th, the convicted sex offender was found guilty of four counts of murder. It was also found that during the course of the murders, Tholmer also committed rape, sodomy, arson and burglary—special circumstances that made him eligible for the death penalty.

Tholmer, however, would not get the death penalty. Convicted of four murders and, in the view of police, responsible for at least eight more, the former shoe salesman was sentenced to life in prison without possibility of parole.

Outside the courtroom, jurors told reporters they voted the way they did because they felt sorry for Tholmer. Explained the jury foreman: "He spent years in state institutions and was deprived of any kind of family background and support necessary for a normal life."

Deputy D.A. Ito was disappointed by the verdict but noted that life in prison would at least serve to protect society.

He was not the only one disappointed. Courtroom observers wondered how a jury could feel anything for a man who had felt so little for his victims.

EDITOR'S NOTE:

Ann Burnett is not the real name of the person so named in the foregoing story. A fictitious name has been used because there is no reason for public interest in the identity of this person.

365

JOSEPH "CUJO" REISS
"I'VE JUST SHOT FIVE PEOPLE!"

by M.J. McCarthy

There's a 140-square-mile area southeast of Pittsburgh, Pennsylvania, locally referred to as the Mon Valley. The area is so named because of the gradually sloping hills that emanate outward from the banks of the Monongahela River, one of two rivers that merge at Pittsburgh's "Point" to form the Ohio.

Like most of this southwestern Pennsylvania region, the Mon Valley, for decades, relied heavily on the domestic steel-making industry for its livelihood. Unfortunately, during the last 15 or so years, production of domestic steel has declined and, proportionately, the communities of the Mon Valley have ceased to flourish.

The spirit of the people in these high-impact employment areas, while perhaps bent, is not broken and there still remains a hope for the future.

Nestled in the midst of the Mon Valley is the borough of Homestead. Once a steel-making town, it is bordered on three sides by similar communities and to its north lie the decaying remains of what was once one of the nation's largest steel-making plants.

Where once the nighttime sky was aglow from the huge blast-furnace operation, all that remains now are a smattering of security lights to hold the scrap hunters at bay.

In the various neighborhood bars, the workers still gather but the mood is noticeably different from the times of great prosperity. What has remained constant is the cohesiveness of the community and, for the most part, you will find that all the patrons in the bar know each other and know each other's business.

Whereas a stranger in the bar wouldn't necessarily be greeted with open hostility, he would be treated as an object of curiosity and most likely not feel welcome.

With the familiarity instilled by these local hangouts, almost any patron can tell you the life story of other patrons in the place. Fathers drink with sons, grandfathers with grandsons. To say that the night-to-night crowd is not transient, is an understatement.

The patrons also know the troublemakers and, when they come into the bar, everyone is alert. Normally nothing happens and the instigator has a few drinks and leaves.

This, unfortunately, was not the case during the early morning hours of March 19, 1988. Trouble came into the bar and, before it left, blood was flowing freely.

It was overcast and bitterly cold that Saturday morning. Evidence of the cold spell and previous

367

snowfalls still lingered on the sidewalks and streets of Homestead. The Friday night crowd at Sportsmans Bar had been considerable, partly because a local disc jockey was playing there, but by 2:30 a.m. Saturday morning, things were winding down.

It was later learned that a phone call had been made to the bar around that time and the message was that "Cujo" was on the prowl and he was looking for someone. The caller went on to say that Cujo was high, mean and carrying a gun.

The call had come from a neighboring bar and it was obviously meant as a warning. It was too late, though, because by the time the call was received, Cujo was already in the bar and stalking.

Sportsmans, like most of the corner bars in Mon Valley, is by no means fashionable in nature. The main bar runs nearly the length of the front room with a smaller room in the back containing a pool table, a few tables and chairs and the restrooms.

On this particular night, the disc jockey was set up in the back room and a small area was cleared for dancing. The majority of the patrons stand in small groups at the bar and mingle freely among themselves and the late arrivals.

Because of the music that night the crowd was a little younger than usual, but there were still many of the older "regulars" present. Until Cujo arrived, there had been little for the doorman (bouncer) to do other than mix with the crowd, talk about recent sporting events and speculate on the future of the steel industry in the valley.

Shortly before 3 a.m., a female patron approached the doorman and stated that she had been in another bar earlier and had seen Cujo brandish a knife while asking around for a certain individual. Further, she told the doorman, she believed Cujo was also carrying a gun and there was a definite possibility of trouble in the Sportsmans. The doorman asked her why she thought this and the reply was, "The man Cujo's looking for is back on the dance floor."

With this information, the doorman approached an off-duty police officer who was standing at the bar. He told the officer the information he had been given and, together, they headed towards the rear of the bar.

Without hesitation, the officer confronted Cujo and, while initially questioning him, he began a quick frisk of the man. He took a long-bladed, wickedly sharp hunting knife from a sheath on Cujo's belt, but his brief search produced no other weapons.

At this point, because of the crowd, the officer asked Cujo to accompany him outside the bar. On hearing this, the doorman thought it best to accompany the officer and the three began making their way out of the bar with Cujo in the lead.

What happened next depends on which of the various witnesses you might ask, but the general consensus is that as the group neared the bar area, Cujo stumbled forward, spinning around at the same time and reaching down toward the top of his boot. When he came up, he was holding a 9mm semiautomatic pistol in his hand and he immediately began to fire.

The first shot struck the off-duty policeman and felled him where he stood. Cujo then turned and pointed towards the doorman but, before he could fire, a girl standing at the bar grabbed his arm and forced it upward. The second shot went harmlessly into the ceiling. A male patron then joined in, trying to subdue the gunman and a violent struggle ensued. When the gunman broke free, those who already hadn't, began diving for cover.

Thomas Cain, the next victim, had the misfortune of exiting the men's restroom when the gunman turned and shot him in the back, killing him almost immediately.

Cujo then began to back out of the bar, passing the area near the front where a vending machine and several video games were located. The third victim, James Craycraft, was standing in this area doing nothing that could be considered even remotely threatening. Without any provocation, Cujo fired into the man's side at point-blank range. The bullet from the 9mm lodged in the man's spine, paralyzing him. The gunman then turned and fired another shot into the ceiling before fleeing out the front door.

An as yet uninvolved patron gave chase and ran out into the street, only to be fired on by the fleeing gunman. The patron heaved a roll of quarters at the assailant and then dove behind a parked car. He did manage to see the gunman flee in an older model car, heading in the direction of the Homestead Police Station. For a moment, the gunman's car slid on the icy road surface and stalled. The car then regained traction, turned down a side street, and disappeared.

Back in the bar, the wounded officer began directing the nearly panicked crowd to call for police and ambulances. Homestead officers were on the scene in minutes as were officers from neighboring communities and several paramedic squads.

While some officers helped the medical personnel, others began taking down the details from the shocked crowd. Over a dozen people readily identified the gunman as Cujo and several supplied the man's last name, Reiss. It took officers only a few additional minutes to develop the man's full name, Joseph Andrew Reiss.

Though only 26 years old, Reiss had already made quite a name for himself, at least as far as the law enforcement community was concerned. Only months after his 21st birthday, Reiss had been arrested for carrying a stolen gun. His adult arrest record revealed an increasingly violent nature and on most incidents of his arrest, a firearm was involved.

Once the wounded men were removed from the bar and the deceased was taken from the scene, the officers concentrated fully on the search for Reiss.

Homestead Police Chief Christopher Kelly, at 3:22 a.m., called for the assistance of the Allegheny County Police homicide squad. Detectives Herb Foote, Bob Lazzaro and Howard Cervone were among the first to respond. They were joined at the scene by several other detectives including John Flaherty and Lee Torbin, as well as Lieutenant Jack Brennan and Inspector Floyd Nevling, head of the county's detective division.

Once at the scene, detectives began to interview witnesses and locate and gather evidence. In the meantime, Chief Kelly's probers had received information that Reiss was living at a residence in the neighboring community of Munhall Borough. Officers were dispatched to check the residence to see if the getaway car was there. The search proved negative for the older model Plymouth with Ohio registration plates.

Chief Kelly's sleuths had already issued local, state and nationwide bulletins, putting a "stop" on the vehicle and its occupant(s).

At 5:40 a.m., the Munhall police located the vehicle parked behind a residence in their borough. In turn they notified the Homestead and Allegheny County Police Department and shortly the house, which sat on a little rise, was surrounded by well-armed officers.

The lawmen identified the occupants of the home and found they were associates of Reiss. When everything was in place, the occupants, four adults and a child, were ordered out into the brisk early morning air. Once all were out, a careful and deliberate search of the residence was made, again with negative results.

While the search was being conducted, one of the adults admitted to detectives that he had been the one who had driven Reiss's vehicle to its present location, at Reiss's insistence.

He initially claimed to have brought the car to this home at approximately 11:30 p.m. the previous evening. One of the other adults, overhearing this comment, corrected him by saying that it was closer to 3 a.m. when he arrived at the home, not 11:30 p.m. Since it was obvious that the driver was attempting to mislead the detectives, he was taken to the Munhall Police Station for further questioning.

Once this individual realized the gravity of the situation, he began to cooperate with the officers and stated that he had been staying with Joe Reiss at a different residence in Munhall. He stated that on Friday night he had been home, alone, as Reiss had gone out and Reiss's wife was at work. He went on to say that Reiss was to have picked up his wife when she 'got off work at 11 p.m., but he failed to show.

Shortly after 11 p.m., Reiss's wife came home and said she had seen her husband's car parked outside a bar. She was mad at him for not picking her up but she wasn't going to say anything because it would only cause trouble.

The man said that shortly after this, he went to bed and was awakened sometime later by Joe Reiss who handed him the keys to the Plymouth. The man said Reiss told him, "Take my car and get it out of here."

The man said he knew Reiss well enough not to question him so he got dressed and left, driving the car to its present location. When asked, the man said that as far as he knew, Reiss was still at the other residence in Munhall.

At about the time that police surrounded the house where the car was located, Chief Kelly and several of his officers had gone to Reiss's residence and spoken with his wife. She told Chief Kelly that she hadn't seen her husband since 11 p.m. Friday night. Armed with this new information, the officers returned to speak with her at 7 a.m.

Detective Howard Cervone conducted the interview of Reiss's wife and on this occasion her story changed substantially.

She again stated that she was to have been picked up by her husband the previous evening but he never showed. She had gotten a ride home with a friend and on the way, she spotted her husband's car in front of a bar. When she got home, she called the bar and spoke with him. He didn't apologize for not picking her up; he simply said that he forgot. She did not pursue the matter.

Reiss's wife said he came home sometime after 11:30 p.m. and he was obviously drunk. She said that she didn't question him when shortly thereafter he announced that he was going out again, ". . . for another drink."

The wife said that after he left she went to bed but was awakened shortly after 3 a.m., by the banging of doors out front of her residence. She said that she got up to investigate and at that point her husband burst into the house and said, "I just shot five people."

According to the wife, Reiss then pushed past her and woke the man who was living with them. He said that he had just shot some people and he had to get moving. He told the man to take his (Reiss's) car and drive it away from the house. He said that he was hoping to buy some time in doing this.

Reiss then went into the living room and made a phone call. Next he went to the bedroom and took a small suitcase and began to pack handguns and ammunition.

The wife was asked if she could remember which guns were taken. She stated that as far as she knew Reiss took a .45-caliber automatic, a .38-caliber derringer, possibly some other handguns and a hunting rifle with a scope. She added that he took "plenty" of ammunition with him also.

Reiss's wife went on to say that he asked her for money and she obliged, giving him $20. He then left on foot without saying more to her.

She was asked who the phone call was made to and she said she didn't know. She was asked where he might have gone and, again, she said she didn't have any idea. She did say that her husband was a member of "The Barbarians" motorcycle gang and they are "all over the place."

Before leaving, Detective Cervone and other officers received permission to search the Reiss residence for evidence or clues that would tell them where he might have fled. The wife gave reluctant permission and among the items, the searchers found a sawed-off 12-gauge shotgun. This illegal weapon was immediately confiscated.

Upon leaving, Detective Cervone asked one final question of the wife of Joseph "Cujo" Reiss. "When he went out last night, after eleven-thirty p.m., did he have a nine-millimeter automatic with him?"

The wife's reply was simple and poignant. "That gun's his American Express. He never leaves home without it."

Checking around outside the property, the officers found Reiss's motorcycle and another vehicle parked inside an adjacent garage. After some brief discussions, it was decided to leave the vehicles there in the hopes that Cujo might return for one of them.

As the detectives and local police developed additional information concerning the suspect, it was followed up quickly. Throughout the course of the morning, interviews were conducted with the suspect's family members and friends in an attempt to determine where the gunman fled. As more and more information developed concerning his membership in the motorcycle gang, additional teletypes and phone calls were made to law enforcement agencies in neighboring states. The lawmen were asked to check the local hangouts of The Barbarians gang in an attempt to locate either the suspect or obtain information on his whereabouts. All of the teletypes carried the suspect's description, including numerous tattoos on both arms. The most distinguishing tattoo was a helmeted Viking head with long flowing hair, the insignia of The Barbarians motorcycle gang.

All of the teletypes also contained a very specific warning to law enforcement officials. "Suspect should be considered heavily armed and extremely dangerous."

Later that first day of the investigation, detectives and Homestead police reinterviewed the suspect's wife and learned that Reiss had numerous biker contacts throughout the tri-state area (Ohio, West Virginia and Pennsylvania) as well as contacts in Detroit, Michigan. Further, they learned that the last place Reiss worked was an auto wrecking yard in Youngstown, Ohio.

With this information, a call was placed to the Youngstown police to check on that location and a new series of alerts were issued locally and nationwide.

Throughout the course of the day, officers continued to check on the conditions of the two victims who survived the shooting spree. The off-duty officer was in good condition and was able to be interviewed. His information concerning the incident was the same as that given by the witnesses.

The other victim, James Craycraft, a 53-year-old retiree, was in guarded condition. The path the projectile had taken through his body before lodging in his spine had damaged several vital organs. He had been subjected to hours of surgery and it would be some time before detectives could speak with him.

Earlier in the day, an autopsy had been performed on 36-year-old Thomas Cain. The cause of death was listed as a single gunshot wound to the back that had traversed through his upper torso, penetrating the diaphragm, liver and heart. The pathologist listed the manner of death as "homicide," a technicality that enabled the officers to secure an arrest warrant for Joseph Andrew Reiss for criminal homicide.

By now, Detectives Foote and Lazzaro had returned to the homicide squad offices of the Allegheny County Police Department and began the laborious task of processing and bagging the evidence that had been collected thus far. Among the items submitted to the Allegheny County crime lab were spent projectiles and casings from the gunman's 9mm pistol. These would be maintained for later comparison should the weapon be recovered.

Throughout the first and subsequent days of the investigation, the detectives and Homestead officers attempted to piece together all the information available on Joseph Andrew Reiss. Photographs of Reiss were obtained from family and friends which were prominently displayed through the local media. The story and photos generated numerous reports of sightings throughout the tri-state area and, though a monumental task, each of the leads was followed up. Numerous biker-types were detained and questioned by police but none proved to be the man sought for the multiple shootings in the Homestead bar.

Over the next week, detectives from Allegheny County, accompanied by officers from Homestead Borough, traveled daily to Ohio and West Virginia and, in cooperation with local authorities, they frequented biker hangouts, especially those where members of The Barbarians were known to patronize.

During these investigative trips, a clearer picture emerged of the individual sought.

Reiss's nickname of "Cujo" had been derived from the Stephen King novel of the same title. King's *Cujo* was a crazed killer-canine that was diabolically clever and exceptionally brutal. Reiss enjoyed the reputation of being a "mad dog" himself and the nickname, according to the bikers, was most appropriate.

The detectives also learned that Reiss was considered an "outlaw" by his brother bikers. By this they meant that he only adhered to the bikers' laws when they suited him. He had several friends among the bikers but none of them would say that they were close to Cujo.

Members of a rival gang that had formed a loose relationship with some of the Ohio law enforcement authorities said they were acquainted with the Barbarian named Cujo. The rival bikers said Cujo was suspected of shooting a rival gang member in the groin, purposely, during a gang fight. They said that Cujo would not be given aid or shelter by either their gang nor any gang that knew him and knew of his reputation. In fact, several of the rival gang members said they were also looking for Cujo and, if they found him first, they would leave him in a place where it would be easy for the police to find him, ". . . or what was left of him."

At the end of the investigation's first week the officers and detectives had exhausted most of their leads. Daily contact was kept with family members of the suspect and they continued to assure officers that they would try to convince Reiss to surrender if he would contact them.

Further details concerning Reiss trickled in, one of which was most interesting to those who were searching for him. Chief Kelly received information that Reiss was once employed by an animal control facility and his job there was to tend to injured, sick or otherwise unadoptable pets. The method used to exterminate these animals was "to shoot them in the head with a small-caliber weapon."

At the end of the first week, police learned that Reiss was to visit a former girlfriend who lived in a county northwest of Pittsburgh. State police joined with detectives from Allegheny County in staking out a rural residence. The stakeout continued well into the night before the lawmen decided to storm the residence. The tip proved false, however, and all the officers left, tired and dejected.

The next tip came from nearby Wheeling, West Virginia, when the proprietor of a bar reported to police that Reiss had attempted to gain entrance to the club "after hours."

The woman recognized Reiss from photos in the paper and on television and, while denying him entrance, told him to come back in a half hour. She then notified local authorities who surrounded the establishment. But Reiss never returned.

Through the Ohio Bureau of Motor Vehicles, the detectives traced the history of the car Reiss had made his getaway in after the shooting. In turn, they spoke with the former owner of the vehicle, himself a biker, who admitted knowing and being friends with Joe Reiss. The biker denied seeing Reiss since Reiss had moved back to the Pittsburgh area. The detectives informed the local authorities who went out of their way to keep an eye on the man.

In a relatively short time, the officers had reason to stop this individual and, during the stop, a receipt was found for a .45-caliber automatic bought out of state. In checking on this weapon, the lawmen found paperwork on two other weapons that had been traded to the gun dealer, one of which was registered to the wife of Joseph Reiss. The next day, Detective Lee Torbin and John Flaherty of county homicide were in a small Ohio town interviewing the man.

After extensive interviewing, during which the man was extremely cooperative, the sleuths believed that Reiss was no longer in the Ohio or West Virginia area.

When they returned to Pittsburgh, a meeting was held with all the investigators. They decided to ask the Federal Bureau of Investigation for assistance and file a Federal Fugitive Warrant.

On March 28, 1988, the Allegheny County District Attorney's Office made a formal request to the United States attorney for western Pennsylvania. In the request, it was noted the crime for which Joseph

Andrew Reiss was sought, the progress of the investigation to date and the belief that Reiss had fled the state.

In closing, it was requested that the U.S. attorney authorize the FBI to search for and apprehend Joseph Reiss under the provisions of the Unlawful Flight to Avoid Prosecution statute.

The U.S. attorney quickly approved the request and the warrant was issued early the next day.

With the FBI entering the investigation, the detectives now had access to a network of agents who specialized in felony fugitive apprehension.

A composite of all known facts concerning Reiss and his affiliations was made and provided to the agents, as well as the best photos of Reiss that were available.

In a short time, calls came in from federal agents requesting additional specific information on Reiss. Detectives became hopeful that the fugitive gunman would soon be found.

On April 20, 1988, Special Agent Bob Garrity of the Pittsburgh office of the FBI contacted county homicide. Garrity's message was that agents in the Detroit, Michigan, office had received information that a biker-type was bragging in a bar that he had "killed a cop" in Pittsburgh. Garrity said he had tele-faxed all available information to the Detroit office and he would keep the county detectives informed of any developments.

On April 21, 1988, at 7:30 a.m., Special Agent Garrity called county homicide again to say that he believed the search for Joseph Reiss, AKA "Cujo," was finally over. He related the following:

381

Late in the afternoon of April 20th, the agents in Detroit received information on Reiss and the photograph telefaxed from the Pittsburgh office. Through investigation, they learned that the man they believed to be Reiss, the man who bragged of shooting the cop, was staying in an apartment in a section of the city frequented by motorcycle gangs. The agents, assisted by Detroit's homicide squad, began a stakeout across the street from the apartment.

After talking with several of the local residents, they tentatively identified Reiss as the man who was staying with a biker and his "lady" in a second-floor apartment in the building. They learned that the biker who normally lived there had been out of town for several days but the visitor and the woman were still there. The visitor had been "high" almost continuously and had, in fact, been bragging about being wanted in Pittsburgh.

Early in the stakeout, the officers found out that the suspect was presently babysitting a five-year-old child. At this point, the lawmen could only wait. They were fairly sure that the suspect had not "made" them so they felt the best action at this time was to wait.

At 10:30 p.m. on the 20th, the stakeout sleuths got a break. The grandparents of the five-year-old came to visit the child and when they left they took the child with them.

As the officers, believing the suspect to be alone, positioned themselves to make entry, the lights of the apartment suddenly went out and they detected movement at the windows. Believing the time to be right, the officers and agents converged on the apartment, but before entry could be made a single gunshot was heard from within. The men quickly withdrew and again attempted to enter the apartment later and effect an arrest.

This time they were successful in getting into the apartment where they found the suspect slumped against the living-room wall, dead from a self-inflicted gunshot wound to the head. A 9mm automatic pistol was found by his side and ballistics tests would later show that this was the same weapon used in the Homestead shooting spree.

Later in the day, on April 21st, the deceased was positively identified by fingerprints as being Joseph Andrew Reiss. His 33-day flight from justice had finally come to an end.

After Agent Garrity's call and the subsequent positive identification, the Allegheny County and Homestead police spent much of the day notifying all the law enforcement agencies involved of the outcome and thanking them for their assistance and cooperation.

When lawmen searched the apartment where the suspect died, they confiscated four handguns, a shotgun and a rifle. The Detroit lawmen were thankful that the suspect decided against taking a stand in that normally crowded neighborhood.

Three days after Joseph Reiss took his own life, he claimed his second fatal victim from the March 19th shooting spree. The 53-year-old victim James Craycraft, who had been paralyzed by the gunman, succumbed to his wounds.

KENNETH ERSKINE
"7 VICTIMS OF THE WHISPERING STRANGLER!"
by Philip Westwood

"Nancy! Nancy, dear, are you there?"

It was 4 p.m. on April 9, 1986. The weather was unusually warm for the time of year, and the beads of sweat on the faces of the two women glistened in the late afternoon sunshine. A sudden breeze caught a piece of carelessly strewn litter, whipped it up over some iron railings, and sent it tumbling down the eight steps that led from the street the front door of the basement apartment outside which the women were standing.

"Nancy! Are you all right?"

The door was open; not wide open, just slightly ajar. It was an old door, dull and unpainted. Its neglect reflected the rest of the street — old, run-down and past its prime. For this was West Hill Road in the south London district of Wandsworth; one of those areas on the south side of the River Thames where, unless you know the place very well, it is unwise to go during the daytime—and downright stupid to go after dark.

"Nancy! Nancy!"

It was clear to the women that Nancy was not going to answer their calls. Maybe she simply had not heard them. After all, Nancy Emms was 78 years old and somewhat deaf. But, conversely, she might be ill or injured and unable to reply. The women decided they would have to go in and investigate.

Carefully, they pushed open the door. A shaft of sunlight streamed into the room. Three cats ran out. Nancy was very fond of cats. She had two of her own, but she would always take in any stray that was in need of food and shelter. Sometimes there were as many as a dozen cats running around her apartment.

The women moved warily through the dingy, squalid room. Nancy looked after her cats well enough, but she didn't bother about herself. Bowls containing varying quantities of cat food were scattered around the floor, and the atmosphere was heavy with that peculiar odor that is pure feline. The carpet was threadbare, and the wallpaper was peeling from the walls. The furniture was the low-quality product of a bygone age, and was occupied by several cats who watched in a slant-eyed half sleep as the women made their way to a door at the far end of the room.

Through the door was the bedroom, and that was where the women found Nancy Emms. She lay on the bed, her arms folded across her chest. She was dressed in her old-fashioned floral nightgown, which was fastened at the neck and reached all the way down to her feet. She was obviously dead, and had about her a look of perfect peace. Only the bruising around her eyes detracted from the impression that she had died a natural death.

The women called for an ambulance, and the paramedics were on the scene within a matter of minutes. They carried out a routine examination — and immediately called the police. It was the faint traces of finger marks around Nancy's neck that caused them to think that all was not as it should be.

Nancy's body was taken away for autopsy, and even hardened pathologists were shocked by what they found. The cause of death was strangulation, but it was not the type of throttling that was usual in such cases. Whoever had killed Nancy Emms had put a hand around her throat and very gently squeezed the life out of her. But before she had been killed, Nancy had been subjected to a violent and brutal rape of the most barbaric kind.

Chief Inspector Mike Duke finished reading the report on Nancy Emms, looked up at the ceiling, and sighed. Whoever the killer was, he was obviously highly dangerous and more than likely to strike again. Nancy Emms had been a 78-year-old spinster who had spent her life working as a schoolmistress and whose only interest since her retirement had been her cats. Being only 4 feet 11 inches tall, and weighing a mere 75 pounds, Nancy would have been unable to resist anyone trying to rob her.

"She was such a frail old lady, you could have held her down with one finger," Duke told reporters at a subsequent press conference. "For anyone to wish to kill her is beyond belief."

Nancy's murder was just one more headache for Inspector Duke and his boss, Detective Chief Superintendent Ken Thompson. Those early months of 1986 had produced a series of murders in that part of London—murders that were particularly disturbing because the victims were all elderly or handicapped people. A blind woman who was so crippled that she was unable to walk had been battered to death in her apartment. Two weeks later, an 82-year-old man had his head caved in with an ashtray as he sat at home watching television. In both cases, the motive was robbery.

But Nancy Emms's death was different. Whoever killed her had not broken into her apartment. There was no sign of a forced entry. So had she known her killer? It seemed unlikely. Nancy didn't really know anyone. It was possible that the killer, knowing of Nancy's fondness for cats, had tricked his way into her apartment by pretending to have found yet another stray for Nancy to take care of.

It was a real puzzler. So Inspector Duke decided to look again in the files of other people who had died under suspicious circumstances during the previous four months. There was one that had certain similarities to the Emms case. On February 4th, John Jordan, a 50-year-old alcoholic, had been found dead in the bedroom of his apartment in the nearby district of Brixton. Though there were no marks of violence on his body, and nothing had been taken from his apartment, police felt that his death had not been due to natural causes. But since nothing could be proven the matter was not taken any further.

A couple of miles away from where Nancy Emms

lived is a large, sprawling collection of apartment blocks known as the Angell Town Estate. Though built as recently as the 1960s, the estate already has about it an air of decay and neglect. Dimly lit footbridges and pathways link one block to the next. Muggers lurk in the dark shadows ready to pounce on anyone brave—or foolish—enough to wander there alone.

In an apartment in one of the blocks—Warwick House—lived Janet Cockett. Janet was a sprightly, lively-minded 68-year-old widow who was not prepared to just sit back and let the creatures of evil take over. She formed a tenants association to protest to the authorities about the conditions on the Angell Town Estate. She bombarded local newspapers with letters and articles warning of the dangers of living there. But nothing was done. Four times Janet was mugged. Still nothing was done. Hers was a lonely battle. Others were too frightened to speak out.

At 1:30 a.m. on the morning of June 9th, a piercing scream echoed round the dark passages of Warwick House. It woke several of the residents from their sleep. Someone was obviously in trouble. But this was the Angell Town Estate. Nobody wanted to get involved. Those who heard the scream turned over in bed and went back to sleep.

Ten hours later, Janet Cockett's 21-year-old grandson paid her a visit. He had a key to her apartment, so he let himself in. He called out to her, but there was no reply. He looked in the kitchen. She was not there.

"Grandma! Where are you?" he called out as he made his way from room to room. Eventually, he reached the bedroom.

"Grandma . . ." He stopped in his tracks. His head shook from side to side as his brain tried to negate the sight that assailed his eyes.

Janet Cockett's naked body lay on the bed. Her head was tilted toward where her grandson stood, and a look of sheer terror filled her sightless eyes. Her mouth was open, as if she were calling him to help her. But she was beyond help. The faint traces of finger marks around her throat indicated that someone had seen to that.

On her chest was a large area of bruising where the killer had knelt on her to hold her down while he slowly throttled her. Her legs were wide apart, a position which led to the suspicion that the killer had done something else to her. This suspicion was confirmed by the trickle of blood that oozed from between Janet's legs and ran down the inside of her thighs before settling to form a bright red stain on the white bedsheet.

Forensic experts examined every inch of the Cockett apartment. As in the case of Nancy Emms, there were no signs of a forced entry. Janet had probably let the killer into the apartment. But, unlike the case of Nancy Emms—where there had been no clues— this time the strangler had not been quite so careful. Fingerprints were found in two places in the apartment. On a plant pot was a thumb print. However, it was so smudged that it was useless. But a palm print on a window ledge was much clearer.

Fingerprints can be checked against the files by computer. But this does not apply to palm prints. They have to be checked the old fashioned way. It is a long and slow process. A photograph of the print has to be manually checked against the many thousands of such prints held in police files. The experts worked non-stop, but it was to no avail. Though clear, the print was simply not clear for a positive match to be made with any print already on file.

The weather grew hotter. As the temperature rose, so did the discernible level of fear among the old people on the streets of south London. It was comparable to the fear experienced by a certain section of the population of east London a century ago when the infamous Jack the Ripper was prowling the dark alleyways of Whitechapel.

Teams of detectives visited the elderly, advising them on simple measures of home security and warning them to be sure that their windows and doors were firmly closed and locked before they went to bed at night. They were told not to open their doors to callers during the daytime unless they were certain as to who their visitor was. But to a determined killer, closed doors and windows are no barrier.

In the early hours of June 28th, at a hostel for the elderly in the Clapham district of London, 83-year-old Emily Yates slept peacefully. Suddenly, her slumber was disturbed by the sound of something gently tapping her window. She turned and looked at the illuminated face of the clock at her bedside. It was 3 a.m. The tapping sound continued. As she became fully conscious, Emily thought that the sound was that of someone throwing pebbles against the window. But who could it be? What did they want?

Without warning, the glass shattered. A large

stone bounced two or three times across the floor of Emily's bedroom before coming to rest by a chest of drawers. Glass fragments cascaded silently down onto the carpet. Emily sat bolt upright in bed. The position of the bed in the room meant that she looked straight at the window that had been broken. The curtains were drawn across the window, so Emily could not see what was going on. But she could hear sounds that told her that someone was unfastening the catch that held the window shut. She tried to scream, but no sound would come from her throat. Her mouth was dry, but the rest of her body was wet with the sweat born of sheer terror. Emily's heart pounded inside her chest.

A short, sharp "click," followed by a long, slow creaking noise told Emily that whoever was outside had succeeded in opening the window. As she watched, the curtains fluttered, and started to draw back across the window.

Outside, it was a clear night. A virtually full moon cast shafts of soft, warm light into the room. Emily's mind was in a whirl. Outside, it was a beautiful night. But inside her room, everything was in turmoil. Who was doing this to her? And why?

Emily became aware of a shape at the window. Silhouetted against the moonlight was a man. He was trying to get into the room. Emily saw his hand. It reached in and took hold of the rail that ran around the foot of her bed. She felt the bed start to move as the man pulled it toward the window. She heard his voice. He spoke very softly—in a whisper. But she could make out what he said. It was, "Kill! Kill!"

Hearing the man's voice seemed to jolt Emily

Yates back to her senses. The terror left her and her voice returned. She let out a scream. It was a piercing scream whose volume was surprising for a woman of her age. It shocked the intruder. He stopped pulling the bed.

From the corridor outside Emily's room came a variety of noises. Doors banged open. Voices called to each other, seeking information on the cause of the cry that had echoed around the hotel. Light switches clicked on, and the sound of feet running along the corridor floor rose to a crescendo.

In the room, all was still. Emily held her breath as she waited to see what the man would do. At the moment he was doing nothing apart from listening to the commotion going on outside the room.

The man seemed to be trying to reach a decision. Had he time to finish what he had started, or should he cut his losses and get out while the going was good? To Emily's eternal relief, the man decided that the risk was too great. Uttering a curse that was barely audible to Emily, the man let go of the bed rail and retreated from the window. In an instant, he was gone.

The people at the hostel tried to comfort Emily. Someone called the police, and within a matter of minutes officers were on the scene. By then it was 3:20 a.m.

Forty minutes later, at 4 a.m., a call came into Chief Inspector Mike Duke's headquarters, requesting officers go to the Sommerville Hastings Home — a home for the elderly situated a short distance from the hostel in Clapham.

Duke and a team of detectives rushed to Sommerville Hastings House. There, they were met by the matron. She had a horrific tale to tell.

Shortly before 4 a.m., she said, the staff had disturbed a man who was prowling along the corridors. When they challenged him, he ran off. The staff gave chase, but the man got away. Nurses decided to check the rooms and make sure that the elderly residents were all right.

One of the nurses opened the door of Zbigniew Stabrava's room. Despite the darkness, she could see that the room was in disarray and the bed was empty. She switched on the light.

Mr. Stabrava lay on his back on the floor. His pajama trousers were down around his ankles, and there was severe bruising in the area of his genitals. His attacker had left faint traces of finger marks on his throat as he throttled the life out of him. In his native Poland, Mr. Stabrava had been a judge. He was a dignified man. But he was allowed no dignity in death as he lay, sadly abused and misused, on the floor of his room. Zbigniew Stabrava was 94 years old.

But in the next room, an even worse sight awaited the nurse. The occupant was Valentine Gleim, a great friend of Mr. Stabrava. Like Mr. Stabrava, Mr. Gleim was Polish. He was 84 years old, and was a veteran of the Polish Army, where he had served with distinction and had attained the rank of colonel.

Mr. Gleim lay on his bed. He, too, had been strangled. The finger marks on his throat were a clear indication of that. But before being killed, Mr. Gleim had been subjected to a vicious homosexual rape.

393

The agony he must have suffered is difficult to imagine.

But at least the staff who had chased after the killer had managed to get a good look at him. They were able to give Inspector Duke and his team a reasonable description. The man was described as being white and between 20 and 30 years of age. He was of medium height and build, and he had dark, curly hair.

The detectives theorized that the killer was a man who often came into contact with elderly people during the course of his work. Maybe he was a mailman or a milkman. Perhaps he had the type of job that meant that he visited their homes, such as a social worker or a health visitor. Alternatively, he could have come into contact with them by working as a clerk involved in the payment of senior citizens' pensions.

The job angle seemed a good one, so detectives arranged to interview and fingerprint everyone in the area whose work brought them into contact with elderly people. It was a long process, and in the end it yielded nothing. Not one suspect was found.

But, back in Clapham, Inspector Duke had found someone else who, like Emily Yates, had come into contact with the killer—and lived to tell the tale.

Jim Watkins, a 78-year-old former engineer, lived in a residential home for the elderly just a few streets away from the hostel on Union Road which was home to Emily Yates. A couple of nights before the attempted assault on Emily, Jim had actually been attacked by the strangler. He had not said anything about the attack because he was afraid that, if he did, the man would return and finish the job. The man believed that Jim was dead, and Jim—who was crippled—wanted it to stay that way. He offered to talk to Inspector Duke only if Duke would guarantee him anonymity.

Duke agreed, and Jim told his story. As he did so, he trembled visibly. Several times, the old man broke down as he relived the horror of that night.

It began when Jim was awakened by the sound of someone moving around in the corridor outside his room. Jim's room had a glass door, so he could see the man quite clearly. He watched as the man approached his door and slid it open. The man came into the room, looked at Jim, and motioned for him to be quiet by putting his forefinger to his lips. Jim reached for a button beside his bed which would raise the alarm. But the intruder was too quick for him. In one movement, he had crossed the room, grabbed Jim by the throat, and pulled him across the bed and away from the alarm button. The attacker sat on Jim's chest, all the time keeping his hand around the old man's throat. His other hand he placed over Jim's nose and mouth so that he could not breathe. Jim thought that his end had come. He tried to scream, but the assailant's hand over his mouth prevented him from making any sound.

"It was a living nightmare," Jim told the detective. "His mouth was whispering sounds I could not make out, except for the words, 'Kill, Kill,' which he kept repeating. He had this terrible grin—like the very Devil."

The man kept pumping at Jim's throat. He felt his consciousness slipping away. Then, suddenly, the attacker pulled Jim off the bed and threw him against the wall. Jim fell to the floor and lay still, hoping that the man would think that he was dead. It worked. The assailant went away.

"I must be the luckiest man alive," Jim concluded. "I've had the killer's hands around my throat, and I've lived to talk about it."

The police were desperately short of clues. But the killer had to be caught, and caught quickly. Why did he concentrate on old people when selecting his victims? Did he have a grudge against them? Or was he simply a copycat killer?

Inspector Duke turned his attention across the English Channel to the city of Paris. For some time, the French capital had been plagued by a maniac known as the "Granny Killer." Over 30 elderly men and women had fallen victim to this serial killer, and French police were making little headway in the case because of a singular lack of clues. It was possible that the London killer was emulating his French counterpart. Their methods were remarkably similar. Maybe one man was responsible for the murders in both cities.

Duke spent several days in Paris, working closely with French detectives and studying all of the evidence they had gathered on the Granny Killer. At first, it all looked very promising. But as each piece of information was carefully examined, the similarities between the Paris and London murders started to disappear. Eventually, it became clear that there was no connection between the two killers. Inspector Duke returned to London, consoled by the fact that one more line of inquiry had been eliminated.

July 8th was a very hot day. The doors and windows of the houses and apartments that made up Clephane Road, in the district of Islington, were thrown open to clear the stifling heat from the tiny, claustrophobic rooms.

There was, however, one apartment on Clephane Road whose doors and windows were closed. Neighbors thought it somewhat odd because the occupant—William Carmen—was a man who liked to be up and about early. He was not a man to lie around in bed, despite the fact that he was 82 years old.

The neighbors knocked on his door, but could get no reply. So someone went to fetch the old man's daughter. She lived a few streets away, and she had a key to his apartment.

When she went into the bedroom, she found her father dead in his bed. At first, she thought he had died peacefully in his sleep. His hands crossed on his chest, and the bedsheet had been pulled up to his chin. But when she looked closer at the room, she knew that things were not as they should be. Pictures had been turned to the wall, and family photographs that stood on a dressing table had been laid face down. One of the dressing table drawers hung open. It was the drawer where Mr. Carmen kept his bank savings book. The book was missing—and so was 300 pounds that Mr. Carmen had withdrawn from the bank two days earlier.

The woman pulled the bedsheets down to the level of her father's chest. She noticed the fingerprints on his neck, and called the police. Fortunately for her, she did not pull the bedsheets down any lower. Had she done so, she would have seen that her father had been anally raped.

Again, the strangler had left no clues. He appeared to have been admitted to the apartment by Mr. Carmen, though none of the neighbors remembered seeing a stranger in the area or noticing that Mr. Carmen had a visitor.

Detectives were still examining William Carmen's apartment when news came in that the strangler had struck again.

On July 12th, neighbors, concerned that Trevor Thomas had not been seen for over 24 hours, called police to his apartment at Barton Court, in Jeffreys Road, Stockwell. When officers broke in, they found the naked body of 75-year-old Mr. Thomas in the bath. Blood on the white porcelain indicated that he had been subjected to a violent homosexual rape. The all-too-familiar sight of finger marks on the throat showed how the callous killer had finished off the helpless old man when his purpose had been served.

The strangler was stepping up his killing rate to alarming proportions. On July 20th, 75-year-old William Downs was found raped and strangled in his apartment on Stockwell's Overton Park Estate. Detectives were particularly shocked by this murder because Mr. Downs, who lived as a recluse, was bedridden. He would have been totally unable to offer any kind of resistance to his killer. How long Mr. Downs's torture lasted is not known. But the strangler, in his frenzy, had made one mistake. He had carelessly left a clear palm print on a wall in Downs's apartment. Detectives set to work to try and match the print against those on file. For two days and two nights, they worked non-stop until, on the afternoon of July 22nd, they found what they were looking for.

To have matched the print, using only manual checking, in so short a time was a tremendous achievement. But it came too late for Florence Tisdall.

There are few events that the British, as a nation, enjoy more than a royal wedding. July 22, 1986, saw just such an occasion, when Prince Andrew married Sarah Ferguson. In houses and apartments throughout the land, people clustered around their television sets to watch the ceremony, and enjoy the pomp and style that a thousand years of history had produced. Even in the humble apartments of Ranelagh Garden Mansions, at Hurlingham, a royal wedding was something that was not to be missed. It was in one of these apartments that Florence Tisdall lived.

Though partially blind and almost totally deaf, 82-year-old Florence was really looking forward to the wedding. She had even had her hair done specially for the occasion. At around noon, she settled herself down in her favorite chair. On the small table in front of her was a tray on which was a pot of tea, her best bone china cup and saucer, and a matching bone china plate which held a selection of cream cakes. Behind her, the open window afforded some relief from the heat of the room.

Outside, only the sounds of a hundred television sets, all tuned to the wedding, disturbed the afternoon air. The only person around was a young man with curly hair who went to the ground-floor apartments. He would look in each window, pause for a few seconds, and move on to the next. When he got to the open window of Florence Tisdall's apartment, he stopped. He saw the elderly woman sitting in her chair. The volume of the television set told him that she was deaf and would not notice his approach. She would be an easy target. He looked around to make sure no one was watching him. No one was. He went in.

Neighbor Tom Dobson found Florence early the next morning. He always called in to make sure she was all right before he went to work. That particular morning she was far from all right.

Her naked body was sprawled across the bed. She lay on her back, with her legs wide apart. The blood that had liberally splattered over the sheets and caked her upper thighs bore testimony to the struggle she had put up before succumbing to the vicious and brutal rape to which her attacker had subjected her. There were finger marks on her throat, but what struck Dobson most was the look on her face. It was a look of sheer horror combined with absolute disgust.

At about the time Florence Tisdall was raped and murdered, detectives at Scotland Yard were matching the print found in William Downs's apartment with those in one of their files. The file was that of Kenneth Erskine, a petty crook who served a prison term for burglary.

The file was sent to Inspector Duke, who studied it closely. It made interesting reading.

Erskine was 24 years old, though his mental age was only 11. He had no home and no job, and slept in the derelict houses that litter south London. The product of a mixed marriage, his parents had kicked him out when he was 16. They had grown tired of his violent behavior. At school, he was constantly fighting with other students—and with his teachers. One teacher had been stabbed in the hand with a pair of scissors when he tried to remonstrate with Erskine. In his early teens, he took to indecently exposing himself to middle-aged and elderly women.

He was sent to a psychiatrist. The idea was to get him straightened out. But it didn't work. Instead, Erskine tried to kill the psychiatrist with a knife. When he was 18, he formed a homosexual relationship with an older man. That ended when Erskine tried to kill the man—also with a knife.

By that time, he was heavily into drugs. He was hallucinating. He believed that he was Lawrence of Arabia. Then, in 1982, Erskine was jailed for burglary. It was in jail that he first demonstrated the only real talent he had. He was an accomplished artist. But his pictures were not of landscapes, or animals, or anything that anyone wanted to look at. At first, he drew pictures of old people. They were lying on a bed. Their mouths were gagged, and knives protruded from various parts of their bodies. In his later pictures, it was impossible to tell whether the people depicted were young or old. They had no heads. Later still, Erskine returned to his theme of drawing old people. This time they had heads. But their bodies were on fire, and their faces had a look of stark terror. All of his work was pinned on the wall of his cell—directly above his bed.

On his release from jail, Erskine lived rough. He

had done so ever since. His only source of income was his Social Security check, which he collected every two weeks from the unemployment benefit office of whichever district he happened to be in at the time. But Inspector Duke discovered that Erskine also had a bank account. It contained 300 pounds—exactly the amount that had been stolen from William Carmen. Also, the account had been opened the day after Carmen had been murdered.

The evidence against Kenneth Erskine was overwhelming. Now the only problem lay in arresting him. Nobody knew where he was. So officers started making a systematic search of the derelict houses of south London. It was a search that turned up several people whom police wanted to question on other matters. But of Kenneth Erskine there was no trace.

So the detectives tried another angle. They knew that Erskine was due to make another unemployment benefit claim on July 28th. At shortly after nine o'clock on that morning, detectives put in a call to the headquarters of the Department of Health and Social Security—the government body responsible for paying unemployment benefit checks—to ask at which office Erskine was due to make his claim on that particular day. In less than an hour, they had an answer.

At 11 a.m., Erskine walked into the office on Keyworth Street, in the district of Southwark, and was promptly arrested.

When questioned about the murders, Erskine claimed to have no knowledge of them. "I have gone in and stolen," he told detectives. "But I don't remember killing anyone. I may have done it without knowing it."

Over the next few months, Erskine was questioned closely not only by police, but also by a team of psychiatrists. They found he had what they described as a hopeless memory. He was unable to retain information for as little as an hour. Of the murders, he had no memory at all.

Officers looked again at several cases of suspicious deaths that had occurred during the early part of 1986. Eventually, they decided to charge Erskine with seven counts of murder and one of attempted murder.

On the cold, clear morning of Monday, January 11, 1988, Kenneth Erskine was led into the dock at the Old Bailey. He was charged with murdering Nancy Emms, Janet Cockett, Zbigniew Stabrava, Valentine Gleim, William Carmen, William Downs, and Florence Tisdall, and with attempting to murder Jim Watkins. It was decided not to proceed with a charge of murdering Trevor Thomas.

During the proceedings—which lasted three weeks—Erskine said nothing. He merely sat in the dock; on his face was that terrible grin which Jim Watkins had described to Inspector Duke as being "like the very Devil." To a hushed court, Jim told his story of the night he encountered the strangler.

Jurors and spectators alike wept as Prosecutor James Crespi described in graphic detail the atrocities inflicted on Erskine's helpless old victims. Several jurors turned their heads away when Mr. Crespi showed them the official scene of death photographs.

A number of eminent psychiatrists, all of whom

had examined Erskine over a long period of time, were called. But none of them could offer any explanation as to what had motivated Erskine to commit such terrible acts. He was simply a killer who liked killing. And all the while, Kenneth Erskine continued to grin. He was still grinning when, on Friday, January 29, 1988, the jury convicted him on all counts.

Passing sentence, the judge, Mr. Justice Rose, told Erskine, "In each case you violated what should have been the safety and security of those elderly people's homes. Not content with killing your victims, you sexually defiled them at or about the time of death."

The judge then sentenced Erskine to seven terms of life imprisonment for murder, plus 12 years for attempted murder. He recommended that Erskine should not be considered for parole until he has served a minimum of 40 years. Still grinning, Erskine was led away to start his sentence.

The sentence of 40 years was the longest ever passed on a murderer in Britain—and the third longest sentence passed this century. Only Arab terrorist Nezar Hindawi, who got 45 years for attempting to blow up an El Al jet, and George Blake, who received 42 years for spying for the Russians, have been given longer sentences.

The chances are that Kenneth Erskine will never be released from prison. By the time 40 years have passed, he will have become so institutionalized that he would be unable to cope with freedom in the outside world. Many people believe that, if Erskine is to remain in prison until he dies, then justice will indeed have been done.

HOWARD FRANK STEWART
"TWO-GUN STALKER ON A MURDER MISSION!"
by Bill G. Cox

For a short period in September 1987, it seemed that bloody murder had settled like a black plague on the southwest Missouri Ozarks. Within a week's time, 10 people were shot to death in murderous sprees. The mass killings were unrelated and the work of different killers, but the marathon of violent death left the normally laid-back residents shaken to their cores. Not only that, the tentacles of one of the coldblooded series of wanton murders would reach out into a Texas city hundreds of miles away and claim four more lives.

Later, officials would speculate that it was the very nature of the rugged area itself that drew desperate and crazed killers. The beautiful Ozarks is a mixture of rich farmland and thickly wooded hills containing remote caves, cliffs and streams.

Conversely, the residents of this rough terrain are of a trusting and independent nature. As one law enforcement officer put it: "People are laid-back. They're not in a hurry. They're just good, fine country folk. Sometimes that attracts undesirable elements. It's the kind of place you can lose yourself in if you want."

Steven J. Vestal, 38, of Conway, Missouri, was one of the easy-going people. Vestal, a field representative for a dairy organization, was known throughout the area as a well-respected family man and a steady churchgoing citizen devoted to his wife and three sons.

On the evening of Wednesday, September 16, 1987, before traveling to his regular weekly choir practice at the Phillipsburg Christian Church, Vestal stopped at his home to deliver a birthday present to his wife. At 6 p.m. Vestal drove away from his home in his 1966 blue Chevrolet pickup. It was the last time his family would see him alive.

When Vestal failed to return home that night, his family checked with the Phillipsburg church and were dismayed to learn that Vestal had not arrived there. This was completely unlike the dependable church member, and his distraught family immediately notified the Laclede County Sheriff's Department.

Sheriff Lawrence Rifenburg, who has been sheriff for 12 years, knew Vestal well. "That's just not Steve," he said of the businessman's strange disappearance.

The sheriff's department issued a missing person's bulletin, and on Wednesday night, county officers and troopers from the Missouri State Highway Patrol searched along county roads, highway and Interstate 44. Their search continued until early Thursday morning without success. It was resumed after daylight and continued throughout the day.

The sheriff told reporters that foul play was suspected. "We're afraid he picked up a hitchhiker," Rifenburg told the press.

Vestal was described as 5 feet, 6 inches tall, weighing 180 pounds and having black hair and brown eyes. He had been wearing a white and navy pinstriped shirt with tan pants when last seen leaving for church in his blue pickup.

Officers located witnesses who had seen Vestal traveling alone in his pickup on a county road near Phillipsburg around 6:30 p.m. Wednesday, shortly after he had left his home. However, other witnesses told officers they had seen a passenger with Vestal, which led investigators to believe he had picked up a hitchhiker.

But Sheriff Rifenburg was puzzled because it was unusual for a hitchhiker to be seeking a ride on a rural highway instead of Interstate 44. And, from all indications, Vestal would not have driven on the interstate but would have stuck to the county route on his way to the church.

While combing the rural roads on Thursday morning, sheriff's officers made a startling discovery. The officers came across a 1980 blue Ford van parked at the side of the road. When Sheriff Rifenburg peered inside the vehicle, he was shocked to see that the interior was drenched in blood.

"There's so much blood on the floorboards that it's not even dry," the lawman said grimly. "It's that deep." From all indications, something terribly violent had taken place inside the vehicle, and if any human being had lost all that blood, there was little hope he could be alive, the officers knew.

The blue van was parked barely inside Dallas County, which adjoined Sheriff Rifenburg's county. The sheriff got on his radio and notified the Dallas County Sheriff's Department that sheriff's officers in that jurisdiction had a problem. He was soon joined in the investigation by Dallas County Sheriff Jerry Cox and investigators of his department.

It was apparent that, while searching for the missing Steven Vestal, Sheriff Rifenburg had discovered the grisly evidence of another violent crime, unless Vestal was in some way linked to the blood-soaked van.

When the officers ran a license check on the van, they learned it was registered to a George Brewer of the rural community of Niangue, in northern Webster County. Following up on this information, officers went to the Brewer residence but found no one at home. They were told by neighbors that George Brewer and his wife, Carol, had two young daughters, who were believed to be in school.

Driving to the school, the lawmen had the youngsters summoned from class to talk to them. The girls told officers that their parents had not come home on Wednesday night, but they didn't know why. The children had not been unduly worried and had not reported the Brewers as missing. The couple had not been seen since about 1:30 p.m. on Wednesday, the investigators learned.

Now, officers from the two counties intensified their search for Steven Vestal and the Brewer couple, fearing that they might be facing three slayings in the area on the same day. Suddenly, violence had apparently struck the peaceful region for some unexplainable reason. At least three members of two separate families were missing under circumstances that led officers to suspect the worst, especially considering the blood-saturated van belonging to the Brewers.

Descriptions of George and Carol Brewer, 43 and 36 years old, respectively, were broadcast.

It was about 5:15 p.m. on Thursday when the Laclede County Sheriff's Department in Lebanon, Missouri, received a phone call from an excited woman. She had discovered a blue pickup in a city park in Lebanon, from which blood appeared to have dripped onto the ground.

Sheriff's investigators sped to the scene, where the woman awaited them at a distance from the blue pickup in the park parking lot. When he looked inside, Sheriff Rifenburg agreed that the witness had had good reason to keep her distance. A man's body was slumped on the seat with his head toward the right side and his knees drawn up.

The officers identified the dead man as the missing Steven Vestal. Preliminary examination disclosed he had been shot in the face and in the back of the head. The bullet fired into the victim's face left an exit wound in the back of the head also. The victim had bled profusely.

The blood had dripped from the bottom of the right door onto the pavement beneath. The truck was parked on a slight slope, and the blood had dripped underneath the vehicle to the left side. Spatters of blood also were evident on the right back side and even on the hubcaps of the wheels, indicating to the investigators that the truck had been driven to the park after Vestal had been shot elsewhere. The pattern of blood on the rear hubcaps indicated that blood had been blown by the wind as the pickup was moving. It looked like Vestal had been dead for hours.

As crime scene technicians took photographs of the vehicle's interior and exterior and made measurements, the sheriff talked to the woman who had found the bloody truck and victim.

"I had brought my son up for football practice and thought the truck was dripping oil when I saw it," the witness related. "Then I recognized it was blood and saw the body inside. Then I screamed."

Scanning the truck and the area for possible clues, the officers found a .22-caliber shell casing on the floorboards of the pickup.

Laclede County Coroner Max Pickering arrived and authorized removal of the body. The sheriff helped the coroner load the dead man onto a gurney and into a waiting ambulance. The body was taken to a hospital in Lebanon for an autopsy.

During the ensuing investigation, sheriff's officers located witnesses who recalled having seen Vestal's pickup in the parking lot of the city park at about 10:30 p.m. on Wednesday. This led investigators to believe the slaying had taken place sometime that evening.

"We don't know what happened between the hours of six-thirty (when Vestal had been seen in his pickup going along the county road) and ten-thirty p.m.," Rifenburg told newsmen later.

Investigators also talked to witnesses who lived in the area where the Brewer van had been found Thursday morning. These people said the van had not been at that location at 4 p.m. Wednesday, but they noticed it parked at that spot about a half hour later. No one had been seen around the van.

Sheriff Rifenburg and the other investigators speculated there was a connection between the blood-drenched Brewer van and the killing of Steven Vestal. They presumed that both George and Carol Brewer also were dead, possibly having been slain by the same gunman who had killed Vestal.

"That leaves about two hours between the time the Brewer van apparently was abandoned and the estimated time Vestal might have picked up a hitchhiker," the sheriff pointed out.

But the big question for lawmen was: Who could be killing off motorists at such a rate?

Considering the known facts, officers surmised that Vestal might have stopped for a hitchhiker or hitchhikers who were the killers of the Brewers. The killer or killers would have walked several miles from the abandoned van before reaching the area where Vestal might have offered a ride, the lawmen theorized.

It also was hypothesized that Vestal had been shot when he noticed blood on his passenger or passengers, or otherwise became suspicious. It was thought the killer or killers were transients, since they appeared to be afoot and no other abandoned vehicle had been found in the area.

Officers continued an intensive search in the area where the Brewer van was found, and, at about 8:30

p.m. Thursday, searchers located the body of George Brewer. The body was stretched out on a gravel bar in a dry creek bed. Examination of the corpse revealed Brewer had been shot once in the face and also in the back of the head. The bullet wounds indicated a small-caliber gun. The shooting appeared to have been execution-style, similar to that of Steven Vestal. Brewer was thought to have been shot in his van and his body then tossed into the dry creek.

With Brewer's body recovered, the lawmen continued to comb the area for the victim's missing wife. They had little hope the woman would turn up alive.

A command post to coordinate the search of the various law enforcement agencies, including the Laclede, Webster and Dallas County Sheriff's Departments, the Missouri State Highway Patrol and the Lebanon Police Department, was set up in the First Baptist Church at Conway. Dozens of local residents also were taking part in the search.

The murders that had struck down members of two families living within a 10-mile distance were the chief conversation in the cafes and stores of the small community. Residents were especially outraged over the brutal death of Steven Vestal, who was well known in town.

One resident summed up the thoughts of his fellow townsmen when he said, "Steve did everything here in the community—sang, preached, played softball and baseball—and was always thinking about other people. It would have been just like him to stop and pick up a hitchhiker, especially if he thought he needed help or something. He was always joking all of the time."

There was other talk, too—about fear. Normally, Conway residents left their homes unlocked, but the killings had changed all that. People were locking their doors and even making sure that a weapon of some kind was handy.

"I'm really scared—I think everyone around here is," said a cashier at a local cafe.

Meanwhile, investigators from the highway patrol's state crime laboratory gathered evidence at the two crime scenes to take back to Jefferson City for analysis and examination.

"Until the results come back from the crime lab, we will not be able to tell if there is blood from more than one person in the Brewers' van," Sheriff Rifenburg said.

The uncertainty about the fate of Carol Brewer came to an end late Friday, September 18th, when the woman's fully clothed body was found halfway down the slope of a ravine in the area where her husband's body and their blood-soaked van had been discovered. She also had been shot twice, once in the face and once in the back of the head. It was believed after examination that the shots had been fired into all three victims from the same gun, probably a .22-caliber pistol.

As officers continued to canvass the roads and highways for possible witnesses who might have seen the killer or killers in the company of Vestal or the Brewers, they obtained the description of a hitchhiker who had been seen in the area on Wednesday, the day the killings were believed to have occurred. Based on the description, officers had an artist prepare a composite drawing to be circulated in the area.

In the meantime, while investigators sought leads in the ruthless slayings, they received information from Nevada authorities who were hunting two escaped felons. The prison inmates, aged 31 and 46, had escaped from the Northern Nevada Correctional Center at Carson City, Nevada in August. Nevada lawmen had received a tip that the fugitives might have contacted someone in Springfield, Missouri, and might still be in the area, which wasn't too far from the sites where Vestal and the Brewers had been killed.

There was one report that said the fugitives had been spotted trying to break into a pickup truck at a service station in the area, but this report was later discounted. But officers continued to be on the alert for the escapees, who, if they had been hitchhiking in the Ozarks, would be suspects in the three slayings.

Almost a week passed with no new leads in the homicide investigation.

On Tuesday, September 22nd, mass murders and the type of killer who commits them were being discussed at a seminar in Corsicana, Texas—a town of some 23,000 residents located several hundred miles from the Missouri Ozarks. The officers attending the seminar lectures had just finished viewing slides showing victims of psychopathic mass murderers when they heard the wail of sirens—lots of sirens. Ironically, the instructor had just commented that "something crazy always seems to happen in towns where I hold these seminars."

The first thoughts of the local officers present

415

were that a major traffic accident had occurred. But suddenly the pagers carried by the lawmen started beeping and blurting the message that a wild gunman was shooting up the town! Detective Gary Youngblood was among the officers who dashed from the seminar to their patrol cars to respond to the emergency alarm.

The unexplained shootings had started at about 1:30 p.m., when a man dressed in camouflage combat fatigues and combat boots walked into Hulcher Services, Incorporated, waving a pistol in each hand.

After asking where the boss was, the gunman strode rapidly to the rear of the building, where foreman Dennis James Wade was working. Another employee who was standing nearby recognized the two-gun man as Howard Frank Stewart, who had worked at the company until mid-July when he had been fired by Wade.

As the witness would later recall to investigators, the gunman didn't say a word. He looked at the witness for a moment, then swung his guns toward Wade and started shooting. As the gunman fired a fusillade of shots into Wade, the witness turned and ran for his life.

The stalking assailant, who had arrived at the business on a motorcycle, didn't linger long. He ran outside and jumped into a pickup owned by the firm. As the driver roared away from the parking area, an employee was on the phone notifying police of the coldblooded gunning down of Wade who lay bleeding from multiple wounds. An ambulance was also summoned.

As reconstructed later by officers, Howard Stewart

drove from the shooting scene to the Western Sizzlin' Restaurant on West Seventh Avenue, apparently looking for his estranged wife, Brenda Kay Stewart, 34. The woman, who was assistant manager of the eating place, wasn't on duty.

Stewart rushed into the restaurant and fired two or three shots into the air from one of the guns he was brandishing, setting off screams of terror from some of the diners. One elderly woman fainted.

An employee approached Stewart and asked him what he wanted. The gunman pointed a gun at her and asked where his wife was. When told she wouldn't be in until 3 p.m., Stewart fired several more shots into the air before leaving.

Rushing back to the pickup he had stolen from the other business, he sped from the restaurant. Stewart collided with another vehicle parked on the lot as he left, but it didn't stop his flight.

By now, police calls on the two separate shooting incidents were flooding the air. The officers who had been at the mass killer seminar were in their units and joining the hunt for the crazed gunman who was shooting up the city.

Stewart headed for a trailer park on Park Row Road, where his wife lived in a mobile home. He screeched to a stop by his wife's trailer and, with two guns in his hands, dashed inside. The gunman found his wife and a man later identified as Edward L. Persons Jr., 30, in a bedroom where they were talking. He opened fire with both weapons on Persons first; the slugs ripped into the man's body from head to foot as the gunman fired 10 shots. The slugs struck the victim in the head, chest and legs.

Then Stewart turned one of the guns, a .22-caliber semi-automatic, on his wife, who had fled into a bathroom in an effort to escape. Stewart fired five shots through the bathroom door, then kicked it down and fired several more bullets into his wife. She slumped over the bathtub.

Stewart then turned and ran from the trailer home. He locked the front door behind him as he stepped onto the porch. He started toward the parked truck, but then hesitated. He could hear the wail of police sirens in the distance, officers would theorize later.

Stewart raised his other gun, a .38-caliber revolver, and fired one shot into his head. He crumpled onto the trailer house porch.

In a 30-minute shooting frenzy that had terrified the town, four people—including the killer—lay dead.

When the police units, Detective Gary Youngblood among them, pulled up at the trailer house, they quickly ascertained that the man on the porch was dead. They also discovered that the pockets of his camouflage suit were filled with ammunition for the two guns found at the scene and apparently used in the slayings.

"He was prepared," Youngblood observed grimly.

The two bodies were found inside the home. Police investigators began photographing the scene and reconstructing the violent events.

Police had been given the trailer house address by employees at the restaurant when they responded a few minutes after Stewart had shot up the place but fortunately wounded no one there. The restaurant workers said Stewart had previously lived with his wife at the trailer house before they had separated in July.

Checking on records of the motorcycle Stewart had left at the first shooting scene, officers learned that he had also been driving a red van.

A short time later, the van was found near Lake Halbert. Looking inside the vehicle, officers discovered two pit bulldogs who had been shot and killed by Stewart. There was something else that caused them to pull up short before entering the van for further investigation: Next to the dogs' bodies lay two items that officers recognized as anti-personnel land mines.

The bizarre scene was made even more weird as they saw that six puppies sucked at the breasts of one of the dead dogs.

Also observed was a wire that hung precariously from the door of the van, making the investigators think the vehicle might be booby-trapped with the two land mines. U.S. Army explosives experts from Fort Hood were summoned to inspect the scene. They found no evidence of a booby trap and learned that the two mines were not armed.

Examining the van interior, the officers noted that Stewart had apparently been living inside the vehicle since his arrival in Corsicana.

Detectives began the job of unraveling the events and possible motive that had launched Howard Stewart on the rampage of killing. In the next few hours, they interviewed residents of the trailer park and other friends or acquaintances of Stewart and his wife. From the various sources they put together a picture of a strange loner with conflicting characteristics of friendliness and coldbloodedness.

They learned that Stewart, 37, was an ex-marine who apparently had been very much in love with his wife but who had been driven by mental demons that spelled tragedy for their marriage.

"He was kind of an odd guy," one neighbor, who had been seated about 50 feet away when the trailer house shootings had occurred, told detectives. "He always wore camouflage. I heard a shot when I was sitting here watching TV but that guy was always going out with a twenty-two and shooting rabbits. That's what I thought it was."

Investigators learned that Stewart had served in the marines in South Carolina for two years, but friends said Stewart told them he had fought in Vietnam, had been badly wounded and had a metal plate in his head. Residents of the trailer park recalled that Stewart preferred to be called "Rambo," after the legendary character of movie fame who mopped up on enemy bad guys.

Stewart had lived with his wife and two sons in the trailer house until about three weeks earlier, when his wife had asked him to leave. She had driven him to the local bus station and put him on a bus to Missouri.

Another park resident, who said neighbors tried to avoid Stewart because of his odd actions, told officers he thought Stewart was mentally ill because of the way he treated his pet pit bulldogs.

"He had a male and a female, and they had puppies," the witness related. "But their teeth were no good. They weren't strong enough, so he beat them

420

all in the head—killed them all."

Other neighbors described Stewart's conduct as puzzling, to say the least. Some said he drank heavily and smoked marijuana. One said he was a "likeable guy and the life of the party who would drink anything, the worst rotgut." A woman recalled that Stewart had given her vegetables grown in his garden, adding, "I've never seen him act violent before."

One man, whose wife worked with Brenda Stewart at the steakhouse, told police that he had drunk coffee with Stewart on the day before the murder rampage.

"He said then he was going to do what he did," the man said, shaking his head in disbelief. "I've been divorced, and I said things I didn't do. I thought he was just saying it because of hurt. He said if he couldn't have her, nobody could have her." The man said he tried to console Stewart and play upon his feelings for the couple's two teenaged sons. He said, 'I feel like I've already lost them, too.' I never dreamed he would actually do it."

Another resident related that Brenda Stewart had known her husband was back in town, and that he had left her a note on Monday saying he was going to California. The witness said Brenda had been afraid of Stewart.

Brenda Stewart was liked by everyone who knew her, her fellow employees told officers. She had been voted one of the best waitresses in Corsicana in October 1986, in a poll by the local newspaper.

"She was kind of a mom to everybody," her boss told lawmen.

As police probed the backgrounds of the other

shooting victims, they learned they had reputations as good, law-abiding people who had fallen into the path of Stewart's destructive mental distortions.

Dennis Wade, 30, who had died in the hospital emergency room after being taken by ambulance from the shooting scene, was married and had two daughters and a son. The family had moved three years earlier from Kentucky to Corsicana, where Wade had become foreman at the company whose business was cleaning up railroad derailments. Friends told police Wade really hadn't planned to work on Tuesday, but he had canceled plans to go fishing on Tuesday because of unforeseen obligations.

Edward "Eddie" Persons, the man shot to death in Brenda Stewart's trailer home, was an oil field worker from Jonesboro, Louisiana, police learned. He had expected to conclude his job on Thursday and return to Louisiana. Persons had met Brenda Stewart at the steak restaurant where he ate. They were mutually interested in pit bulldogs and he had been discussing taking two puppies back to Louisiana, officers were told.

Police recovered .22-caliber shells from the shooting scenes. Autopsies were ordered on the four bodies, which would be sent to a Dallas forensic crime laboratory for that purpose. Bodies of the two pit bulldogs found in Stewart's van also would be sent to the lab so the slugs could be recovered for comparison with the bullets in the human victims.

Continuing their interrogation of people who had known the strange-acting Stewart, detectives quizzed two witnesses who disclosed a startling statement made by Stewart on Tuesday morning before he went on his murderous mission.

Stewart had told the acquaintances that he had earlier killed three people near Lebanon, Missouri, where some of his relatives owned property. He had added that he didn't have much time because he was wanted for the three murders in that state.

Knowing that Stewart had come back to Corsicana from Missouri, the Corsicana police quickly got on the phone to Missouri authorities. They learned from Sheriff Rifenburg of the shooting deaths of Vestal and the Brewers in that area on September. And from the information provided by the sheriff, it certainly sounded as if Stewart could have been responsible for the three killings. One glaring similarity: All three Missouri victims had been shot with a .22-caliber weapon as disclosed by the shell casings found by the crime scene technicians.

Plans were made for Sheriff Rifenburg to fly to Corsicana, bringing the .22-caliber shells and other evidence to Texas for comparison with the slugs in the Corsicana mass slayings.

Rifenburg told the Texas officers that he knew Stewart, who had lived in the Lebanon area for two or three years. The sheriff didn't think Stewart matched the description of the hitchhiker seen on the day of the killings there, at least in one sense. The hitchhiker had been described as having long hair. Stewart's hair was short and his hairline receding.

But the Corsicana detectives recalled that among the items found in Stewart's van was a wig, which Stewart could have been wearing in Missouri, they theorized.

Sheriff Rifenburg and his investigators set out to pin down Stewart's activities during the time he was known to have left Corsicana by bus in mid-July for Lebanon until his fateful return to the Texas city. They learned Stewart was known in the area, having lived with relatives near Lebanon previously for about two years. Again, Missouri people described him as a loner, a drifter and slightly odd.

Investigators went to the farm near Lebanon, which Stewart had visited before returning to Texas, and interviewed relatives. Relatives related that Stewart had left the place on Wednesday morning, September 16th, after an argument with a relative about his alcohol and drug problems.

Stewart had been carrying an orange backpack and a gun when he left that morning, hitchhiking, the officers learned. He had returned to the relatives' house at about nine o'clock that night. He was apparently depressed by events of the day, telling the relatives that a man who stopped to give him a ride had driven off after Stewart put his backpack in the vehicle.

Stewart told his relatives he had been given three different rides that day. One man had brought him back to Lebanon, from where he had walked the four miles to the relatives' home, according to his story to his kinfolks.

Stewart had done some practice shooting at a tree the next day, walking into town for two boxes of shells.

On Friday, relatives had conceded to Stewart's wishes to return to Texas. They had put him on a bus for Corsicana, where his wife and children were, the

424

relatives told officers.

Officers collected .22 shell casings from the spot where Stewart had practiced shooting on Thursday, for comparison with the shells from the Lebanon murder scenes.

On September 23rd, Sheriffs Rifenburg and Cox and two investigators from the Missouri State Highway Patrol arrived in Corsicana. They conferred with the Texas detectives and took custody of items found in Stewart's van. Among the items were the wig, a brown cap and a shirt, which the Missouri lawmen said matched clothing worn by the hitchhiker seen on the day of the three Missouri slayings. They also were given shells from the Corsicana murder scenes.

Several days after ballistics and laboratory tests had been completed in Texas and in Missouri, Sheriff Rifenburg and Corsicana Police Chief J.J. Ryzman held press conferences confirming that Howard Stewart had been identified as the killer of the three Missouri residents (Vestal and the Brewers) as well as the Corsicana victims.

"He's the guy," Ryzman said. "Everything checked out perfectly."

Ballistic tests had shown positively that the .22-semi-automatic pistol used to kill the Corsicana people was the same gun that had fired the shots into the Missouri victims, Ryzman and Rifenburg said.

Sheriff Rifenburg said, "We're confident Howard Franklin Stewart is our killer. The ballistics did match up in the Texas and Missouri cases. There was only one killer. The case has ended."

The shell casings taken from the site where Stewart

had practiced shooting at a tree matched the shells found at the Vestal-Brewers slaying scenes, as well as those from the Corsicana shootings, the officers added.

Also, lab tests had matched one of Stewart's boot prints with a boot print found on Vestal, apparently left on the body when the killer kicked the victim, said the officers. Stewart's fingerprints also were identified on at least one of the vehicles driven by the Missouri murder victims, Rifenburg said.

The murders of Steven Vestal and George and Carol Brewer were marked closed, based on the evidence examined, the Missouri officers said.

HOWARD UNRUH
"FANTASY OF DEATH"
by David Redstone

He tagged along with his artillery group at the fringes of the European theatre, moving from Italy to Belgium and France, then through Austria to the finish in Germany. He came out without a scratch and, even more remarkable, without any particular notice from anyone in his outfit. He had been an unknown quantity through it all, and as such, "Mr. X" describes him for the time being better than his name, which most men easily forgot.

He had exchanged letters off and on with a girl back home in Camden, New Jersey, but the correspondence had lapsed because nothing deep lay behind it, as far as he was concerned. But when he returned to civilian life the girl called him up so many times, he felt obliged to ask her out. Outwardly he was presentable, being young—about twenty-seven—rather tall, dark-haired, soft-voiced, and exceedingly polite. They met at church socials, or went to a movie on a Saturday night, and he was always well behaved. He never tried to kiss her. He didn't even hold hands when they were alone.

Bashfulness in a youth is a challenge to most young girls. She resolved to overcome it. One night, when they were saying good night at her door, she took his arm and drew him toward her.

"Why don't you kiss me?" she asked. "Unless," she added with a little smile, "you don't want to, really."

He wanted to, he said, though he hadn't exactly meant that. He wished he wanted to; that would have been more truthful. She was a nice girl; others said she was pretty, though he hadn't thought of her quite in that way. She waited. Why was he hesitant?

On impulse, she threw her arms around him and before he realized what was happening he felt her lips on his. A moment later she was running up the steps. She called good night after him, smiling secretly, as if confident that from now on she wouldn't have to hint again.

But he never came near her after that.

He resented other things, too. He disliked the jobs he had strayed into for brief periods. More and more he began to hate his surroundings, his neighbors and for that matter, strangers who passed him in the street. Everyone seemed bent on annoying him in trivial ways. The woman in the house next door was always shouting at him to close the gate. The kids on River Avenue said things, usually in whispers. Actually, they hardly knew him and paid no attention to him. To them, as to the fellows in his outfit, he was an unknown quantity — Mr. X.

He took courses at Temple University, in Philadelphia, under the G.I. bill. He hoped to become a pharmacist. But after a short while he realized that he wasn't the least interested in the subject. He began to cut classes. He went to movies and sat through shows twice over, content to sit alone in the darkness. But he couldn't escape the intensity of his feelings about people in general — always present, deep-down, slow-burning resentment of everyone's attitude toward him. It wasn't right. It was unjust.

On Monday, September 5th, 1949, he was away from home all day, in Philadelphia. He dropped into the Family Theatre on Market Street late in the evening and saw a double feature — *I Cheated the Law,* and *The Lady Gambles*. His mind was not concentrated on the screen characters nor on the action, which had its high points; he was concerned, as always, lately, with himself: the wrongs inflicted on him by others and his forbearance with people's rudeness and spite.

A mood came over him that had been mounting over the months since his return to Camden, until now as he sat alone, a consuming rage gripped him. He would find a way to free himself of this injustice! He stumbled out of the theatre and struck out aimlessly along the street, arms stiff at his sides, fists clenched. In time, he realized how late it was, and headed for the bus stop. It was nearly 3 A.M. when he alighted from the bus in Camden.

River Avenue was silent as he stood watching the bus recede in the distance. He remained for a moment near the corner drugstore at 32nd Street, trying to decide whether to walk through the empty lot from River, or to get into his house by way of the druggist's side gate. The two houses adjoined each other but there was only one entrance to the second-story flat where he lived with his mother, and this was at the rear. He chose the druggist's gate on the side street and let it slam shut after him with a loud bang. As the iron bolt clanged against the post, from somewhere above a woman's voice shouted:

"Can't you be more quiet!"

He stopped, glared up at the darkened window, trembling with rage. Then he went into his own house next door.

Before going to bed, he scribbled on a slip of paper,

429

"Wake me up at eight o'clock," and left it on the kitchen table where his mother would see it.

At eight o'clock the next morning his mother called him. He took care in dressing, choosing his best dark suit, a white shirt and bow tie. He prepared a hasty breakfast for himself while his mother dressed, then went downstairs to the basement. He was gone some twenty minutes. When he came back, he turned on the radio in the living-room and stood there toying a while with the dial.

It was 9:15 when his mother appeared at the door. She glanced toward the radio where she had expected to see her son but he wasn't there. She heard no sound in the room other than the voice of an announcer reporting the weather for Camden and vicinity. She took one step inside the door and suddenly drew back. An upraised arm had been awaiting her entrance, and something metallic gleamed and swept downward, narrowly missing her head. Had it reached its mark it would have killed her instantly.

A scream escaped her lips. She ran down the stairs, terror-stricken and sobbing. Out in the street, she glanced helplessly this way and that, then hurried away toward a neighbor's.

A few doors from the drugstore, John Pilarchik, a shoemaker, was tapping away at a half sole. He had been at work since 8:30 and the shelf of footgear awaiting his skill would last him well through the week. John didn't talk much to customers. Conversation, with nails in one's mouth, was precarious.

He barely glanced up when the front door opened at 9:18. But this man didn't appear to be a customer. He had something in his hand but it wasn't a pair of shoes.

John never knew exactly what it was because the object exploded in his face with a deafening roar and he passed on into the unknown.

Clark Hoover, the barber next door, was industriously snipping the blond hair of Orris Smith, aged six, who was seated on a hobbyhorse specially designed for children's haircutting. In a chair close by sat Orrie's mother, chatting with Mrs. Daniel Voutier whose little boy was to be next on the hobbyhorse. The barber was about to nod good morning in the direction of a man who had just quietly entered when, from a distance of two feet, a .45-caliber bullet crashed into his brain. His body was still falling while a second bullet sped into the back of little Orrie's head. The child tumbled off the horse into a reddening pool, and Mrs. Voutier, screaming frantically, clutched her own baby in an attempt to shield it with her body. Meanwhile, Mrs. Smith, sobbing hysterically, lifted her dead son from the floor and stumbled dazedly, unbelievingly, into the bright daylight of River Avenue.

The barber-shop wall clock said 9:20. Three murders had been committed in the space of two minutes.

James J. Hutton, the insurance man, was about to enter Cohen's drugstore. He did not live in the neighborhood but was well known here. His home was in Westmont, not far away, and he had come down to East Camden especially early, so as to finish his rounds by five. Today, September 6th, was his wife's birthday, and he had planned to give her a surprise. He was startled at the approach of a man who pointed a German Luger at him. The other calmly said, "Excuse me, sir," and killed Hutton on the spot with a single bullet.

Maurice Cohen happened to be looking out of his drugstore window and saw Hutton drop to the sidewalk.

He saw the gunman step neatly over the corpse to enter the drugstore. Cohen ran to the staircase and shouted a warning to his family above. Turning, he realized he was being pursued and he began to run up the stairs. He could hear the panting breath of the man behind him. Cohen's son Charlie, twelve years old, was on the landing. At his father's orders he went out of the window onto the roof from where he made it easily to the ground. Rose, the druggist's wife, sought refuge in a clothes closet. The druggist's mother, a woman of sixty-eight, was still asleep in one of the bedrooms.

Cohen was attempting escape by the same route his son had taken, and had gained the sidewalk when the bullet caught him. He fell headlong and died instantly. Three shots followed in quick succession, shattering the door of the closet where Rose had hidden. It opened, and her dead body fell forward into the room. The old lady, Rose's mother-in-law, was putting on her robe, wondering what sort of commotion was going on in the house — the shouting and screaming and banging — until a stranger entered the room, leveled his gun, fired, and the old lady toppled over dead.

Seven murders in the space of slightly under six minutes.

The sun appeared from a cloud drift, bathing the highway with warmth and casting points of brilliant light from one glinting object to another, on the chromium ornaments of cars that passed, on window panes and tinplated gutters on the edges of roofs. Young Alvin Day, twenty-four, in a delivery truck which he had just parked, was a veteran of some of the most violent hand-to-hand fighting in World War II. He had often laughingly remarked to his mother that the Germans hadn't ever been able to make a bullet with his name on it. He wasn't yet out of his truck when he faced Mr. X and in a matter of seconds lay dead on the pavement.

Charles Petersen, a youth of eighteen, crossing the road from where he had left his father's car, felt stabs of pain at thigh and ankle which brought him writhing to the ground. Luckily for him, the bullets had not found vital spots. From scores of telephones in the 3200 block, residents were frantically calling police, ambulances, doctors. Mothers were screaming at their children to get them indoors. Shopkeepers were locking and barricading their doors. The news echoed from throat to throat that a madman more deadly than a rattlesnake was loose in the neighborhood.

In the American store, a grocery on the corner of 32nd Street opposite Cohen's, the manager had the presence of mind to snap the bolt of his door and to herd the half-dozen women customers to places of shelter. Those inside saw the quietly moving killer try the door, then move on.

All life had deserted the sidewalks on either side of River Avenue; the field was in possession of one man alone, until a bakery wagon drove up. The driver, Roxy De Marco, heard the crack of a pistol and the thrum of a bullet just above his head. For once the killer had missed—the first time. It was now 9:25 according to witnesses.

Helga, the young bride of Thomas Zegrino, was sorting garments in her husband's cleaning shop two doors beyond the barber's. Some of the customers who had left their clothes had attended her wedding just three weeks before. A dress she now held was stained with the wine drunk during a toast to her future happiness. Suddenly a deeper stain dyed the fabric as she collapsed and the garment dropped from her lifeless hand.

Nine murders — and still the time was running less than one minute for each.

No more than two seconds after, little Tommy Hamilton, two years old, appeared at the window of his parents' home. His head made a perfect target. Mr. X's bullet hit him squarely between the eyes, killing him instantly.

Just before this, Frank Engel, proprietor of the cafe beyond the lunchroom, had seized a P-38 automatic from under the counter and, with a friend named Kirk, had rushed upstairs to a window facing the highway. He passed the gun to Kirk, saying, "You kill him." But Kirk's hand was unsteady. Impatiently, Engel grabbed the gun. "I'll kill the son of a b—-!" he muttered. He fired and saw the gunman stop short, waving his Luger from side to side as if to cool the barrel, then move on, limping a little, toward the corner of 32nd Street.

The traffic light just then turned red, bringing a sedan to a halt. Inside were Mrs. Helen Wilson, at the wheel, and beside her Mrs. Emma Matlack, a woman of sixty-seven — Mrs. Wilson's mother. A nine-year-old boy, Johnny Wilson, son of the younger woman, sat in the back. The seconds ticked on to 9:29 as a tall figure approached the sedan. The destination of the three in the car was a doctor's office less than a mile away; they were to learn the result of tests made for Mrs. Matlack a week before. A terrible shock was in store for the family. The doctor was prepared to announce that Mrs. Matlack would die of cancer within three months.

But this news was destined to be withheld from them. Mr. X calmly raised his gun and fired three times through

434

the open window of the car. Mother and daughter both died in a matter of seconds. The third bullet hit Johnny. He too died. Johnny was No. 13.

An observer checked his watch after hearing the three shots. It was a few seconds past 9:29.

Thus in a few seconds over eleven minutes, thirteen murders had been committed by one man — a record, so far as I have been able to find out — unequalled in any country on earth in modern times.

And then, at 9:30, the killer tried to add to that record. Mrs. Madeline Harrie, in her living-room at 942 32nd Street, just around the corner from the drugstore, screamed as a strange visitor walked into the house and began shooting. Mrs. Harrie's son, Armond, seventeen, tried to grapple with the intruder and was struck on the head with the pistol and shot in the arm. The woman fell with a bullet in the shoulder and dazedly watched the assailant searching the rooms for more victims. Leroy, a younger brother of Armond, had hidden himself under the bed. The youngest, Wilson Harrie, was one of the persons barricaded inside the grocery store.

Several neighbors watched the killer leave the Harrie porch and they saw him spit from the side of his mouth before taking careful aim at the grocery window. No one was hit this time. After two or three more shots the gun clicked emptily and the madman, for such he seemed to be, disappeared through the druggist's side gate for a fresh supply of ammunition, it was assumed, and no doubt rightly.

At the time, everyone in the vicinity was wondering why the police hadn't arrived, not realizing during the shock of events how swiftly things had happened. And now sirens rose shrill on the air as police in cars and on motorcycles came racing up the highway. Fully three-score officers invaded the area, swarming in with riot guns, tommy-guns, shotguns and tear-gas equipment. They had located the killer at a second-story window and were rapidly closing in—and not without danger—because he had apparently obtained more ammunition and was taking pot-shots at any and all. Regardless, police came on by a series of sprints, from point to point, taking risky shelter in order to draw his fire and enable others to gain the roof, if possible.

For several minutes the crack and flame of guns sounded like a full-scale battle—and battlefield it surely had become, with the clanging of ambulances and the shouts and the gathering up of a dozen bodies and the pools of blood in the street. There were actually not enough litters for the fallen. And in the midst of all this, a telephone had begun to ring in the house where the killer had taken refuge.

Philip R. Buxton, a city editor on the Camden *Evening Courier,* eager to verify reports that flooded his desk, had looked up a phone number—Camden 4-2490 W—and decided to try the connection. It was then 9:58 A.M. He almost gave up, after persistent ringing, when the party answered. The following conversation, among the strangest ever recorded, is given verbatim:

Is this Howard?
Yes, this is Howard. What's the last name of the party you want?
Unruh.
What do you want?
I'm a friend. I want to know what they're doing to you.

436

They haven't done anything to me yet. But I'm doing plenty to them.

How many have you killed?

I don't know. I haven't counted. Looks like a pretty good score, though.

Why are you killing people?

I don't know. I can't answer that yet; I'll have to speak to you later. I'm too busy right now.

Thus ended one of the world's strangest phone conversations, considering the circumstances. What kept Mr. X — or Howard Unruh — busy during the next few minutes was tear-gas vapor sent in by the Camden police. His eyes had flooded and his throat was choked. He fired once more, blindly, but the pistol clicked hollowly. Meanwhile, Police Officers Charles Hance and Everett Joslin had followed through after hurling tear gas into the room and were the first at hand for capture. They heard Unruh's gasping plea:

"Don't shoot. Please don't shoot!"

Patrolman Hance ordered him to come all the way out with arms upraised. Other officers joined in to grab the killer. Unruh put up no resistance at all, and showed no trace of excitement or even fear He was taken down, faced against a wall where he was searched for weapons. A six-inch jackknife and a tear-gas pencil were removed from his pockets. Though blood dripped from his clothing, he didn't complain of a wound. The police at first assumed that one of their bullets had hit him, because round after round had been poured into the apartment, riddling the windows and walls, and it was a wonder Unruh hadn't been killed by one of these bursts.

Questioned at police headquarters by Chief Prosecutor Mitchell H. Cohen, who sought Unruh's motive for this hideous murder rampage, the captive stated simply:

"They were picking on me."

"Who?"

"Everybody. For months they've been bothering me. I knew that some day I would kill them all. Last night, while I was in the movie theatre, I decided to do it in the morning."

He then spoke of a gate he had built the previous week which, he said, someone had torn down. It was a fact that he had had some slight dissension with the Cohen family next door about access to the yard of both properties. The enclosure was fenced in and a gate, as has been stated, on the druggist's side was the only access to the Unruh apartment from 32nd Street. Other than this, one had to go around the opposite side, through an empty lot, which, after a rain, became a muddy puddle. The Cohens didn't object to the Unruhs using the side gate so long as it wasn't slammed late at night. But Howard Unruh repeatedly slammed it hard, or else he left it wide open.

On a couple of occasions Mrs. Cohen had called to him: "Hey, you—can't you be more quiet with that gate?"

What he resented most, he told the prosecutor now, was the "Hey, you." He brooded over that phrase. After all, he had an identity—Howard Unruh was his name.

But what was his grievance against all those others slain—infants, women, total strangers? And why had he shot down Hutton, the insurance man, who had been his friend? In fact, Hutton had just put through a policy transfer for him as a favor and had come down especially to tell him the good news.

Many more questions were put to him by Prosecutor Cohen, by detectives, by eminent psychiatrists, but Howard Unruh's answers had become vague. The consequences that he might suffer did not disturb him, nor did he show the slightest remorse for what he had done.

Police had meanwhile recovered other weapons belonging to him, other than the deadly Luger. Down in his basement, Unruh had built a target range where he practiced shooting regularly. He owned knives, revolvers and a collection of seven rifles, with a store of ammunition. This was not in violation of Camden County law.

Late in the afternoon, Unruh was brought to Cooper Hospital to be X-rayed, and thus doctors located the small-caliber bullet that had entered the left buttock at a downward angle and lodged inextricably in the spine.

More than seventy-five witnesses offered testimony to what they had seen and heard on the morning of the massacre. Among these was Freda Unruh, mother of the slayer. Howard would have killed her too, she said; she had narrowly escaped, running then to her neighbors, the Pinners, in the next block, to tell them that her son was behaving strangely. She had wept and had been on the point of calling up her relatives when the first shots sounded. Then she had fainted—because she knew Howard had his pistol that morning.

As a reporter for TRUE DETECTIVE, I went to Camden to gather what facts I could, firsthand. I went to the scene of the tragedy and spoke to Frank Engel in his tavern. I found young Charlie Petersen limping on a cane; he showed me where one bullet had gone through his ankle. He introduced me to Wilson Harrie, who reported his mother and brother Armond well out of danger from their bullet injuries. Mrs. Joseph Hamilton appeared from her doorway with a baby carriage — she was the young mother of Tommy, the two-year-old child who had been shot dead through the window. A daughter was born to the Hamiltons on October 6th, just a month after her boy's murder.

I didn't have the heart to approach Thomas Zegrino, bereft of his bride three weeks after the wedding. His face was drawn and his eyes hollow, for he came home each day to a silent, empty house. He had expressed the wish that it might have been he that Unruh had killed instead.

Of all the people I met here, not one would have seen justice in allowing Unruh to live.

Yet, as Prosecutor Mitchell Cohen told me in his office, the decision was not his to make. Four noted psychiatrists had submitted a unanimous report after a month's continual observation, saying that Unruh was mentally deranged. They classified his malady as: *Schizophrenia of the catatonic type, with marked violent paranoiac tendencies*. It was their judgment that he be committed to the Trenton State Hospital for the insane. This is where Unruh is at present.

The prosecutor promised the citizens of Camden that as long as he remained in office, and as long as he lived, he would fight any attempt to release the patient into society.

Soon after this announcement, the Camden County Court ordered Samuel Unruh, fifty-eight, father of Howard, to pay $15 a week to the State for his son's maintenance at the institution. He had been estranged from his wife, Freda, many years and had visited Howard (and a younger married son) only seldom. He didn't know how he was to furnish the money, as he had to pay $21 a week to his wife under a separation agreement, and $10 a week to the Government in income tax arrears. That would leave him, he said with $11.95 a week to live on, if he were to pay the $15, and who could live on that amount per week?

Army records pertaining to Pfc. Unruh disclosed nothing that would have predicted his violent behavior. He had not taken part in combat to speak of. He was never sick and had no medical history. At the end of the war he was given the Good Conduct Award.

Incidentally, those who understand German will have been aware of the fact that Unruh, translated, means *unrest*.

As a result of the Unruh case, the New York *Journal American* started a campaign to have all World War II veterans turn in their souvenir weapons, resulting in the turning in or rendering harmless of more than 10,000 such weapons in the New York City area.

Joining the fight to remove dangerous weapons from incompetents was the Middlesex County, New Jersey, grand jury. This body urged passage of a State law requiring the registration of war souvenir pistols and revolvers and added that such registration should be accompanied by "proper screening of individuals to eliminate many senseless and unneccessary deaths."

CHARLES STARKWEATHER
"11 MURDER VICTIMS FOR THE YOUNG LOVERS!"
by Randall Shanley

It is doubtful that anyone has ever compiled statistics on the subject, but almost anyone familiar with police affairs will tell you that the ulcer rate among homicide detectives is high. A sense of urgency is as much a part of their lives as breathing or eating or sleeping. In no other branch of law enforcement is there so much pressure to catch the criminal in a hurry.

The reason for this is obvious, for it must always be assumed that if a man has killed once, he will not hesitate to kill again; even when he faces a death penalty, the slayer knows he can be executed only once, no matter how many people he murders.

These pressing considerations are ever-present when a homicide investigator is working on a case, be it a common grocery store stick-up killing which excites little comment in the press, or a spectacular murder of some prominent personage which makes headlines. In some cases, however, the pressure is greater than in others.

Thoughts of the type of slayer known as a "mad-dog killer," for instance, give a homicide detective nightmares. The mad-dog killer is one who seems possessed by a blood lust, one who kills again and again—at random, senselessly, indiscriminately—anyone unfortunate enough to cross his path.

America has seen few, if any, mad-dog killers worse than Charles Starkweather, a 19-year-old punk from Lincoln, Nebraska, who affected the nickname of "Little Red."

The only police record against this kid was a minor one, a complaint by his father that the youth had allowed a girl friend to borrow the family car and the girl had cracked it up. Among his contemporaries, though, Little Red was a VIP, a tough, obnoxious brawler who had frequently clobbered adversaries twice his size, even if he had to resort to knife-fighting to down his man.

Sometimes this is a phase through which kids pass and go on to lead respectable lives. Charles Starkweather was not one of them. Late in January of 1958, he embarked on an orgy of senseless, sadistic blood-letting and murder that shocked the entire North American continent and even impelled the governor of Nebraska to call out the National Guard to protect the terrified citizenry.

With him every step of the way on his incredible crime spree was a shapely, precocious 15-year-old girl friend with whom Starkweather was enjoying a flaming romance—Caril Ann Fugate, also of Lincoln.

For Lincoln police, the case began when one of the girl's relatives complained on Saturday night, January

25, 1958, that Caril Ann wouldn't let them into the family home in the Belmont district where the teenager lived with her stepfather, Marion Bartlett, her mother, Velda, and her half-sister, Betty Jean, two and a half years old. Detective Frank Soukup and Patrolman Donald Kahler were sent to investigate. It was a few minutes after 10 p.m. when they knocked on the door of the Bartlett house. Their insistent knocking finally brought Caril Ann to the door.

She looked like she had just gotten out of bed. She was wearing a filmy negligee over a nightgown. She was dark-haired and petite, obviously quite young, but her scanty attire clung to softly rounded curves which clearly indicated she was fast blossoming into womanhood.

"Is everything all right here?" Detective Soukup asked. "Your brother-in-law called headquarters and reported that you wouldn't let him or your sister into the house."

Caril Ann's dark eyes flashed annoyance. "I wouldn't let him in because everybody here is down with Asian flu," she snapped impatiently. "The doctor told me not to let anyone in. Besides, my sister had her baby with her. I'd have been crazy to let them expose the kid."

There was no reason to think the matter was anything other than a routine intra-family misunderstanding. Detective Soukup reported to the shift commander, Captain Joe Harbaugh.

Nearly 36 hours later, at 9:20 a.m. on Monday, January 27th, another relative of the family appeared at the police station in person. She was in a highly excited state. Referred to Assistant Chief of Police Eugene

Masters, she told him she had just been out to the Bartlett home in Belmont, and Caril Ann flatly refused to allow her into the house.

"I pleaded with her," the woman said tearfully. "I begged her to let me talk to the folks through the door, but she wouldn't let me. I called out to little Betty Jean, but she didn't answer me."

An aide brought Assistant Chief Masters the report filed by Detective Soukup on his investigation of the first complaint on the Bartletts the previous Saturday night. After studying it briefly, Masters assigned Detectives George Hansen and Ben Fischer to accompany the relative to the Bartlett home.

There was no sign of life around the place when they arrived. Detective Hansen knocked repeatedly, but there was no answer. Fischer tried the back door and reported it was locked. As Hansen opened the screen door to try the front doorknob, a note fell to the step. It read, "Stay away. Everyone is sick with flu." The signature was, "Miss Bartlett."

Fischer found a ground-floor window unlocked and at the relative's insistence, he climbed in, then went to the front door and admitted the others. A search through the house disclosed it was empty, save for a frisky little mongrel dog which wagged its tail happily and followed them around. They could find nothing amiss. The house was warm, and they could hear the oil furnace working. The beds appeared to have been slept in recently and were unmade. The whole house had the appearance of neglect, as though no housework had been done recently, but the illness of its inhabitants could explain that.

There was absolutely no sign of struggle or violence.

The relative was still unsatisfied, but sheepishly conceded she had probably worried needlessly. "I guess I got too excited," she said. "They must have gone to the store to do some shopping."

The officers drove her home, and reported to Assistant Chief Masters. Their report was appended to the Saturday night report by Detective Soukup.

In the meantime, the brother-in-law of Caril Ann Fugate, who had instigated the first visit to the Bartlett home, was still perturbed by everyone's inability to make direct contact with the family. At about half-past three that same afternoon, Monday, he decided to drop around to the Bartlett home again and have another look around. If the family had been shopping that morning, they certainly should be home by now.

He took with him a young friend. They found the house still deserted, but they climbed in the same window through which Detective Fischer had gained access to the home that morning. The mongrel pup was whining piteously, so they fed it and gave it water. The brother-in-law could not understand why no one was around.

"In the first place," he said, "I can't figure out why—if they were all so sick—everybody went shopping, if that's where they went. Maybe a couple of 'em might have gone out, but I can't see all of them going."

He was on the verge of leaving, when he had an idea. "I just remembered," he said. "Bartlett's always fiddling around the chicken house in his spare time. Let's take a look out there."

It was bitterly cold and the sky was a drab winter gray as they walked to the low-roofed chicken house that stood some 20 yards behind the Bartlett home.

The brother-in-law commented that it seemed unlikely a man just getting over the flu would be out there in such weather.

They opened the door of the chicken house and had to duck as they entered through the low entrance. When they raised their heads, they paused briefly to let their eyes adjust to the dimly lighted interior. Then, suddenly and simultaneously, both men gasped in horror.

The brother-in-law's hunch had been correct. Marion Bartlett was in the chicken house, but not for the reason he usually went there. He was dead. His body was carelessly wrapped in old rags and shreds of feed sacking, and it was frozen stiff.

The hastily telephoned report of the grim discovery swiftly brought a procession of official cars to the house in the Belmont district. Among those who gathered there, in addition to Assistant Chief Masters who headed the city police contingent, were Lancaster County Attorney Elmer Scheele and Captain Harold Smith, commanding a squad of investigators from the Criminal Division of the Nebraska Safety Patrol.

The frozen state of Marion Bartlett's body made it difficult to conduct a detailed examination of it, but several bullet wounds in the head were immediately apparent. Later laboratory examination established that these were made by a .22 caliber weapon. In addition, there was a profusion of knife wounds in the victim's upper body.

The officers were still engaged in examining the body and the surrounding area when one of Captain Smith's men who had been ordered to conduct a thorough search of the property burst into the chicken house.

"Captain, we've got a couple more bodies!" he announced breathlessly.

He led them to an abandoned outhouse no more than five yards behind the chicken house. Velda Bartlett's body, loosely wrapped in a filthy old quilt, lay half-propped in a corner. Death had come to her in much the same fashion as it struck down her husband—the small bullet wounds in the head, the savage knife slashes on the body.

A different fate had been reserved for the baby, 2 1/2-year-old Betty Jean; the infant's throat was slashed from ear to ear, the small body clumsily stuffed into a brown corrugated carton which once had held canned goods.

Both these bodies, like that of Marion Bartlett, were frozen as solid as blocks of ice.

When the investigators and the coroner were finished with their brief on-scene examination, the three bodies were ordered removed for autopsy. The coroner warned the officers, however, that the post mortem report would be delayed, since it would be impossible to begin the autopsies until the bodies had been thawed out.

Assistant Chief Masters and Sergeant Gerald Tesch of the State Safety Patrol took charge of the joint investigation. The first question they wanted an answer to was, Where was Caril Ann Fugate, the only member of the family still unaccounted for? An intensified researching of the house, grounds and outbuildings failed to reveal any trace of her, although the searchers momentarily expected to come upon her bloody and frozen body.

But if the killer of her parents and half-sister had slain Caril Ann, too, then he had either done it elsewhere or had taken her body with him. An all-out effort was immediately ordered to get a line on the girl.

Relatives provided police with a list of her friends, acquaintances and schoolmates, of places she frequented, and detectives ranged over the city attempting to pick up some lead to the pretty teenager's whereabouts.

Within two hours they had an answer, but exactly what it meant was not immediately clear. At half-past one that afternoon, a stream of probers learned, Charlie "Little Red" Starkweather had been seen with Caril Ann when he went to the home of a friend to pick up his souped-up hot rod, a black 1949 Ford. The informant said Red and Caril were carrying a couple of suitcases.

Masters and Tesch immediately broadcast pickup bulletins for the young couple. Charles Starkweather was described as five feet five inches tall, weight about 140 pounds, with a mop of unkempt red hair cut in a fashion much in favor with teenagers — short on top but long in the front, back and sides. Starkweather was said to wear thick-lensed glasses without which he "couldn't see beyond the end of his nose." He was bowlegged and pigeon-toed and walked with a rolling gait, almost a swagger. When last seen he was wearing blue jeans, a black leather motorcycle jacket and cowboy boots.

Police Chief Joseph Carroll ordered a check to see if Starkweather had a criminal record. He found only the complaint from the youth's father about the boy lending the family car to Caril Ann, who had smashed it up. After that dent, it was learned, Charles left the family home and rented a furnished room, but his landlady had locked him out three weeks before for nonpayment of rent.

Detectives interviewing young people who knew Red Starkweather quickly gathered information to round out details of his character. Charles was the third of seven children. His parents were respectable, law-abiding, hard-working people. The rest of the children were polite, courteous, well-mannered. Charles was the exact opposite.

He always had a low boiling point, a temper that flared violently at the slightest provocation, often imaginary. He once was expelled from grade school for fighting. He was a high school dropout at 16 after a hectic couple of years that saw him involved in wild brawls several times a week, frequently with classmates far bigger and heavier than he was. Due to his ferocity and lack of respect for the rules of a fair fight, he rarely lost a battle, and he had the reputation of being "a bad guy to tangle with." Reportedly, he would never hesitate to use a knife. He drank heavily and could not hold a job.

Some of his chums told of a habit Starkweather had developed in recent months; he was fond of yelling obscenities at total strangers, daring the object of his abuse to "make something of it." He was enthusiastic about only three things—comic books, hot rods and hunting—and he was said to be a crack shot, despite his weak eyes.

"Charlie used a gun to make him somebody," a friend told detectives. "At first he used it only to hunt game. He got so he could put a bullet right through the head of a squirrel. But sometimes he'd start blasting at nothing at all. He just loved to shoot."

Nothing that investigators learned about Charles Starkweather inspired any optimism that he might be innocent of involvement in the deaths of the Bartlett family; but if he was implicated, the evidence strongly suggested that Caril Ann Fugate also was involved. Yet the savagery of the murders made this seem incredible.

It was learned that the Bartletts had vehemently disapproved of Caril Ann going out with Little Red, but this hardly seemed a powerful enough motive to kill three people, including an infant less than three years old. If the couple was innocent of these crimes, however, why had they fled? Where were they?

Police were now virtually certain that Caril Ann had not been slain, that she was traveling with Charles as a willing companion. The autopsies finally established that the three murders had been committed no later than January 25th, two days before she was last seen with Starkweather. The victims might even have been slain a couple of days earlier than the 25th. At the very least, the girl must have been aware of the disappearance of her family. At the worst, she may have had guilty knowledge of their massacre.

The bulletin for the pickup of the young couple was now broadcast nationwide. Until, or unless, subsequent developments proved otherwise, Lincoln police and the Nebraska Safety Patrol homicide investigators were proceeding on the assumption that they were dealing with at least one mad-dog killer.

The autopsy reports established that cause of death for both Marion and Velda Bartlett was the bullet wounds in the head. Their bodies also had been mutilated with a sharp instrument, probably a knife. The baby, Betty Jean, had died from a skull fracture believed to have been caused by a blow from a pistol butt. Apparently her throat had been cut as an afterthought.

The pathologist's estimate of the time of death made it virtually certain that all three were already dead when Caril Ann spoke to Detective Soukup and Patrolman Kahler at the time of the first police visit to the Bartlett home on Saturday night.

Technicians found a wealth of Charles Starkweather's fingerprints in and around the Bartlett home, along with those of family members. A door from inside the house, which had been removed from its hinges, was found near the outhouse. It apparently had been used as a stretcher to carry the murder victims to the outbuildings.

The Nebraska Safety Patrol was manning roadblocks thrown up at key intersections on highways in a 50-mile radius of Lincoln. In the city, meanwhile, detectives were conducting a methodical interrogation of every person known to have had any contact with either Charles Starkweather or Caril Ann Fugate.

The manager of the trucking company where Marion Bartlett worked reported that he had not come to work for a week. The manager said someone—a male voice—had telephoned that Bartlett was ill with the flu. The caller did not identify himself; the executive had assumed it was a member of the family.

It was late Monday night before police picked up the first lead on the whereabouts of the missing couple. A gas station owner, whose place was eight miles south of Lincoln on Highway 77, reported that a couple answering the fugitives' description had stopped there a little after 2 o'clock that afternoon.

"They bought 45 cents worth of gas," he said, "and had a tire repaired. The boy bought two boxes of .22 rifle cartridges and a box of shells for a .410 shotgun. The girl bought some candy bars. The boy also asked for some ammo for a .32, but I didn't have any. Before they drove away I spotted a .410 shotgun on the front seat of the Ford they were driving."

Additional roadblocks were hastily mounted in the area south of Lincoln, but no further word of the teenagers was heard until late the following afternoon. Morton Hooker, who owned a farm near Bennet, some 13 miles south of Lincoln, heard about the search on the radio and called police. He told them he had pulled Starkweather's car out of the mud the day before, Monday.

Hooker knew Starkweather, so there was no mistake. The youth had often hunted in the area, he disclosed. Hooker said he came upon the black Ford mired near a storm cellar on the grounds of an abandoned school. Starkweather and a young girl were trying vainly to push the car onto dry ground. The farmer hauled it out of the mud with his pickup truck.

In the light of developments which came to light soon after this incident, the farmer has reason to be eternally grateful to his guardian angel. He was one of the very few to cross the path of Charlie Starkweather who lived to tell the tale.

The next lead came on Wednesday morning, the 29th, when a Bennet garageman who also knew Starkweather reported seeing a 1949 Ford sedan that might be the fugitives' parked in the driveway of the August Meyer farm. He said Charles often hunted there.

Investigation by Patrolman Vernon O'Neal proved that the Ford in the driveway was Starkweather's hot rod. O'Neal found six spare tires in the sedan, also two road maps, one of Kansas, one of Missouri. There was no sign of life around the farmhouse, not even a wisp of smoke from the chimney, although the temperature was hovering around the zero mark.

A double set of blurred footprints led from the car to the front door of the Meyer farmhouse, suggesting that the car's occupants might have found refuge there. But since the pickup order had stressed that Starkweather was a crack shot, armed and dangerous, O'Neal deferred direct action till he radioed news of his discovery to Captain Harvey F. Nash of the Safety Patrol. He was ordered to stand by till reinforcements arrived. He didn't have long to wait.

Lancaster County Sheriff Merle Karnopp soon arrived at the Meyer farm with six deputies. Lincoln Police Chief Carroll sent ten men. Five cruisers of the Safety Patrol brought 20 troopers under command of Colonel C.J. Sanders.

Reporters, photographers and crews from a couple of Lincoln television stations followed the lawmen to the scene. Neighbors, attracted by the commotion, also hurried to the farm. A couple told Sheriff Karnopp they had tried to telephone August Meyer that morning, but got no answer.

Keeping in mind Starkweather's reported prowess with a rifle, the lawmen approached the farmhouse with extreme caution. A deputy was sent to a nearby

454

farm with orders to keep trying to telephone the Meyer place, and if anyone answered to stall him.

Officers were deployed to surround the farmhouse. At a signal, they closed the ring slowly, then halted. At this point, as possemen covered him with fingers on triggers of rifles, shotguns and submachineguns, Sheriff Karnopp stepped out alone and fired nine tear gas shells through the farmhouse windows as he advanced. At the same time, Safety Patrol Sergeant Tesch rushed the rear and kicked open the door of a small washroom.

He didn't have to look any further for August Meyer. The 70-year-old bachelor farmer lay on the floor, his brains blown out by a blast from a .410 shotgun. A thin trail of blood led from the washroom, which was detached from the house, across the back porch and into the kitchen. It appeared that the old man was slain there, then dragged to the spot where his body was found.

The inside of the house was in wild disorder, drawers pulled out and their contents scattered. The whole place appeared to have been thoroughly ransacked. Neighbors who were familiar with the house were asked in to look around. They told the officers that Meyer's .22 rifle was missing. Two 12-gauge shotguns were found on Meyer's bed.

Technicians from the crime lab lifted several sets of fingerprints which were established as those of Charles Starkweather and Caril Ann Fugate. Despite the disorderly state of the house's interior, detectives could find no evidence of a struggle from the old man.

Sheriff Karnopp put into words what the other officers were thinking. "I don't doubt that Starkweather—

and perhaps the Fugate girl—are more than just witnesses. They're killers. I'm sure now that Starkweather murdered the Bartletts. He's the man we want. Meyer makes the fourth killing he's committed."

As subsequent developments proved, Sheriff Karnopp was only partially correct. August Meyer was not the fourth person Starkweather had murdered. He was the sixth. Two more, already lying dead in Lancaster County, had not yet been discovered.

On January 27th, two days earlier, a 17-year-old youth named Robert Jensen had gone out on a date at eight p.m. with Carol King, 16, one of his classmates at Bennet High School where Jensen was president of the junior class. He was driving a blue 1950 Ford with twin radio antennae on the rear fenders.

"We'll be home early," Carol King told her family as they left.

But Carol did not get home early. Neither did Bob Jensen. They didn't get home at all that night. The next morning, after mutual checking, the worried parents called the Nebraska Safety Patrol to report both youngsters missing. Jensen's car bore Nebraska license plate number 2-8743, they said.

Carol King was a young beauty who looked more mature than her 16 years. She was a cheer leader, active in many other school affairs, and a fine student. Both were extremely popular. Both were regarded as responsible youngsters of fine reputation.

A group of Bennet townspeople were aiding in the search for the missing youngsters. Barely a couple hours after old Gus Meyer's body was found, another farmer, Karl Ericson, was with such a group combing an area about a half-mile northwest of Meyer's farm when he spotted fragments of torn schoolbooks near an old storm cellar. Searching further, he found a small patch of something that looked like blood at the edge of the cellar door.

Ericson, fighting back a rising foreboding, tugged open the cellar door. The steps were covered with blood. At the bottom of the steps lay the bodies of Robert Jensen and Carol King. Jensen was fully clothed. Most of the girl's clothing had been stripped from her.

Report of the new murders was relayed to the Meyer farm and officials hastened to the storm cellar nearby. Other than the torn school books and bloodstains, the only other physical evidence found was a few .22 caliber shells picked up along the road in the vicinity.

The search of the area was conducted, with disappointing results. There were no witnesses to be questioned, but lawmen talked to residents living in the sparsely inhabited region, in case someone might have seen someone, or something that might be helpful. No one had. Photographs were taken of the victims and the surrounding area, and the bodies were removed to a mortuary for autopsy.

No one was surprised when the postmortem report stated that both Jensen and Carol King had been killed by .22-caliber bullets fired into their heads. But the report also stated that Carol had been the victim of a bestial, unnatural sex attack.

Sheriff Karnopp refused to elaborate. Neither would Safety Patrol officials or any other officers approached by newsmen. They would say only that Charles Starkweather had to be caught and that they were bending every effort to that objective.

457

But Starkweather remained at large and near-panic gripped the 125,000 people residing in Lancaster County, not to mention others living in adjacent areas. Reserve law officers were summoned to duty and road-blocks were thrown up everywhere, even at country crossroads. Parents kept children home from school and made them stay in the house. Men in isolated districts stayed home from work to protect their families, keeping loaded weapons close at hand.

The press now openly called Charlie Starkweather a "Mad-Dog Killer." Some headline writers making a play on his nickname of Little Red, dubbed him "The Red Dog Killer," and news of his murderous odyssey catapulted him into headlines throughout the country. Tips poured into Nebraska police agencies from everywhere. Most of them proved worthless.

By a weird combination of circumstances, even our then President Eisenhower became involved in the far-flung manhunt for Starkweather and his sexy girl friend.

The first of those circumstances was the death, on January 26th, of the president's brother, Arthur Eisenhower, at his home in Kansas City. Ike flew to the funeral services a few days later, but bad weather forced the pilot of the Presidential plane Columbine to land at the Naval Air Station at Olathe, Kansas, 27 miles from Kansas City.

The Navy provided a caravan of staff cars for the Presidential party, which was escorted on the trip to Kansas City by a sirening motorcycle escort of a couple dozen state police. Citizens in the countryside through which the official cortege roared, unaware of the change in the president's itinerary, leaped to the conclusion that Mad-Dog Killer Starkweather was being chased by police. Someone telephoned this information, reporting it as a fact, to a radio station in Olathe, which promptly interrupted its program with the bulletin that Starkweather was streaking across Kansas with the law in hot pursuit.

Hours passed before the confusion was cleared up and the public convinced that it was all a mistake.

In Lincoln, meanwhile, Prosecutor Scheele filed first-degree murder charges against Charles Starkweather and Caril Ann Fugate in connection with the murder of Carol King. Then the FBI entered the case when U.S. Commissioner C.M. Pierson issued a warrant for their arrest for unlawful flight to avoid prosecution.

But despite the most gigantic manhunt mounted in the State of Nebraska in recent history, officials admitted at noon on Wednesday, January 29th, that they were no closer to capturing the fugitives than they were when the first pickup bulletin was issued days before. They would soon learn, however, that Starkweather's blood lust was still raging as hotly as ever.

Late that Wednesday morning, a relative of C. Lauer Ward, a prominent Lincoln businessman, became concerned when Ward failed to appear at his office to keep an important appointment. He could not get any answer to telephone calls to Ward's home in the exclusive County Club district, so he finally drove out to the handsome residence on 24th Street.

He rang the doorbell again and again. He could hear it ringing, but no one came to the door, a fact which caused him concern. Mrs. Ward should have been home. So should the Wards' housekeeper, Mrs.

Lillian Fencl. He walked to the rear of the house, where he found the back door locked securely, as was the front door. The garage doors were open, but Lauer's 1956 black Packard sedan was not in its accustomed place. In its place stood a 1950 blue Ford. Ward's relative drove to the nearest telephone and called the police.

Assistant Chief Masters sped to the Ward home with half a dozen detectives, closely followed by a squad of FBI agents armed with submachineguns. From its license plate, Masters immediately identified the blue Ford in the Ward garage as the car of the murdered Robert Jensen. That was enough for Masters.

"Hit the front door," he ordered, after deploying men to surround the house. A couple of burly shoulders crashed the door and broke it in.

As their momentum carried them into the foyer the officers almost fell over the body of C. Lauer Ward. He lay sprawled on the floor, a .22 bullet wound in his temple, a deep knife wound in his back.

Lawmen swarmed through the house, but they didn't find Charles Starkweather or Caril Ann Fugate. They did find, in an upstairs bedroom, the horribly mutilated bodies of Mrs. Clara Ward and her housekeeper, Mrs. Fencl. They were fully clothed. Their hands were bound behind their backs. Rough gags had been stuffed into their mouths. Neither woman had been shot. Both had died from multiple stab wounds.

An alarm was broadcast for the Wards' Packard, which Starkweather and his girl apparently now were driving.

Detectives questioning nearby residents learned that Charlie Starkweather once had worked as a helper on a sanitation truck which collected garbage in the neighborhood. He may have gotten to know the Wards but why he chose them as victims, rather than any of the other wealthy residents of the Country Club district, could not be explained.

A house-to-house search was already under way in the area between Lincoln and Bennet. Now Sheriff Karnopp ordered every county officer to active duty and Governor Victor Anderson, with whom C. Lauer Ward had conferred the night before he was found murdered, mobilized 200 troops of the Nebraska National Guard to assist in a full-scale search of Lincoln. The sheriff also requested and got reinforcements from adjacent counties. At the peak of the search, more than 1,000 men armed with rifles and shotguns were on posse duty. The Safety Patrol was manning more than 100 roadblocks.

It seemed utterly impossible that Starkweather could escape this mammoth dragnet, but the people of Lincoln and Lancaster County were terror-stricken.

The Herculean effort of Nebraska authorities was in vain, for Charles Starkweather had fled the state. At the height of the manhunt, he was 500 miles away, tearing through Wyoming. Fourteen miles west of Douglas, Wyoming, a big courageous man named Joseph Sprinkle had the misfortune to meet Nebraska's Mad-Dog Killer.

Sprinkle, an agent for an oil company, was driving along the highway when he noticed a Packard at the edge of the road parked in front of a 1956 Buick. He saw a young girl in the back seat of the Packard. She was crying.

Thinking there had been an accident and that he

might be able to help, Sprinkle stopped. As he got out of his car, he spotted the bleeding, bullet-riddled body of a man lying on the front floorboards of the Buick.

At the same instant, a bespectacled, wild-eyed young fellow carrying a .22 rifle suddenly appeared from behind the Buick. His eyes, behind the thick lenses of his glasses, had the look of a punch-drunk fighter. His red hair seemed to have been smeared with some black substance, as if in an effort to darken and disguise it.

He aimed the rifle at Sprinkle's head and snarled, "You—I can't get this damn emergency brake off. Help me, or I'll kill you!"

Sprinkle leaned into the Buick and bent over the brake, and the youth reached across him as if to help. Sprinkle took advantage of the split-second opportunity to straighten up swiftly and snatch the rifle from the youth's hand.

With his free left hand, Starkweather swung at the big man's jaw, but Sprinkle hung on and tripped the young redhead. Starkweather crashed to the ground, but managed to pull Sprinkle down with him. They were struggling furiously, rolling on the road, when another car pulled up. In it was Deputy Sheriff Bill Romer of Casper. Romer pulled his car to a screeching halt and leaped out.

But as he started toward the two men grappling over the rifle, Caril Ann, who had been screeching her head off in the back seat of the Buick, suddenly ran to him and threw her arms around him.

"He's going to kill me!" she screamed. "He's crazy! He's just killed another man. I've seen him murder ten people."

"Who's going to kill you?" Deputy Romer asked.

"Starkweather," Caril Ann yelled. "For God's sake, arrest him!" She clung to the deputy like an octopus.

If Romer could have shaken her loose he probably would have collared Starkweather then and there. But as he tried to get free, Sprinkle managed to get the rifle away from Starkweather, who promptly sprang to his feet, raced to the Packard and roared away down the highway to the west.

Deputy Romer, finally freeing himself from Caril Ann's clutches, ran to his patrol car. On his radio, he called back to Douglas and advised Converse County Sheriff Earl Heflin and Police Chief Robert Ainslee that Starkweather was fleeing westward in the Packard. Then he radioed ahead to Division B of the Wyoming Highway Patrol at Casper, requesting roadblocks.

Then he joined Sprinkle at the Buick to examine the murdered man in the front seat. Papers in the slain man's wallet identified him as Merle Collison, 37, a shoe salesman. Deputy Romer counted nine bullet holes in him.

Questioned by Deputy Romer, Caril Ann said, "The Buick was parked at the side of the road. The driver was sleeping. Charlie decided we should change cars. He killed the man, but he couldn't release the emergency brake."

Taking the girl in the patrol car with him, the deputy now headed west in pursuit of Starkweather.

Caril Ann, still half-hysterical, couldn't stop talking. She seemed desperately anxious to convince him she had had nothing to do with her boyfriend's murderous rampage.

"I was just his hostage," she insisted tearfully. "I was too scared to try to get away."

Referring to the killing of her mother, stepfather and baby sister, she said, "By a ruse, he kept me in the house for six days. I didn't know my family was lying dead in the outbuilding."

Her protestations of being an innocent victim did not sound convincing to Deputy Romer. They had gone about 20 miles when they saw the black Packard racing toward them at a speed of at least 100 miles per hour. Starkweather probably had spotted a roadblock and was doubling back in an effort to elude capture. The fugitive roared past Romer's patrol like a rocket.

Minutes later he flashed by the cruiser manned by Sheriff Heflin and Chief Ainslee. Ainslee swung around in a screaming U-turn and took after him. The cruiser was doing 115 miles an hour when it overtook the Packard at the Douglas city limits.

The chief tried to crash the Packard from behind. For a moment he managed to lock the bumpers of the two hurtling cars and it looked like they had Starkweather at last. But in the next instant the cars became disengaged as they jounced over a bump in the road and the Packard was free again, racing toward the business section of Douglas, the cruiser with Sheriff Heflin and Chief Ainslee close behind. By some miracle, the two cars managed to clear the busy district without crashing into another car.

As they raced out of the east end of Douglas Sheriff Heflin began firing his .30-.30 carbine at the Packard's tires, but the high speed made them an almost impossible target. Nevertheless he kept up a steady fire that must have been unnerving to Starkweather trying to control the Packard, which again was racing in excess of 100 miles per hour.

The sheriff's rifle fire blasted out the Packard's rear window. He could see where the three bullets had punctured the rear end of the car.

Then, quite suddenly, when they were some five miles east of Douglas, Starkweather braked his car to a screeching halt right in the center traffic lane of the highway. Ainslee drove his footbrake to the floorboards to avoid hitting him.

Guns in hand, the two officers were out of the cruiser in an instant. Starkweather burst out of the Packard, staggering in the roadway, one hand clutching his bleeding right ear. Tears streamed down his face and he was nearly hysterical.

"Get your hands up!" Sheriff Heflin shouted.

Starkweather only continued to babble. Heflin snapped off two shots at the redhead's feet and again ordered, "Get your hands up!"

Starkweather got the message. His hands went high above his stained red hair. "For God's sake, help me," he pleaded whiningly. "I'm bleeding to death. Your bullet splintered the windshield and the glass slivers cut me."

He truly believed he was dying. The sight of his own blood terrified the youth who had mercilessly slain at least ten persons. But for the fearful tragedies he had wrought, it would have been ludicrous — the full extent of Starkweather's wounds was a cut ear lobe.

They clapped a pair of handcuffs on the pint-sized killer and took him to the Converse County jail in Douglas. Caril Ann arrived a few moments later with Deputy Romer. The lovers were locked up in separate

465

cells and Nebraska authorities in Lincoln were notified of the capture of the Mad-Dog Killer and his sexy paramour.

From the stolen Packard, officers retrieved a .28-caliber pistol and a keenly honed hunting knife. In a suitcase they found a white shirt with C. Lauer Ward's name inked in the neckband, a satin shirt initialed C.L.W., four handkerchiefs, five pairs of socks and a pair of cream-colored corduroy trousers.

Starkweather regained his bravado after a doctor had put a band-aid on his ear. "I should have shot you both," he said to Chief Ainslee and Sheriff Heflin. "You never would have got me if I hadn't stopped the car."

"You've killed ten people," Chief Ainslee said evenly. "Isn't that enough?"

"Ten?" Starkweather said, with a boastful smirk on his face. "That's all you know. I've killed eleven!"

Blandly, he told how he held up the Crest Service Station in Lincoln on December 1, 1957, and took $160 from attendant Robert Colvert at the point of a 12-gauge shotgun.

"I made him drive me in my Ford to a county road. He tried to grab the handkerchief I had over my face. I told him to get out of the car and then I blasted him in the back of the head."

He added details which checked with Lincoln police records, which still carried the Colvert killing as unsolved.

Nebraska officials flew to Douglas and, after a conference, Converse County Attorney William Dixon agreed to waive jurisdiction in the Collison killing and release the prisoner to Nebraska. Starkweather also agreed to waive extradition. He seemed to enjoy his role as a national celebrity, albeit a notorious one.

"I always wanted to be a big-shot criminal," Starkweather said cockily, "but I never thought I'd be this big a one. I wasn't mad at anyone. I just wanted to be somebody."

But the multiple killer had a scare in store for him. He actually trembled when he was told they planned to fly him back to Lincoln.

"Fly?" he echoed in a quavering voice. "Are you guys crazy? I'm not going up in a plane. It's too dangerous."

They finally agreed to take him and Caril Ann back to Nebraska by car. Back in Lincoln, in the presence of Prosecutor Scheele, Sher. Karnopp and Assistant Chief Masters, Starkweather dictated a confession that filled 231 typewritten pages. He showed not a whit of remorse for his bloody crimes.

He said he had killed the Bartletts on January 21st. "I went to the house that day while Caril Ann was in school. I got in a fight with Mrs. Bartlett and she slapped me twice. Naturally, I belted her back. The argument was about me dating Caril Ann. When the old man took her side and came at me I shot them both. Then I cut them up a little." Then the baby, Betty Jean, began to scream, he said. So he killed her, too.

Charles and Caril Ann decided to get out of the Bartlett house on January 27th, after a relative threatened to get a search warrant unless they let her in. They headed for the Meyer farm.

"Meyer must have heard the radio reports about me," Starkweather continued. "He met me at the door with a gun. So I blasted him with my shotgun and

467

dragged his body to the outside washroom. After that we headed toward Bennet and my car got stuck in the mud. That young couple came up and asked if he needed help."

Starkweather said he and Caril Ann got into Bob Jensen's car at his offer to drive them to a garage. "Then I ordered him to drive over to that old farm cellar. I took what money he had on him and told them to get out and start walking.

"At the time Caril Ann was holding a gun on them, too. I shot the guy and the girl started to run. Then I shot her and threw their bodies in the cellar."

He and Caril Ann then drove back to Lincoln in Jensen's car and went to the Ward house. "I remembered the place from my garbage-collection job. I remembered he had a good looking Packard."

Ward was out when they arrived. They forced their way in when the housekeeper answered their ring, then bound and gagged her and Mrs. Ward. "I stabbed them to death," Starkweather said mildly. "Then when Ward came home around six p.m. I shot him in the head. Then I stabbed him with my hunting knife to make sure he was dead. After that I took his car and we headed for Wyoming."

Finding the shoe salesman, Collison, asleep in the Buick outside Douglas gave Starkweather the idea of changing cars again. It seemed too good an opportunity to pass up. "But he put up an awful argument," the redhead said. "I had to shoot him nine times."

In the interrogation of Caril Ann, she stubbornly clung to her story of being an unwilling witness to her boy friend's murder spree, that she was merely his "hostage." Investigation showed, however, that she

468

had made no attempt to take advantage of numerous opportunities when she could easily have escaped during stops at restaurants, service stations and the like.

On February 4th, she and Starkweather were arraigned in Lancaster County Court, Judge Herbert Ronin presiding. Each pleaded not guilty to charges of first-degree murder. They were ordered held without bond.

The trial of the murderous lovers in May, 1958, ended in verdicts of guilty for both. On May 24th, Caril Ann Fugate was sentenced to life imprisonment in the Women's Reformatory at York. Charles Starkweather was sentenced to death in the electric chair, and his execution date was set for December 17th. A series of appeals, however, delayed his date with the executioner.

When the United States Supreme Court declined to review his case, Starkweather's last avenue of appeal was exhausted, and his execution was rescheduled for June 25, 1959. At 12:05 a.m. on that date, Nebraska's infamous Mad-Dog Killer paid the supreme penalty, in the electric chair at the state penitentiary, for the wanton, senseless murders of 11 innocent people.

Caril Ann, meanwhile, after the initial shock of facing life imprisonment was over, managed to adjust admirably well to her existence behind bars. So well, in fact, that late in the summer of 1972 she was the subject of a one-hour, in-depth nationwide TV interview, filmed at the prison. All indications were that the process of rehabilitation was succeeding in her case, but whether she is being considered for parole in the near future was not disclosed.

EDITOR'S NOTE:

Morton Hooker and Karl Ericson are not the real names of the persons so named in the foregoing story. Fictitious names have been used because there is no reason for public interest in the identities of these persons.

APPENDIX
ADDITIONAL COPYRIGHT
INFORMATION

"Massacre at the University of Texas," *Official Detective*, November, 1966.

"2800 Volts for Indiana's Multiple Killer," *Master Detective*, August, 1981.

"Eight Girls, All Pretty, All Nurses, All Slain," *True Detective*, October, 1966.

"Holiday Horror on a Ferry Boat," *Official Detective*, December, 1986.

"The Serial Killer Snuffed Two More," *Front Page Detective*, April, 1987.

"Stop the Madman's Murder Mission!" *Front Page Detective*, April, 1987.

"17-Year Track of the Family Slayer!" *Master Detective*, February, 1990.

"Four Executions by the Rampaging Psycho!" *Front Page Detective*, June, 1987.

"A Maniac's Rage Claimed 15 Lives!" *Official Detective*, January, 1987.

"The 'Animal' Is Loose! He's a Rapist! He Has a Woman Hostage!" *Official Detective*, January, 1987.

"Hunt for Phantom Strangler of Seven!" *Front Page Detective,* March, 1987.

"Weird Twist in the Marshfield Massacre!" *Official Detective,* October, 1988.

"The Man with a Rage to Kill!" *True Detective,* June, 1988.

"I'm Going Hunting Humans!" *Front Page Detective,* March, 1990.

"Horror of the Hungerford Massacre!" *True Detective,* February, 1988.

"Rampaging Sex Starved Strangler!" *Inside Detective,* January, 1987.

"I've Just Shot Five People!" *Inside Detective,* November, 1988.

"7 Victims of the Whispering Strangler!" *Front Page Detective,* February, 1988.

"Two-Gun Stalker on a Murder Mission!" *Front Page Detective,* September, 1988.

"Fantasy of Death," *True Detective,* August, 1950.

"11 Murder Victims for the Young Lovers!" *Master Detective,* February, 1973.